the lust for blood

JEFFREY A. KOTTLER

the lust for blood

why we are fascinated by
DEATH, MURDER, HORROR, and VIOLENCE

Prometheus Books

Essex, Connecticut

Prometheus Books

An imprint of Globe Pequot, the trade division of
The Rowman & Littlefield Publishing Group, Inc.
4501 Forbes Blvd., Ste. 200
Lanham, MD 20706
www.rowman.com

Distributed by NATIONAL BOOK NETWORK

British Library Cataloguing in Publication Information Available

Library of Congress Cataloging-in-Publication Data

Kottler, Jeffrey A.
    The lust for blood : why we are fascinated by death, murder, horror, and
violence / by Jeffrey A. Kottler.
        p. cm.
    Includes bibliographical references and index.
    ISBN 978-1-61614-228-5 (hardcover : alk. paper)
    ISBN 978-1-63388-948-4 (paperback : alk. paper)
    1. Violence—Psychological aspects. 2. Violence in mass media. 3. Popular
culture.
HM1116 .K68 2010
303.6—dc22

                                                              2010030412

Contents

Preface

When I was of impressionable age, perhaps ten or eleven, I remember going to the usual Saturday matinee with my grandfather. We saw a scary movie, *Horrors of the Black Museum*, that had something to do with a mad killer seeking some sort of revenge. He was on the loose, wiping people out in very creative and revolting ways. I remember one person looked through a pair of binoculars and when he held them up to his eyes, spring-loaded spikes went through them. Before I could recover fully from that bloody spectacle, another victim lay down on a canopy bed, where a guillotine had been set up above. It chopped off her head. There must have been a dozen other spectacular kills, but those are the only ones I remember.

Now, here's the problem: I had a canopy bed.

That night when it was time to go to sleep, I refused to lie on my bed and insisted instead on sleeping on the floor. By the next day, I was determined to never sleep in my bed again as long as that canopy lurked above me. In spite of my protests, my parents would not relent. They insisted that since I "made my bed" (meaning I went to see the horror film against their wishes), I had to sleep in it.

After some consideration, I decided that I could reverse my covers so that my feet lay underneath the canopy, but at least my head would be spared. I am ashamed to admit that I slept that way for the better part of a year before the fears abated.

Even the most primitive marketing campaign (such as this film that terrified and haunted the author as a child) capitalizes on interest in the forbidden. It offers to "put you in the picture," thereby heightening excitement and arousal, as well as piquing your curiosity: "You can't resist it!"

You'd think I would have learned my lesson, but I also remember the effects of seeing the movie *Halloween* when it first came out. At the time we had a hot tub sitting outside on our patio. It was a beautiful thing, made out of redwood and heated to a perfect 103 degrees. It would have been lovely to soak out there and watch the stars at night—and I was more than eager to do so if someone else would join me. But even in my twenties I was a scaredy-cat and wouldn't go in the tub by myself for fear that I would be attacked. For some reason, it didn't occur to me that the killers in these movies had absolutely no compunction about going after pairs or groups of people at the same time.

I know that I'm not the only one who feels disturbed by horror movies. There was that famous shower scene in *Psycho*, which took ten continuous days for Alfred Hitchcock to shoot to his satisfaction. Janet Leigh, the actress who played the shower-scene stabbing victim, was so traumatized by the murder enactment that she stopped taking showers altogether, only baths, and always with the curtain open. Even more interesting, this was a form of "secondary trauma" since Leigh had a body double who did the nude shower scene (the actress Marli Renfro was herself raped and murdered in real life a few years later).[1]

Soon after my experience with *Halloween*, I went to see another John Carpenter movie, *The Fog*. I settled in my seat, popcorn on my lap, and as soon as the fog rolled in, the scary music cued, and some type of creatures lurked just out of view, I finally asked myself: "What the hell am I doing here? I *hate* this feeling of being terrified. I paid money for this experience. I could be somewhere else, doing anything else, but I *chose* to subject myself to this suffering. What's up with that?"

I have been wrestling with that question for the past thirty years, trying to come to terms with my love-hate relationship with horror and violence. I am ashamed and feel guilty about enjoying war movies and any-thing with automatic weapons and a high body count. I feel like a hyp-ocrite that I preach nonviolence in my work, devote my life to projects that prevent verbal and physical violence in families, and yet . . . and yet . . . I derive such pleasure from viewing violence—at a safe distance.

Like many people, I enjoy action movies, reading suspense novels, and watching true-crime dramas unfold on television. I also slow down like most motorists whenever there is a car accident, hoping to catch a glimpse of something horrifying, or at least to satisfy my curiosity. It has always bothered me that I don't understand this attraction that runs so counter to my most cherished values. It almost feels as if the urge overpowers me and I am forced to look against my will.

I am a psychologist who specializes in researching why people behave the way they do. The projects I have undertaken in the past have usually been about subjects that not only appeal to my intellectual curiosity but also my deeply personal motives to understand a part of myself. While part of my interest is purely scientific in wanting to understand deviant behavior so that I can prevent future crimes, I admit, with a certain hesi-tation, that I am also attracted to the darker side of human depravity.

Although I am a relatively nonviolent, sensitive guy, prone to avoid direct confrontation whenever possible, there is a part of me that really enjoys watching others in the midst of conflict, especially when it leads to bloodshed. This is true whether I am watching a fight break out in a hockey arena or a bar. Furthermore, I know that I am not alone.

While the motivation to write this book was, in part, based on scien-tific curiosity, I have an intensely personal motive to understand my own dark side. I am curious about why the subjects of death, violence, and murder attract so much attention.

Perhaps we should start at the beginning.

THE IRRESISTIBLE APPEAL

"How was school today?" I asked my sixteen-year-old son the moment he walked in the door.

He looked at me—half amused, half irritated—by the rather benign inquiry. Questions in any form were off-limits as far as he was concerned. They were intrusions into his privacy, his very right to control his parents' access to his life.

Perhaps he felt sorry for me this afternoon, or more likely, he just couldn't help himself because he was so excited by something that had happened at school.

"It was okay," he answered my question, but with a little hitch at the end that was an invitation for me to probe further.

Like a fish that has just started to nibble on the line, I was very careful not to spook him. Just a few gentle wiggles of the bait, urging him to continue at his own pace.

"Just okay?" I echoed his last remark. Then the really hard part: wait patiently and act unconcerned. If he wanted to tell me, he would; if not, any amount of pressure and he'd be in his room in a flash.

I continued looking through the day's mail, as if I had all the time in the world. Finally, unexpectedly, that little-boy smile I recognized all too well emerged on his man-sized face.

"It was pretty cool."

What was pretty cool? I wondered. I knew I couldn't ask directly.

"Oh, yeah?"

"Yeah," he jumped in immediately. "This fight broke out in the lunch room. These two girls went at it. One of them is a cheerleader and she was mad because the other girl was after her boyfriend or something."

I nodded encouragingly, not at all sure I wanted to hear the rest but still feeling delighted that at least he was talking to me.

"A bunch of us jumped up on the table so we could see better and the two girls were swinging like welterweights. One girl, the bigger one, almost got her blouse ripped off. She was getting her butt beat by the cheerleader. We were all screaming at them. It was so cool."

"You mean," I asked him in spite of a warning that this might shut him up again, "that it was a good day in school today because you saw a fight?"

He looked at me as if I was some kind of idiot. "Of course, Dad!" He shook his head, as if to say that I was truly beyond help.

"It's all we were talking about the rest of the day. The bigger girl had to go to the nurse's office. The cheerleader who kicked butt is usually in my fifth-hour class but she was suspended."

Even more complete and vivid details tumbled forth. Clearly, this brutal conflict that had been publicly enacted was absolutely riveting for the other kids. My son went so far as to admit that the single distinguishing feature that makes for a good day at school is when a good fight breaks out.

I was appalled by this realization about my son and his contemporary values—that the prospect of seeing a fight, a display of brutal violence, was so entertaining that it absolutely diminished anything else that occurred. Then, before I became too judgmental, I noticed where my attention had been devoted during the previous hour—scanning the paper and magazines about the latest celebrity death, even rereading vivid passages that described the condition of the body and the exact means by which the death had occurred.

I thought about all the television shows and movies my son and I had seen together, especially the ones we enjoyed the most. In fact, our one solid criterion was to choose a film that had automatic weapons to be sure it would grab and keep our attention. Car crashes and explosions were even better.

Then I started considering other samples of this behavior—the vicarious enjoyment of, or at least the irresistible attraction to, acts of death, mayhem, and violence. I thought about the real reason some people go to hockey games (to see fights) or to car races (to see crashes). I mused about the strong appeal of true-crime books, especially anything to do with serial killers or mass murderers. Every new killer on the scene attracts his own share of groupies, fans, or spectators who can't get enough details about the grisly crimes.

More recently there has been an influx of increasingly more graphic and violent video games in which participants can vicariously kill, maim, and torture people in a far more active role than just as a spectator. And this is hardly just a brief flirtation considering that the average American kid now spends an incredible seven and a half hours per day sitting in front of a television, computer, or mobile screen.[2]

We can wring our hands over the demise of contemporary values, the prevalence of violence in the streets, as well as on television, movies, and the Internet, but the truth is that many of us are drawn to acts of murder, violence, horror, and crime in a way that we can't explain, or even understand. It is a phenomenon disturbing enough that every health organization under the sun has come out with strong statements decrying the toxic effects of violent entertainment on our youth.[3]

What is the appeal, after all, of seeing a horror movie? By any stretch of the imagination, the experience is hardly pleasurable and, in fact, is often quite painful. Do people look like they are having fun while watching a monster, human or otherwise, stalk and dismember hordes of innocent victims? Not any more than people appear to enjoy eating spicy foods. By any objective measure, what people describe happening in their mouths as they munch on a chili pepper, or what happens in their chests when they watch a horror film, is excruciating pain. Yet, there is an attraction we feel for the sheer stimulation of the experience, not unlike the appeal of a roller coaster that gets the juices flowing and the senses heightened.

Whether self-serving or not, movie directors claim that there is a distinct difference between violence on the screen and blood spilled for real. After all, movies are fake and just entertainment. Increasingly, however, the boundaries between what is real and unreal are difficult to decipher. New technology makes it possible to rearrange or even create images that are virtually indistinguishable from actual events. Computer simulations, virtual reality, special effects, and perceptual manipulations now make movies so real that what is proclaimed as documented truth has been faked in such a way to fool experts. The question isn't whether movie violence is different from watching the real thing, but rather, what is it about the action that people find so intoxicating?

The lust for blood that we can witness in every facet of the world—from the media we watch to the scenes that unfold in everyday life—is a paradox of human existence. We are attracted to that which repulses us the most. We are drawn to the exact scenarios that we find most horrifying.

What is the appeal of watching a horror movie or television show, or reading a horror book, when the audience appears to be in such discomfort and pain? There is something undeniably attractive about violence in the way it captures attention and holds our curiosity. Image © Andresr, 2009. Used under license of Shutterstock.com.

Inescapably, we are led to wonder what is within each of us that attracts us to violence. And we are left to come to terms with what this means.

There is a deep-rooted fear in many people of losing control, believing that just because they might entertain violent fantasies (as almost everyone does), enjoy watching brutal sports or movies, or follow lurid crimes, that somehow they are at risk to someday slide into acting out their impulses. Nothing could be further from the truth, especially for anyone who actually worries about this scenario, given that true sociopaths are missing a conscience or the slightest concern about anything other than getting caught.

As it turns out, there are some very good reasons why horror and violence have such appeal. In spite of complaints about the degradation of the very moral fiber of our society as a result of pervasive violence in the media, research has generally not supported the notion that playing violent video games or watching violence on television, in movies, or at sporting events necessarily leads to aggressive, antisocial behavior. On the contrary, there is some evidence that the kind of emotional arousal that takes place is actually quite constructive in helping us to deal with fears and express impulses that might otherwise lead to self-harm or danger to others. It is a complex phenomenon that we will examine from multiple angles.

As we explore the fascinating world of spectator violence, whether in true-crime stories, suspense fiction, slasher or disaster films, homicide or accident scenes, wrestling or cage fighting, or any of the other contemporary manifestations of "gladiator" spectacles, it is important to understand not only why these experiences have such appeal, but also what we can do to appreciate the meaning of them in our lives—without guilt and without shame. Even if it is inevitable that violent entertainment will always be a part of our culture, the key question we will examine is related to how such behavior can lead to the promotion of greater peace, cooperation, and kindness in the ways we relate to others in our daily lives.

INVESTIGATING THE MYSTERY

I am fascinated by the forbidden, not only as a psychologist but also as someone with his own unusual proclivities. I once wrote a book that involved interviewing people about what they do when they're alone, mostly to reassure myself that I'm not that weird because of my own behavior, the least of which is that sometimes I like to talk to myself in strange voices.[4] I have since completed other research projects and books about forbidden subjects in the practice of therapy like the practitioners' own inner struggles, feelings of failure and uncertainty, as well as the ways these are transformed by their clients.[5] I've investigated the subject of creativity and madness, again because of an intensely personal fear that someday I might go crazy.[6] I've also been intrigued with the ways that travel experiences can be so powerfully impactful, much more so than traditional therapy, and how to make those changes endure over time.[7] So it seemed natural for me to take on the subject about which I feel most uncomfortable and insecure.

The main question we will be addressing in this book is, Why do we have such an irresistible attraction to violence? What is the appeal of sensational murder trials such that people actually stay home from work to watch the lurid details unfold? What is the enticement of horror movies in which the viewer is subjected to the most vivid enactments of dismemberment and blood lust? Why is it that the best predictors of a new movie's success are a high body count and spectacular explosions? Why do people slow down at the scene of an accident and hope to catch a glimpse of a body? Why do spectators act horrified when someone is killed in the boxing ring or during a car race, even though secretly they were hoping to see the most violence possible? Why are the most popular spectator sports such as football, mixed martial arts, and hockey designed to maximize violence? Why do true-crime books and detective novels that trace the careers of serial killers and mass murderers sell so well? What is the attraction that most of us feel toward the spectacle of violence and murder? The questions go on and on. This book is an investigation of the phenomenon as to why human beings lust for blood.

We are at heart voyeurs. People like to watch mayhem and murder, although all the while we protest how horrible it is. We are drawn to human depravity—as spectators. We may not feel disposed to commit savage acts ourselves, but we love to hear stories about others who have done so. Better yet is to see pictures or watch movies. These are creations specifically designed to elicit extreme fear responses—monsters terrorizing villages, predators stalking victims, aliens wrecking havoc, creatures seeking blood, or all-too-human characters torturing innocent victims. Then there are all the forces of nature that have been made into the subjects of films or written into books—earthquakes, tornadoes, tsunamis, floods, plagues, volcanic eruptions, global warming, fires, each one threatening the destruction of humanity.

Based on a series of interviews with a wide variety of experts, prominent psychologists and psychiatrists, media researchers, criminologists, homicide detectives, executioners, movie producers and directors, celebri-

At the heart of this investigation is the question as to why we are so drawn to watch spectacles of violence, with all the accompanying discomfort, anxiety, and displays of evil and inhumanity. Successful movie franchises such as *Halloween*, *Hostel*, *Scream*, *Saw*, and others all appeal to the innate human desire, perhaps even need, to examine death from multiple angles—all from a safe distance.

ties, convicted murderers, serial killers, victims of violent crime, as well as "consumers" of all kinds of entertainment violence, I explore what it is about this subject that has drawn such a wide audience. While there have been many such investigations undertaken to explore the motives of perpetrators, and the effects of violence on victims, very little has been written about the vicarious thrills that most of us enjoy as consumers of violent acts. Even less is understood about why there are such different reactions to watching violence. Whereas some people can't stand even the slightest exposure without feeling sick to their stomachs, others can't seem to get enough of the stimulation.

Yet this is not a book about the deviant but about the normal, average person who enjoys, even against his or her will, getting close to the most forbidden, perverse, dark side of destruction and evil. Ultimately, it is a book with an optimistic message that it is entirely possible for people to watch and enjoy violence as entertainment and yet still practice the highest level of morality with respect to their behavior, valuing compassion, empathy, respect, and caring for all people.

From the gladiator days of ancient Rome to the contemporary spectacles of football, hockey, or rugby, humans have lusted for opportunities in which they can observe acts of violence on a consistent basis. It has become part of the civilizing process of human evolution that we now pay people to simulate wars in arenas so we don't have to fight with competing tribes ourselves. Yet far beyond the vicarious appeal of symbolic war, bloodshed in almost any form is both horrifying and mesmerizing.

It is one of the genuine mysteries that still confront scientists and contemplative individuals alike: What is it about the most dark and depraved side of human existence that draws us in? In *The Lust for Blood*, I address those questions through the voices of serial killers who reflect on their groupies and fans, as well as through the narratives of the most civilized, and also honest, consumers of violence, who were willing to say out loud what so many of us think and feel.

NOTE ON THE INTERVIEWS CONTAINED IN THIS BOOK

Much of the material for this book has been collected during the past twelve years. Several collaborators and research assistants helped me conduct interviews with various law enforcement professionals, media experts and researchers, incarcerated criminals, perpetrators of violent crime, as well as a host of everyday people who enjoy various forms of violent entertainment. Except when otherwise indicated, I have used fictitious names and changed identifying information to preserve the anonymity of those who were interviewed.

I am grateful to all those who helped with the research and production, as well as shared their stories. I wish to thank my agent, Claire Gerus, and my editors, Steven L. Mitchell and Joe Gramlich, who were involved in every aspect of the book's development. I also wish to thank the following individuals for their help with the project: Ellen Kottler, Jason Moss, Laura Triplett, Andi Stein, Jeanne Lightly, Jonathan Keim, Chris Carlino, Sloane Costello, Erika Medina, Kimberly Jackson, Nancy Fishman, Maria Lazcano, Amanda Rinehart, Sarah Valenzuela, and Bruce Chambers.

Chapter 1

Paradoxes of Violence

I t is that time of day when the heat and humidity are so suffocating it is difficult to draw a breath. No matter, he thinks. It is the way of things.

He is out for a walk with some friends, just hanging out and trying to stay cool. He is enjoying the companionship and the exercise, stretching his legs a bit. He is walking with a steady gait but then is momentarily distracted. Something is rustling in the bush. While his friends seem alarmed, he unconcernedly ventures ahead. Their chatter abruptly ends.

Suddenly, he sees the shapes of blurred movement. Before he can react, or even figure out what is going on, he feels an excruciating pain near his neck. Then he feels others tearing at his flesh, literally pulling him apart. The agony is unbearable, but he can do nothing but lie there immobilized. His testicles and ears are ripped off. Large gashes appear in his stomach and back.

As he begins to pass out, he notices his friends in the background watching this torture with horror and fascination. They seem paralyzed, unable to move and unwilling to help. They watch the bloodlust continue, never averting their eyes for a moment, as their friend is systematically disemboweled, his spine severed, and feet torn off, eventually dying of shock and blood loss.

When the band of savages runs off, the victim's companions remain to inspect the carnage. They just lost a valued friend, but they seem more concerned with the smell of death and how pungently it lingers.

This ambush in the Ngorongoro Crater of Tanzania takes place among two rival clans of spotted hyenas, although it could have easily been a description of what has happened repeatedly in the jungles of our own inner cities or battlefields. This is true not only with respect to acts of ferocious violence but also in the behavior of the spectators who stood riveted by the mayhem. The events described, documented by Hans Kruuk in his study of African predators,[1] illustrates the type of lust for blood present throughout the animal kingdom, human animals included. Among a number of other mammals, including chimpanzees, gorillas, and lions, murder is also common—usually with witnesses making no attempt to intervene. Often this is not because they fear personal injury from such intervention, since a dozen bystanders could certainly restrain a few violent killers, but because they seem to accept that such murder is none of their business. They watch with discomfort, agitation, but also riveted fascination.

WHISTLING IN THE DARK

The killer is calm and methodical. There is no drama in his actions. He slices small bits of skin off the writhing victim with a casualness that might be associated with reaching into the cupboard for a snack. Indeed, he is eating the various body parts that he cuts off his prey, still alive but beyond the point where she can scream any longer. Every time she whimpers, the killer looks up in annoyance, then resumes his consideration of where he might extract his next bite of flesh.

There is blood everywhere. It runs in streams down the ravaged body. It lies pooled on the floor and on the table where the killer is enjoying his meal. There are spatters of red on the walls and ceiling. Most alluring of all are the blood spots that mar the blinding gleam of the rather large steel bowie knife.

You watch this scene unfold with a mixture of revulsion and rage. You feel sick to your stomach and very sorry that you agreed to watch this film. For a moment, you consider leaving and even look for the fastest route out of the darkened theater. But there is something that holds you in place, some unforeseen power that keeps you cemented to your seat. You could very easily look away from the putrid, sickening violence on the screen, but for some reason you can't explain, and frankly would rather not think about, you watch the nightmare continue until the end.

When the lights of the theater are turned on, you are startled by the intrusion of reality. You check your body parts and all is well: you have survived! There is also a lingering uneasiness you feel, not only about the horror you witnessed on the screen, but also by your own varied reactions to what you saw. Spiders, rats, snakes, ghosts, aliens, zombies, vampires, werewolves, monsters in the night, always in the night, and death, especially death, impending death most of all, is what cranks up the tension, gets the juices flowing, and reminds you that you are still very much alive.

This reminder is important considering we are likely the only creatures that are distinctly aware of our eventual, impending death. It is our consciousness that is our greatest gift and yet our most terrible burden. From the time we reach the approximate age of three or four, we learn that our tenure in this existence is limited. Dread is our constant companion. Existential philosophers have given a special name to this intense apprehension we feel about our own demise: *angst*. This is the free-floating anxiety that often crops up when you least expect it, when you hear the tick-tock of the precious seconds of your life ticking away with each beat of your heart. Your heart, after all, is just another muscle in your body, one that is slowly wearing out with each contraction.

Death is ever present in the back of your mind and the center of your spirit. It is so emotionally terrifying for most people that it lays at the core of literature, art, drama, film, and other entertainment. There is no subject more riveting because it is *the* topic that concerns you most, wondering how long you have to live and what happens after you die.

If you were really honest with yourself, there is something about watching a horror film, reading a crime novel, or viewing violence on television that is strangely stimulating. Then there are the times you are driving on the freeway and see an accident scene on the other side of the road; without thinking, you slow down and try to catch a glimpse of what happened. Sure, you are not a violent person by nature, and you are the first to admit that this world would be a lot better off if people resorted to more peaceful means to satisfy their desires. Still, there is something about vicarious violence that seems irresistible and riveting. Most people can't quite explain the attraction, and may even exhibit strong will to resist it, but the intense curiosity and interest still lives within. Even more surprising is that the interest in violence is hardly limited to macho men or adolescent boys.

Isabel Pinedo, a film scholar and avowed feminist, attempted to reconcile her commitment to peace and women's empowerment with her love of "slasher" movies like *A Nightmare on Elm Street* and *The Texas Chainsaw Massacre*. How, she wonders, did a good Catholic girl become so addicted to horror films, the gorier the better? Why, she asks herself

Television shows (*Dark Shadows, True Blood, Vampire Diaries, Moonlight*), movies (*Dracula, Twilight, New Moon, Buffy the Vampire Slayer, From Dusk to Dawn*), and books (*Interview with the Vampire, Nice Girls Don't Have Fangs, Eclipse, The Strain*) about vampires are only one example of the fascination that audiences have with monstrous serial killers who stalk and murder helpless victims. The myth of vampires has special appeal because of their immortality, special powers, overt sexuality, and typical physical beauty. Image © Bliznetsov, 2009. Used under license of Shutterstock.com.

even more perplexed, does the genre that debases and defiles and diminishes women instill "such a powerful source of pleasure for me and for others, but especially for women?"[2] The burgeoning proliferation of movies, books, and television shows about vampires, creatures of the night that feed on helpless victims, has a special, forbidden allure to many women.

Very few people feel neutral about the subject of entertainment violence—either you like it or you don't. For those who feel the pull, it is something that defies easy explanation. Those who have a higher need for arousal and sensation seeking are more likely to be the ones most attracted to this media.[3] These individual differences in the desire for new experiences and different forms of stimulation have something to do with the interest in violent entertainment.

THE STRANGE ALLURE OF HORROR

Human beings are about the only inhabitants on the planet that deliberately inflict cruelty on others, that relish the opportunity to do so, and without apparent gain. Paradoxically, we are also unique in our capacity for compassion and altruism. This conundrum has puzzled philosophers and scientists for centuries and was a major sticking point for Sigmund Freud in his attempt to reconcile what he considered the masochistic and sadistic nature of human beings.[4] Yet there is increasing evidence that our lust for blood is instinctually based, biologically programmed, and reinforced by stimuli in our environment, especially with regard to the presence of blood as a signal that we have been successful predators and thus able to survive.[5]

We are all sadists at heart, argued Aristotle, Freud, and famously, the

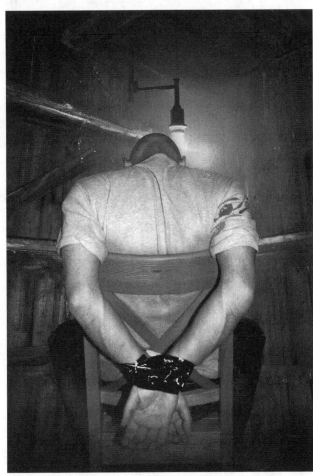

Human beings are capable of remarkable cruelty in the ways they will subject others to intentional pain and torture, not only to extract information or exact punishment, but for the pleasure derived from others' suffering. Yet it is the same capacity for empathic connection that makes it possible for people to feel such vicarious arousal from watching violence inflicted on others, or alternatively, to feel compassion, love, and caring for those who are at risk. Image © 2009. Used under license of Shutterstock.com.

Marquis de Sade. All sensations, even those that are painful, can become pleasurable as a function of their pure stimulation of the nervous system, as well as awareness of the fragility of life. When we are able to put some distance between the violence and ourselves, as in entertainment media, there is a blurring of the boundaries between pain and pleasure, between horror and fascination. It is the detachment and awareness that the video game, movie, or scene from a vampire tale is not real that permits indulgence in the most forbidden thoughts and feelings.

Some of the most disturbing psychological experiments have confirmed the ways that people are capable of extreme cruelty if they feel they have permission. Philip Zimbardo's studies in mock prisons showed the ways that ordinary people can become quite sadistic in certain contexts, especially if given permission by an authority figure to do so. This phenomenon was highlighted even more dramatically in other studies by Stanley Milgrim, in which men in white lab coats told participants that it was perfectly okay to shock their partners (paid actors)—who were screaming in agony—even to the point of death. As much as we might shake our heads in disgust at what took place in real prisons, concentration camps, or the Coliseum of Rome, we are far more capable of violence and cruelty than we are willing to admit.

It is also peculiar the ways we subject ourselves to horrifying experiences, albeit vicariously, but are at a complete loss to understand what drives us to do so. Whether among hyenas or humans, there is a legacy from ancestors that makes us hyperalert to violence and its aftermath. There is something about the prospect of bloodshed that people find both compelling and intriguing. One feminist scholar, who rails against the depersonalization and oppression of women as victims in violent media, reluctantly admits she is also a fan of them: "I am irresistibly drawn to horror movies and simultaneously repulsed by them."[6] It is the rational mind, the reflective thought asking, "What the heck am I doing watching this stuff?" that triggers the revulsion; it is a baser instinct that draws us into the vicarious experience in the first place.

Violence in general, and murder in particular—especially grotesque killing—is a form of escape from the drudgery of our lives. It is entertaining precisely because it is so different from anything else we experience on a daily basis. On some level we hunger for action and excitement that is missing in our routines. This isn't so much because the ways we spend our time is without purpose, or even passion, but the result of genetic programming that prepared us to function as thoroughbred racehorses rather than pack mules.

The neurological, endocrine, and muscular systems of the human body are exquisitely designed to tune into potential violence and danger, and then respond decisively. Certain emotional responses—fear, for example—are hardwired into our bodies. In the face of mortal danger, the fraction of a millisecond that it takes to send a warning from the brain to the large muscles used to fight or flee may still be too slow. That's why, in addition to the electrical signals that are launched through the neurological system, there is an even more efficient biochemical messenger that can be routed through the endocrine system. This option doesn't really even need the brain to interpret or translate what is happening—you just react, almost instantaneously, to a perceived threat. Even babies are born with this startle response, which is activated when they hear loud noises, for example.

For our ancestors who confronted the constant threats of predators and warfare, to react hesitantly would have resulted in a very short lifespan. We are all the products of spectacularly violent ancestors who survived and procreated largely because of their ability as stalkers and killers; their peers who were more peacefully inclined were wiped out by the likes of Vlad the Impaler, Genghis Khan, Ivan the Terrible, Hernándo Cortés, Francisco Pizarro, Alexander the Great, Joseph Stalin, or Adolf Hitler. We each hold within us the capacity to respond violently and swiftly to any threat or problem that confronts us. The problem today is that although we've retained the taste for violence that would have once saved our lives when facing a saber-toothed tiger or hostile enemy, we no longer face those situations in which the lust for blood remains functional—unless you work as a soldier or a professional fighter.

People who can afford it will pay huge sums of money for big-game hunting in which they experience the thrill of the hunt that has all but vanished from contemporary life. In addition to hunting large animals, they will pay premium fees to kill rare or endangered species. There are even reported cases in Cambodia of opportunities to shoot a cow with a bazooka or rocket launcher for the bargain price of three hundred dollars (which includes videos being posted on the Web).[7] For those who don't wish to leave home, "crush videos" are becoming the rage, in which you can watch naked women in stiletto shoes stomp mice or kittens to death.[8]

For most of us, about the only real-life physical danger we encounter on a daily basis is crossing a busy street or negotiating rush-hour traffic. Still, the hunger for risks is so strong that many people deliberately put themselves in harm's way in order to satisfy their need for stimulation. In fact, adventure-based travel is one of the fastest-growing segments of the entertainment industry, largely designed to feed public interest in minimal-risk, controlled excitement. That is why we pay good money to ride roller coasters, jump out of airplanes or off cliffs, or watch movies that really make us jump out of our skin.

For those without the courage to fight on a real battlefield, or the time and resources to finance an expedition to Everest or a hunting trip to Africa, we must make do with vicarious thrills. Thus tales of blood and violence, or better yet—realistic visual enactments—whether on the football field or movie screen, capture our interest in ways that few other experiences could touch. And this began from the earliest age with bedtime stories featuring witches, goblins, and monsters, or tales around the campfire that describe ghosts and demented killers on the loose. Throughout the ages, children have been indoctrinated into the violent legends, myths, and stories that have been passed on from one generation to the next.

SATISFYING CURIOSITY

Not only did biology predispose us to become aroused by violence and death, but so, too, are we culturally programmed to respond that way. We are bombarded by paradoxical messages that we should act peacefully and yet we are constantly teased and enticed by media images of aggression. The best predictor of a show's or a film's success is its budget for special effects, body count, and displays of violent action. Even supposedly educational vehicles, like the Discovery Channel, are watched most avidly when they show real-life predators trapping and eating their prey.

There are functional reasons why we should be curious about death and feel drawn to watching violent struggles unfold. These are potential object lessons so that we can learn from others' misfortunes. Based on what is observed, there is a belief that we may be able to prevent something similar from happening.

Whether the spectacle is a car wreck on the side of the road, a news report of a serial killer on the loose, a true-crime book, or a movie featuring mayhem and murder, there is a natural curiosity to make sense of what happened to the victims. At an instrumental level, the presence of death sparks three basic questions that we feel driven to consider:

1. What happened to this person?
2. How did it happen?
3. What can I do to prevent such a thing from happening to me?

Among the most popular shows on television are those that depict predators chasing, capturing, and killing their prey. The Discovery Channel, Animal Planet, and National Geographic Channel feature dozens of such programs, including *Rogue Predators*, *Predator X*, *Predators in Action*, *Most Extreme Predators*, *Killer Dolphins*, *Piranhas Attack*, and *Shark Attack*. There is something that is both mesmerizing and horrifying about watching victims hunted and devoured, reminiscent of the ways that humans used to live and survive hundreds of years ago. Image © Mogens Trolle, 2009. Used under license of Shutterstock.com.

Dead bodies are magnets for the curious, not just because we are morbid and perverse, but also because we are trying to learn from what occurred. In the very conversation in which this theory was discussed, a bunch of us were sitting around digesting our food and talking about current events. When one man offered his explanation for why people slow down at car crashes or crane their necks at crime scenes, before he could even finish, others jumped in with stories of death they had encountered.

The group had been on the verge of breaking up. Yawns everywhere. Hands were reaching for coats. People saying good-byes. Then, whammo, one lady starts telling the story of a murder in her neighborhood.

"I can't believe it," she said in reverent tones. "It was on my same block!"

She was asked a dozen questions. What happened? Why was this neighbor singled out? Could it have been prevented in some way?

At the heart of these inquiries were some very tired people, on the verge of going home, who stayed an extra hour just to talk about victims of murder. What they were actually doing, however, was following genetically programmed instructions that lead us to study disaster and death in any form so that we might protect ourselves better in the future.

After hearing the story of the murdered neighbor, one of the listeners announced: "Well, from the sound of things, this house was broken into because it presented a good target. That's why I leave a light on all the time."

Of course, this person was almost literally whistling in the dark. She was deluding herself into thinking she could prevent future harm by merely taking a few precautions. This conception, known as the "Just World theory," is favored by those who don't believe that violent acts (at least by strangers) are often random and irrational; they believe that the victim somehow did something that invited misfortune.[9]

"If only she hadn't taken her garbage out so late at night," one person argued.

"Yeah," agreed another. "And I would never have opened my door in the first place."

There is indeed a marked preference on the part of some people to believe they can prevent future harm by studying the tragedies of others. While this may be a strong motive for becoming a student of violence, it is by no means the only attraction we feel to the subject. It may seem rather obvious that murder is a terrible crime, the most awful thing that can be imagined, but our curiosity about it is directly related to the huge stakes involved: "When you kill someone," reminds evolutionary psychologist David Buss, "you not only take away everything they have, you take away everything that they ever could have in the future."[10] As if that isn't enough, when someone dies, the very survival of his or her family is put into serious jeopardy. In the olden days in some cultures, the deceased's children and mate might be put to death because they would be a burden on the rest of the community. No wonder, then, that there is a strong motive, if not a secret pleasure, in learning about what happened and why.

Clearly, there is something titillating about looking at anything that is novel, much less forbidden. Except to pathologists or homicide detectives, death is certainly an unusual circumstance, literally a once-in-a-lifetime experience. There is nothing more mysterious, or more unknown. There is no subject more alluring, especially if we can experience death as spectators. Furthermore, we are exposed to so many violent stories during childhood that it is no surprise that the interest continues throughout life.

SOFTENING DEATH'S TERROR

Each of us lives with the certainty that we will someday cease to exist, at least in this world. It is both our greatest fear—and greatest gift. The "gift" part is related to the *idea* of death, which ultimately motivates us to live with greater passion and intensity knowing that our time is so precious. It is also through surrogate bloodshed, observing others' suffering and demise, that we come to terms with our own mortality.[11]

There are all kinds of theories and hypotheses about what happens after our physical demise, but the ultimate answer to the mystery is only supplied to those at the point when they can no longer share it with those who are still living. Regardless of whether you believe in heaven or hell, reincarnation, or that we simply become food for worms, death represents the end of something. That something, which we call mortal life, is mostly cherished, and what lies beyond is unknown; for most of us, that prospect is terrifying.

What do we do with that fear? Denial is a preferred option: pretend you will live forever. When that no longer works—and it *is* time-limited—the next alternative is to grab onto a belief system that offers the prospect of a better (or at least another) existence in the hereafter. There are those who have perfect, unwavering, unassailable faith in the certainty of life after death, and that is indeed a tremendous comfort. But for most people there are whispers of doubt: death remains a frightening uncertainty.

To add to the mystery, death is largely shielded from us. Corpses are quickly covered. Bodies are buried or burned as soon as possible. When someone's "remains" are viewed, it is almost always in a tidied-up form, with even the facial expression carefully sculpted. Mourners are encouraged to "move on" as best they can. Most people rarely encounter direct experiences with someone dying. Yet the subject is almost always on our minds.

Every birthday brings you closer to death. Every breath you take, every beat of your heart, represents a loss of finite energy. Your body is wearing out this moment, bringing you closer to your own end. Stay with this thought for a moment and notice the immediate fear and uncertainty welling up inside you. There is a great temptation, a powerful urge, to just bury such thoughts altogether.

Given how significant thoughts and feelings about death are in our lives, it is not surprising that we would have a strong interest in the subject in all its manifestations. Since death has been so sanitized and sheltered in daily life, people often struggle with what to do with their uneasy reactions. Some prefer to close their eyes to it altogether.

I was walking down the Strip in Las Vegas on a morning exploration and I was astonished to see a man, obviously keeled over from a heart attack, lying in the middle of the sidewalk. I stopped and saw clearly a death grimace on his face and a body contorted into a shape that could only mean his spirit was no longer home. What surprised me most about the incident, seeing my first, real dead body outside of a funeral service, was that hundreds of other people were walking by without a glance. Some even stepped over him and continued on their way. I can only assume they thought he was drunk and passed out, but I think it more likely they just closed their eyes to the reality of what was present. It was just too intense and scary to see death that close up. Here was a big chance for anyone to really see what he or she finds so curious, and it seemed to be more than they could handle. Me too. I hurried away from there as fast as I could run.

Yet later that day, those same passersby would watch death in safer contexts, one degree removed from its vivid reality. As much as we might

There is a peculiar attraction/repulsion to viewing images of the dead, especially those who have been subjected to horrific cruelty. In this photo from the Buchen-wald concentration camp, a truckload of bodies was about to be incinerated when the camp was captured by US troops. The actual witnesses to this carnage often broke down in sobs, vomiting, and trauma, yet many felt they had a responsibility to bear witness to the horror so as to tell the world what happened. Notice your own complex reactions to viewing this photo, and other images like it, including horror, sadness, revulsion, curiosity. You turn away, or turn the page, and yet feel an urge to peek at it again to make sure it is as horrible as you first thought. Photo courtesy of US National Archives and Records Administration, College Park.

wish to avoid death, there is an irresistible compulsion to sneak glimpses of it when it feels safe to do so. "It's not easy to live every moment wholly aware of death," writes existential therapist Irvin Yalom. "It's like trying to stare the sun in the face. You can only stand so much of it."[12]

In an interview with Yalom, I asked him what draws people to deliberately choose experiences that force them to look at death in the most gruesome forms possible on-screen or in books. He nodded his head, also intrigued with the question, but he struggled to make a connection. Finally he referred to a passage in his book that he felt had particular resonance: "Because we cannot live frozen in fear, we generate methods to soften death's terror."[13]

One of the most prevalent ways for desensitizing yourself to apprehensions related to death is to face the fears in controlled doses, on your own terms. And that is exactly one benefit of observing violence, whether in the form of photographs, movies, books, or sports. It is yet another paradoxical aspect of our subject that, whereas encountering violence or associations with death in real life are often devastating experiences that produce lasting trauma, watching violence as a spectator is often viewed as interesting if not entertaining.[14]

WEANED ON VIOLENCE

Before written words were invented, the earliest humans were already recording stories of violence on the walls of their caves. The dominant motif was to present narratives of the hunt or battle scenes, memorializing a particularly successful killing. Cave dwellers would sit around the fire and tell stories of demons and supernatural forces, mostly to scare the hell out of one another. These tales eventually became what we know as myths, legends, fables, and ghost stories. Their intended purpose, besides entertainment, was to come to terms with mysteries and conquer fears.

Humans are raised on tales of violence from the moment they hear their first stories. Little Red Riding Hood is about a child being stalked by a serial killer wolf who wants to rape and devour her. Hansel and Gretel, one of the most popular Grimm's fairy tales, is about a child who is being fattened up before he is cooked and eaten by a witch. *The Legend of Sleepy Hollow* features a boogieman on horseback. Even parents get into the act, threatening their kids in a teasing way, "You're so cute, I'm going to eat you up!" The children are then told to say their prayers before they go to bed: ". . . if I die before I wake, pray the Lord my soul to take."

Movies like *Creature from the Black Lagoon*, even with their primitive special effects, haunted children into many sleepless nights yet also launched their ongoing interest in rediscovering the fear they felt.

Horror writer Stephen King remembers *Creature from the Black Lagoon* as the first movie that had any lasting impact on him. He was seven years old. What the movie did for him, other than haunt his sleep (and launch a career), was grab his attention so completely and hook his emotions so totally, that he chose to ignore the hokey monster suit worn by some underwater stunt guy.

Horror movies provide the same sort of thrill as a scary amusement park ride. Rationally, you know it's perfectly safe, yet you can't help but scream as your guts get turned inside out. Just like a terrifying ride, one appeal of horror is that when the lights come back on, the book is completed, or the show's over, there is a tremendous feeling of relief. Not only did you survive the ordeal with all your body parts intact, but the only noticeable casualty is a little popcorn grease on your fingers.

According to Stephen King, "The business of creating horror is much the same as the business of paralyzing an opponent with the martial arts—it is the business of finding vulnerable points and then applying pressure there."[15] And what is more vulnerable, he asks, than going after the ultimate pressure point—our own mortality?

Like probing a wound, we can't resist getting close to the edge of what we fear the most. This is not only true, King argues, with respect to death, The Big D, but also the nature of evil. Why is it abnormal or forbidden, he asks further, to have an interest in these subjects? Why do people assume that someone must be unbalanced, perverse, or even demented because he or she enjoys horror? Nightmares may not be fun, but they are memorable. Likewise, horror may not be exactly enjoyable, but it is stimulating.

The average child, before reaching the age of eighteen, has witnessed thousands of murders and ten times as many acts of violence on television. That figure would double, or even triple, once movies are added in as well, especially with the increasing popularity of blockbusters with high body counts. To further entice the interest of young children, toys are marketed as tie-ins to movies, but these movies are so violent that these same children are not allowed to see them. One such example, the alien invasion film *Starship Troopers*, featured mutant creatures resembling giant bugs that impale humans through the chest and then suck their brains out. Although this R-rated film was not considered appropriate for children under the age of seventeen, there were nevertheless action figures available—killer bugs that children can use to re-create the carnage on the screen.

We are thus saturated with violence from the earliest age. We see death every day on our televisions and movie screens. We read about death and violence in papers, magazines, and books. Cable news stations broadcast a barrage of images every minute of the day from the latest war, suicide bombing, atrocity, genocide, homicide, suicide, kidnapping, or terrorist attack. Yet all the time we devote such considerable attention to lurid stories of murder, crime, violence, and death, this lust for blood is ridiculed by social scientists and politicians who claim that we are all slipping into irredeemable perversity. Most people seem to agree, considering that somewhere between 75 to 90 percent of people polled believe that violence is excessive in the media and should be significantly reduced—even though the demand by the public for such programming is greater than ever.[16] And on some level, such critics are correct since viewers heavily into television news, particularly news shows that focus on crime and violence, tend to look at the world as a more dangerous, suspicious place and grossly overestimate the amount of crime in the world.[17] They are hyper-vigilant, mistrustful toward strangers, and look over their shoulders, constantly expecting the worst in others. This is not exactly conducive to a cooperative, supportive, peaceful community.

REALITIES OF VIOLENCE

Violence is discussed within the context of entertainment and amusement, a leisure activity that is for the consumption of those who are feeling bored or want to be further stimulated. As you'll see, such activities and media can be quite enjoyable and satisfying, as well as functional, in helping people to deal with fears, anger, aggression, not to mention some fairly strong instinctual drives. However, before we delve into the entertaining and engaging aspects of violence for those who are watching, I must acknowledge that we are dealing with a subject that is really about human suffering. This is true not only for the direct victims of bullying, assault, rape, abuse, murder, and intimidation, but also for their family members and loved ones. In the United States there are ten violent crimes and two murders every hour, a new victim of assault every seven seconds.[18]

The whole idea of violence spans so many different forms and meanings. There is the violence of childhood as in bullying and playground fights, escalating to gang activity, robbery, rape, assault, child abuse, spouse abuse, and homicide. Then there is violence on a larger scale with battles, massacres, genocide, terrorism, riots, hate crimes, piracy, rape, assassination, torture, human sacrifice, and executions. Finally, there is the kind of sanctioned violence that is created for entertainment purposes, which is one focus of this book. In addition, the whole texture of violence is difficult to define. Is psychological abuse a form of violence? What about torment in which the protagonist is manipulated and played with, like a cat does with a mouse? How about if the violence is offscreen and not actually shown (the sound of a gunshot)? What if the violence is presented as part of an artistic masterpiece (as in the films *The Godfather, Schindler's List, Hotel Rwanda,* or *Saving Private Ryan*) that earns an Academy Award?

I want to present just one case to bring this into closer emotional focus. One of my graduate students, now preparing to be a psychotherapist, described what it was like growing up in a home where her father was always just on the verge of a violent outburst that put all their lives in jeopardy. "We use to pray in a circle in the living room," Bridget remembers. "Oh, dear Lord, please keep the demons away and project us. I remember saying this over and over and feeling so terrified I couldn't sleep. My mother would tell me to go in my room and not come out again no matter what I heard."

This was all part of the preparation for when her father returned, drunk, incoherent, and very out of control. "I would lie in bed and hear the sounds of the beating. When I couldn't stand it any longer, I'd peek out my door and find my mother curled into a ball on the floor, her clothes torn and bleeding everywhere. Then I noticed my father standing there with a hammer in his hand. I pleaded with him to stop. I begged him to leave us alone. He was killing my mother right before my eyes and there's nothing I could do to stop him."

Bridget paused for a moment, remembering the events with a clarity that signaled she would live with these memories forever. "My father threw the hammer down and then jumped on top of my mother and began strangling her. I tried to pull him away and begged him not to kill her. It was only after my mother passed out that he backed off. But then he started yelling at me, warning me not to say anything to anyone or I'd be sorry. He just threw a bunch of towels and bleach at me and told me to clean up the mess. I never said anything to anyone about that until now."

Bridget finds that the weirdest thing is that her father would never touch her. Instead, what he would do is torture her by beating up her mother and her brothers. He knew how much it bothered her to see violence, and so he used that against her. "He beat my brothers until they were bloody and he always made me stand there and watch. I try to get those memories out of my mind, but I still hear them crying and begging. Even when I was the one to get in trouble he'd punish me by hurting them and telling me it was all my fault."

Bridget's story struck me powerfully during the time I was studying all the ways that violence can be so enticing and entertaining. It acted as a reminder that however alluring it can be to watch violence from the safe distance of a television, movie, or video screen, violence usually implies that one being is hurting another, often in painful ways that leave lifetime scars.

One of the many paradoxes related to this subject is that the enjoyment of watching violence takes place at the expense of others' pain. Even humor often has an edge to it in which the joke is at the expense of someone else being mocked. It would appear as if we literally thrive on the misfortunes of others, especially when the demotion, self-destruction, or failure presents additional ways we might take advantage and consider these opportunities.

THINGS THAT GO BUMP IN THE NIGHT

Paradoxes related to this subject abound. It is interesting that the same negative feelings, such as dread and fear, that are elicited by horror and violence are also experienced as enjoyment. While almost everyone agrees that peace is a very good thing, we still remain avid consumers of violence. We are horrified by the sight of blood, yet nevertheless drawn to it. The same mother who shelters her children from any exposure to harm devotes much of her discretionary time to reading true-crime stories. The same guy who argues that he is completely nonviolent still enjoys watching mayhem on the screen. People complain about violence in sports like hockey, boxing, and football, yet feel cheated if there is no serious blood spilled. The same people who argue passionately against the death penalty nevertheless may try to catch a peak of a public execution—or a dead body lying trapped underneath a wrecked car.

Sean, a veterinary medicine student, was working late one night in the surgery area where students had been practicing their skills. He wandered into the walk-in cooler and was absolutely terrified, on the verge of a heart attack. "I've gone to plenty of horror flicks, but I've never been so shocked. It was huge and horrible, an eviscerated beast that looked like it had been torn apart by some alien creature."

Sean was frozen in this freezer, utterly at a loss whether to move closer, run, or scream. "The smell and sight assaulted me in a way nothing had ever before. It was like a malevolent being that was about to attack and my senses were on full alert status. I have never been so terrified in my life."

After calming down and investigating further, Sean discovered that it was an elephant carcass that had been donated to the school for research purposes. It had died from human tuberculosis and would be receiving an autopsy.

"The really weird thing was that as soon as I could gather my senses, I ran full tilt to find a friend of mine working in another part of the facility. I wanted to show him the cool thing that I'd found and he couldn't wait to see it. It was still pretty shocking and gruesome, but this second time I was extremely curious and not nearly so repulsed."

That is the paradox of feeling simultaneously repelled and attracted by death and horror. Sean explains his reaction as a kind of morbid curiosity. "It's against the law to do the violent things we see in movies, so we find other ways to satisfy this basic human curiosity to study corpses, disasters, and homicides. It's just too bad we can't be more honest about this urge to understand."

Many people thrive on the kind of emotional stimulation that comes from surprises and shocks like finding an elephant carcass in the freezer or a mad killer who jumps out of shadows in a movie. Look around you during any horror film in which aliens drip slime, the living dead decompose, or psychopathic murderers chop up victims, and you will see people in the throes of pain *and* pleasure. Horror writers like Stephen King see as their main job in life "to scare the shit out of little kids after the sun goes down."[19]

As much as we might be repulsed by sickening images on the screen or in the pages of books, on some level there is delight in the arousal they create within us. Your heart is pounding. You look between split fingers to see if it's safe, unable to resist when you hear the sounds of screaming. Your neurological and endocrine systems are churning out juice at a feverish pace, not trusting other parts of your brain that say *This isn't real.*

The civilizing process has muted all forms of emotional expression over the millennia, aggression and violence most of all. Spectator sports from gladiator days onward were designed to provide vicarious outlets for citizens to release pent-up needs for battle and competition that have been programmed into our psyches and hardwired into our systems. With few opportunities in contemporary life to exercise the tools of violent aggression that were once necessary for survival, the best we are offered are ritualized arenas—football or hockey arenas, boxing or wrestling matches, car and horse races like the chariot races of ancient times. We are encouraged to experience the thrill of participation—but by watching at a safe distance.

Many people hunger for more excitement in their lives. They are bored with their jobs, burned out from their routines, stuck in patterns that are repeated over and over again. Most of daily life is programmed according to entrenched habits, most of which are designed to keep us comfortable and predictably safe. This is quite unlike the good old days when life was fraught with danger from starvation, marauding enemies, and predators. Death was a constant companion with life expectancy in the mid-twenties. Now we no longer partake in direct combat except in ritualized or symbolic ways—negotiating a deal, making a sale, debating an opponent, playing chess, tennis, basketball, or a video game. Even more common is to let others do the work on our behalf in the form of professional athletes who represent our hometown on the playing field. We bask in the "reflected glory" of our designated combatants and even feel a surge of testosterone during victory.

RECONCILING THE PARADOXES

It is not that we are hypocrites but rather that our reactions are so complex and multidimensional. It really isn't a matter of either liking or disliking violence as entertainment (although there is tremendous diversity in its relative attraction), but rather that most of us feel ambivalent and con-

fused about the urge to peek through our fingers. There are instincts operating here, as well as reasoned moral judgment. "We are frightened by
death, by things we don't understand, and by things that go bump in the
night," observe media researchers.[20] We might know that there is a monster lurking in the closet, but we can't help ourselves and have to take a
look. We have "this strange human craving for the pleasure of feeling
afraid," commented no less a writer than Virginia Woolf.[21]

Director Arthur Penn, who made a number of extraordinarily violent
films such as *Bonnie and Clyde* and *Missouri Breaks*, confessed his own
paradoxical reactions to violence: "I don't like to fight, but I'm intrigued
by watching people fight and seeing it happen."[22] Intrigued indeed—
enough so that he created what is considered one of the most arresting
visual experiences in the history of cinema, the final gun battle from
Bonnie and Clyde when Faye Dunaway and Warren Beatty are ambushed
in super-slow motion. *Bonnie and Clyde* was so controversial that it was
the first time a film was ever featured on the cover of *Time* magazine.

The inescapable but disturbing truth of our subject is that we all have
a dark side and the potential to hurt others. What separates killers from
the rest of us is that they *act* on their impulses, whereas most people only
think about fantasies of revenge or retribution.[23] Among the reasons why
there is such a fascination for violence as a form of entertainment is that it
provides a kind of vicarious gratification that can actually *prevent* destructive or antisocial behavior.

Perhaps the ultimate paradox is that until we come to terms with our
own lust for blood, we will never understand the irresistible attraction for
violence. Without such awareness, it will be very difficult for us to create
a more peaceful existence in which murder and mayhem do not so dominate our lives.

Chapter 2

From Roman to Contemporary Gladiators

The two combatants face off, their short swords used as crutches to prop up their shaking legs. They are drenched in sweat and bleeding from several gaping wounds along their torsos. One of them has dropped his shield to the ground, unable to support its weight with a shoulder that appears dislocated after a fall to the ground. They have been fighting each other for the past fifteen minutes, already exhausted, but the crowd will not let them rest for long. There are thundering screams calling for continued action.

The Coliseum is packed as tightly as any modern football stadium, tens of thousands of spectators enjoying a Sunday afternoon. Hawkers are selling food, drinks, and souvenirs. Noblemen, senators, families, and young children are all in the stands, watching with riveted attention the action below them.

The gladiator with the wounded shoulder is left-handed, giving him a distinct advantage just as baseball pitchers and tennis players enjoy today—most fighters were unaccustomed to parrying the strikes of the opposite hand. Yet even with this benefit, he looks wasted and defeated, blood streaming down his body. Although their sword arms and legs were protected with light armor, gladiators were essentially fighting in their underwear so as to avoid concealing any blood wounds or entrails that might ooze from a strike. After all, the crowd was there to see as much gore and violence as can possibly be created in the show. The combatants had been trained and instructed to draw out the battle as long as possible, to add flourishes to their attacks, and to land as many stabbing wounds as they could to draw blood.

There are cries from the crowd to finish off the wounded combatant, screaming "*hoc habit*," but his opponent appears reluctant. It is not friendship nor compassion that fuels this hesitance—he knows well how much time and expense was invested to train a fighter. Whatever bloodlust would be satisfied by a killing would be paid for later. Still, the people want their death scene. It wasn't enough to watch the animals being slaughtered in the initial bouts, hundreds of bears, bulls, lions, leopards, tigers, even a rhinoceros, all imported at great expense from Africa. And all this was after the noon intermission, in which close to eight hundred slaves and accused criminals were tortured and put to death for the thrill of the audience. Citizens were granted a relatively quick death—a simple beheading or a few hacked limbs—but the slaves and captured prisoners were crucified, burned at the stake, or literally torn apart by starved lions or panthers.

The heat has become insufferable in the stands, over 90 degrees in the Italian sun, the stink of blood and thousands of decaying corpses and body parts strewn across the ground. Yet the packed crowd waits impatiently for the main event—the gladiators paired against each other with complementary weapons, a short sword and oval shield against a warrior with a net and trident.[1]

There had been a gladiator rebellion the year before, led by Spartacus and his slaves, who managed to hold off and defeat the Roman legions for almost two years before their eventual slaughter. Six thousand of their survivors were crucified and left to die, nailed to crosses, a lesson to any others who would dare such disobedience. The road into Rome was literally lined with tortured bodies on display. It was as if they were billboards advertising to all the world that this was the epicenter of the most horrific and excessive violence ever imagined, a virtual Disneyland of mayhem and cruelty—all for the entertainment of its citizens.

GIVING THE PEOPLE WHAT THEY WANT MOST

Most historians are seemingly appalled by the brutal displays of violence during the Roman games, describing them variously as "scandalous," "monstrous," "a torture chamber," "callous, deep-seated sadism," and "debauched popular entertainment." Before an audience of screaming fans, thousands of prisoners would be crucified, slaves would be fed to wild animals imported from Africa, and combatants would be forced to fight to the death.

Critical of his colleagues who don't mind describing the practices of ancient Rome but can't bring themselves to explain the reasons why the games were such a raging success among the populous, historian Fik Meijer offers several possible functions that gladiators served, some of which still operate today in our own versions of entertainment violence.[2] We may not be big on human sacrifice or honoring the death of our most prominent citizens by spilling more blood to appease the gods, but violent sports and spectacles today have become a form of release, just as they were in the Coliseum or medieval jousting tournaments. They also represent the great cultural values of the time—courage, chivalry, strength, and dominance. For Roman emperors, the games also represented a symbolic display of their power, demonstrating all too clearly how they controlled life and death for humans and animals alike. Meijer also makes the point that it is difficult, if not unfair, to examine behavior of two thousand years ago and hold it to the moral standards that exist today. After spending years studying the practices and rituals of the games, he admits, "Who am I to say that, no matter what the circumstances, I would have been capable of resisting the appeal of the Coliseum?"[3]

It was when Rome first became urbanized, attracting thousands of free citizens, immigrants, slaves, and the vast military complex, that blood sports were invented for public consumption.[4] With all those people crowded together, at one point approaching close to a million inhabitants, there needed to be some way to keep them satisfied and engaged. For as long as they could remember, Rome had been at war and violence had been a way of life. Now, during relative peace, the natives were getting restless.

As originally conceived, the gladiatorial events were a private affair, organized by noblemen to honor their sons killed in battle. Several pairs of fighters would fight to the death, until the blood of one was spilled, believing that this would help the deceased during the challenging journey to the ever-after.

After Caesar was assassinated on the Ides of March, 44 BCE, the political stability of Rome began to teeter on the verge of collapse. Those who were trying to inherit the power needed a way to win public approval: their successful strategy involved feeding the populace violence to appease them, elevating gladiatorial combat from funeral settings to entertainment for the masses. This was a turning point in the creative construction of violent spectacles. Chariot races eventually filled venues to standing-room only, the crowd screaming for crashes. Various forms of combat, execution, slaughtering, sacrifice, torture were put on display for public consumption to feed their bloodlust. In particular events during the reign of Emperor Augustus, as many as twenty thousand gladiators fought to the death and three thousand wild animals were slaughtered. Bigger stadiums were built to hold as many as fifty thousand spectators at a time; this is all the more incredible when you consider the whole population of ancient Rome in the first century BCE was only about a half million inhabitants (similar to a Green Bay Packers football game). And this strategy worked! The politicians were never more popular.

Although often slaves of the lowest class, or captured prisoners, noted gladiators became sports heroes similar to what exists today. They were revered by fans for their skill and brutality and became objects of considerable lust by women who created fan clubs. Some would pay huge fees for the privilege of having sex with a prominent gladiator; others became quite aggressive in trying to seduce them, just as occurs today with prominent sports celebrities.

Once semi-psychotic rulers like Caligula and Nero came to power decades later, the games reached new heights of violent brutality, in part motivated by the crazed bloodlust of the emperors and also demand by an increasingly desensitized public that became bored with the usual spectacles. During one series of games that occurred a bit earlier in Roman history, Pompey had over six hundred lions and four hundred leopards slaughtered—after they were done mutilating thousands of Christian or slave prey. Women were introduced into the act, as were realistic reenactments of famous battles. Spectators were packed so tightly into the stadiums that when one amphitheater in a "suburb" of Rome collapsed under the weight of all the people, thousands of people died in the tragedy. They experienced, firsthand, the death fascination that had drawn them there.

The close connection between violent punishment and entertainment

This painting by Jean-Leon Gerome, *Pollice Verso*, remains one of the most vivid and realistic depictions of gladiatorial combat in ancient Rome, even though there are some inaccuracies in the weapons displayed.

was advanced considerably by some of the most bloodthirsty rulers of this period. Caligula quite enjoyed torturing senators who opposed him, not just to establish his authority but because it amused him to have excuses to inflict pain. Sometimes he would enter the arena himself to face opponents who had blunt weapons just so he could join in the killing frenzy. A century later, Commodus organized boxing matches for his entertainment, but instead of wearing cushioned gloves, he had them filled with lead so that combatants could inflict the most damage. Cruelty thus became institutionalized in Rome, and the games were used to desensitize soldiers and citizens alike to the blood spilled in war.[5]

THE WORST THAT COULD BE IMAGINED MADE THE BEST ENTERTAINMENT

During the height of the gladiatorial spectacles there were over two hundred amphitheaters scattered around the Roman Empire, some of them capable of holding over two hundred thousand people for the chariot races or a quarter of that for the executions or fighting contests.[6] And as the spectacles become more commonplace, there was a public demand for greater bloodlust requiring progressively more brutal entertainment. A bear and a bull might be chained to each other and forced to fight to the death. A lion would be matched with a leopard for a death match, then buffalo against a rhinoceros. When that grew tiresome, a lineup of a hundred slaves, clothed in only loincloths, would be prodded to run around the stadium, chased by the next in line who held a sword or spear with the instructions to hack the defenseless man to death; his reward is that he was then the next in line to flee, chased by the next man in line. Finally, the last one left would be executed, all to an adoring, cheering crowd. It is absolutely staggering the depths of depravity and brutality that inventive minds could create to increase the levels of sickening violence, all to feed the crowd's lust for blood.

Warning: please cover your eyes for this next description (or at least read through your fingers or skip the paragraph altogether). In perhaps the most revolting "game" created for public entertainment that I discovered, selected women were brought into the Coliseum for suitable punishment. In one account of a new "event" that occurred in the southern region of the empire, a naked woman accused of criminal activity was tied to the back of a bull, which was let loose, closely followed by a leopard that eventually ripped the woman to shreds as she sat astride the bucking animal screaming horrifically. An even more disgusting display (it's not too late to skip the rest) involved reenacting the myth of the Minotaur, the half-human, half-bull creature. A woman would be covered in a cowhide and tied down on her knees, her vagina smeared with the blood of a cow in heat, and then a raging bull would be let loose to rip her to shreds while raping her. Whatever you can possibly imagine is the worst possible thing that human beings could ever do to a fellow human was enacted in the amphitheaters for the pleasure of the crowd.[7]

Talk about audience participation: in the gladiatorial games the crowd was very much a part of the whole experience. "Right from the start of the fight," describes historian Fik Meijer, "people in the crowd make themselves heard. They were not simply enthusiastic spectators, cheering and jeering, but to some degree were also participants in the fight, since they would be involved in the final outcome."[8] They may have felt powerless in their daily lives, frustrated that they lived in poverty or couldn't advance themselves above their class, but while attending the games they could literally make their voices heard to determine life or death for the combatants. They made their judgments based on the courage and honor they witnessed on stage and whether they felt sympathetic toward a particular combatant's performance. If displeased, a hoarse chorus would roar out among the crowd, screaming, "Slit his throat! Slit his throat!" Then there would be another scream of approval after the blood was spilled, the audience feeling damned pleased with themselves.

Keep in mind this wasn't just one or two bouts but dozens of them, one after another, all day long, interspersed with comedy acts, more executions, and animal slaughters. The killing went on from morning until night, sometimes several days in a row, with tens of thousands of putrefied, hacked bodies, animal carcasses, and viscera piled up just outside the stadium walls. It was quite a logistical nightmare to dispose of all the dead. They would burn as much as they could, throw piles of bodies into the river, arrange funerals for the most well-known fighters, or just haul away the corpses and dump them into a ravine. Some of the meat was saved to feed the animals still in captivity, waiting their turn for slaughter; other portions were doled out to the poor as rations, although it was sometimes unclear whether they were given human or animal carcasses since they were all mixed together. Meanwhile, hunters were sent deeper into Africa to capture more and more exotic specimens such as rhinoceroses, crocodiles, and giraffes.

It is impossible to get our heads around the very idea that human beings could be so cruel and bloodthirsty. We can blame the crazy emperors, or the greedy entrepreneurs who staged the spectacles, just like today we can blame the media for broadcasting or publishing unrestrained violence, but in all fairness they were serving public demand. If the public was disappointed in the mediocre level of violence on display they might very well riot. Believe it or not, accept it or not, but such cruel and bloody sport has been around as long as humans have been on the planet.

Certainly there were protests among those who felt that blood sports were immoral and should be banned. Indeed, there were brief periods in which religious leaders protested the violence and rulers temporarily suspended the games, but these intervals didn't last very long. In addition to the increasing influence of Christianity, eventually it was economic considerations that made it far too expensive to stage elaborate spectacles.

Historian Kathleen Coleman wondered how it came to be that the Roman "middle class" became so desensitized to what were such exaggerated spectacles of brutality, suffering, and horror. Why did they react with such blasé amusement instead of revulsion? She offered several possible explanations.

1. Violence was sanctioned by the state. The government sponsored and funded the games, and it was considered not only unpatriotic but seditious to criticize the practice.
2. Bloodlust was combined with festivals and feasts, a social activity for the elite that was later emulated by the populace.
3. The violence represented rituals steeped in tradition. From the earliest age children were socialized to play at war.[9]

It is certainly not unusual in human history that people would seek to hunt and kill one another—to enslave, murder, torture, and control. But what was so significant about the Roman version was how much people liked to watch. And similar to the Romans, we "educate" our children to enjoy a degree of violence. We wean them on stories of murder and torture in fairy tales. We tell them scary stories about the headless horseman of Sleepy Hollow or the evil witch of *Sleeping Beauty* or *Wizard of Oz*. Then we put them in front of televisions to watch cartoons of characters beating the heck out of one another, all for laughs. Finally, they graduate to video games in which they can take on villains in simulated combat.

"The Roman public was as fickle as our own," notes one theater critic. "Like channel switchers, they frequently left one event for another and demanded diversions capable of withstanding all competition."[10] In all aspects of experience, whether travel, food, sex, and yes, violence, humans crave novelty, variety, and greater intensity. We are sensation junkies looking for all possible ways to induce maximum stimulation. This can be produced artificially through drugs or as the result of totally unique sensory experiences.

ENTERTAINMENT PREFERENCES EVOLVE

The Coliseum in Rome, once the proud home to the most gruesome and violent spectacles ever created, now lies in ruin. Malaria, plague, and other diseases wiped out a significant part of the population. Earthquakes reduced some of the walls to rubble. Building materials were plundered by thieves. Finally, centuries of neglect reduced the remnants to a shell. There is nothing left but ghosts of all those who were murdered in order to feed the public hunger for entertainment violence.

After seven centuries, gladiator games died out in a single generation, to be followed by the next stage of popular entertainment. Another venue, the Circus Maximus, was constructed to house chariot races, eventually expanded to hold an amazing 250,000 spectators, greater than the capacity of three football stadiums. I'm not by any means implying a cause-effect relationship, but it so happens that entertainment violence became moderated at the time that real killing moved into the streets as Rome fell into chaos. By the fifth century, political assassinations, riots, coups, and civil war between factions were commonplace. During a single year, 455 CE, Emperor Valentinian III eliminated a rival, General Aetius, who had just defeated Attila the Hun. Several of the general's followers then killed Valentinian. His successor, Petronius Maximus, was killed by an angry mob soon after his ascension. It would seem that the citizenry of Rome no longer had an outlet for their frustrations and aggression, so they took it out on their political figures who had previously bribed them with food and entertainment spectacles.

Fast-forward to our own era. Two gladiators, ripped bodies gleaming with oil and bulging muscles, enter an arena to the sounds of music blaring (hip-hop rather than trumpets). The crowd is going wild, screaming for their respective hero. "Kill him," someone yells in a hoarse voice. "Take that fucker down!" Others shout him down with their own cries for victory.

Whether in boxing, wrestling, or the mixed martial arts ring, the rituals related to displaying enactments of violence have been passed down from generations. Designated gladiators, whether chosen based on their professional fighting skills, economic need, or lower status, are put on display to act out the bloody spectacles that are no longer a part of our daily life. They have become relegated to ceremonial forms of entertainment to feed the public interest—and need—to watch people attempt to destroy one another in the most violent and dramatic ways possible.

What is truly remarkable is really how far we have come in moderating bloody spectacles of public entertainment. We still have our coliseums and stadiums where chariot races (NASCAR), gladiators (football, boxing), and animal contests (bullfights, dog fights, and cockfights) are still wildly popular, but increasingly greater controls have been enforced during the past millennium to protect cruelty against animals and the safety of combatants. And more often, the masses are turning to their own simulations in the form of video games, war enactments, television dramas, movies, and even game shows that pit one gladiator against another.

It is interesting in our own culture how we have transformed the bloodlust in public entertainment from watching combatants actually kill one another in stadiums to now doing so during simulations in movie theaters. There have been six different versions of the story of Spartacus, the escaped gladiator who organized the slaves to defy Rome. There have been dozens of other gladiator movies (and television shows, such as *American Gladiator, Spartacus: Blood and Sand*) made over the years, including *Gladiator* starring Russell Crowe. It was produced with a budget of over $100 million and generated five times that amount in worldwide ticket sales. That's half a billion dollars that audiences paid to watch combatants go after one another with swords, axes, spears, and other implements of torture.

It is clear from this discussion that the lives of human beings, from the very beginnings of our existence, have been saturated with violence. In fact,

Gladiators are almost as popular today as they were during ancient Rome. Just as boxing, wrestling, and cage fighting represent more controlled versions of combat for entertainment, reenactments of gladiator sport and times continue to attract huge audiences. Starz cable channel achieved its biggest hit ever with its version of *Spartacus*, which is described as a "gore-and-sex spectacle" composed of the winning formula: "part *300* [an ultraviolent gladiator film], part Harlequin bodice-ripper, and part soft-core porn."[11]

our very continued existence, as offspring of ancestors who survived, is based in part on survivors who managed to outwit and outfight their brethren. Those who were the best hunters and killers, the most adept in battle, those who could effectively eliminate rivals, were afforded greater resources, food sources, and the best opportunities for mates. Keep in mind that until fairly recently, in the last few hundred years or so, only the most physically fit and violent specimens, the alpha males, were allowed to procreate with the most desirable and attractive females. The losers, the weak, the ones who were not as skilled in fighting and killing, were banished, exiled, or ignored—but their genes did not continue on to the next generation.

Among most other animals, this survival of the fittest and most violent continues to be the dominant scheme to control perpetuation of the species. Males who are at the top of the food chain are those who attract the most attractive females; most have multiple mates, whereas those at the bottom of the hierarchy live off scraps and will not be permitted to have a partner. Historically speaking, it is the characteristic of dominance that ensures the best possible opportunities. While this only partially explains the appeal of the gladiatorial and other violent games, there are quite different factors at work explaining the historical use of human and animal sacrifices as entertainment or religious rituals.

FOOD FOR THE GODS

I mentioned previously that gladiatorial sport in ancient Rome had its beginnings as a form of human sacrifice to honor deceased noblemen. It was actually not uncommon that a dying dignitary would specify in his will which of his slaves he wished to fight to the death so that they might accompany him on his journey to the ever-after. Yet human sacrifices have been a part of almost all cultures and religions from earliest times.

Among all forms of violent entertainment for the masses, human sacrifice has the distinction of ritualized murder in the name of religious beliefs. Whether undertaken to satisfy the demands of the Christian God, the Muslim Allah, Jewish Yahweh, Hindu Kali, Norse Oden, Moloch, Satan, or Zeus, vulnerable victims (children, prisoners, slaves, virgins) were murdered in order to sanctify a construction project, protect a business deal, bless a harvest, condone a battle, or honor the dead. "If the killers view their act as necessary to affect some metaphysical result, it is sacrifice," writes Michael Newton in a study of psychohistory, "whatever uninvolved bystanders may decide after the fact."[12] He is referring to the consistent attempts by various religious scholars, historians, and politicians who deny that human sacrifice was ever part of their traditions.[13]

Blood sacrifices once served similar purposes as the violent sports, to provide an outlet for the community to displace aggressive energy—and appease the gods. Aztec temples became the venue for high entertainment under the guise of religious ceremonies in which spectators would identify strongly with both the victim and the wielder of the knife.[14]

In a typical sacrificial ceremony victims were forced to climb the tall pyramids with thousands in attendance, watching with baited breath. The priest would then cut open the chest of the victim, reach inside, pull out the still-beating heart, and offer it to the sun while onlookers cheered. The victim's body would then tumble down from the top of the pyramid, after which it would be prepared as a scrumptious meal for the priests.

When one historian studied the history of human sacrifice among the Aztecs and other cultures, he described his experience attending one ritual for research purposes.[15] Initially he felt considerable apprehension and dread, but then felt intense excitement, and ultimately, relief at the realization that it wasn't him on the chopping block.

There are all sorts of justifications for killing human beings in front of an audience. As we've seen, the Romans did it for pure spectacle. However, this practice of sacrificing "lower" species of humans for the benefit of the higher orders has been practiced from the very beginning of our occupation of this planet. Almost all the ancient religions decreed it was important to make the gods happy by killing people to bring prosperity or a special blessing. Sacrifices were used to consecrate a new building or structure, to

An Aztec priest is depicted pulling out the heart of a victim during a ritual to appease the gods. It was reasoned that since the gods made a sacrifice to give humans life, to provide food and warmth, it was only fair that the gods be fed as well—with human blood. During a single year, 1487, it is estimated that over 20,000 captives were murdered in public ceremonies.[16]

ask the gods for favors, or to pay them back with someone else's life. When gods were viewed as generally entertained and appreciative of violence, offerings would be routinely given to satisfy the projected bloodlust.

In the Old Testament, there are all kinds of references to this practice. But going much further back in time, there is evidence in which cave dwellers routinely killed others out of the belief that it would bring them good fortune or prevent a disaster. Christians, Jews, Muslims, Hindus— you name it and there is some sacrificial practice part of the religious tradition. The Old and New Testaments provide several examples of attempting to appease a wrathful god by providing human fodder. In Exodus Abraham was asked to sacrifice his son, as were the Israelites ordered to do so with their firstborn sons. King David killed seven people to end a famine and ensure that the next harvest might be plentiful.

We've already covered the sacrificial excesses of Roman times, but it's worth noting their example has been repeated throughout history.[17] The Phoenicians and Carthaginians were fond of sacrificing their children. The Celts enjoyed burning their victims alive, although they grew more inventive over time, ritually mutilating women, as well as cutting off body parts to bury in the foundations of their construction projects. The Vikings preferred hanging sacrifices to promote fertility of the land. Slavs employed beheadings to show their gratitude for a prosperous season or successful battle. Then the Inquisition launched a whole new age in sacrificial practices, introducing cannibalism and progressively more creative forms of torture. Moving further south to the African continent, the blood of virgins was mixed into mortar when new palaces were built. On and on throughout every culture in the world, from the Mongols, Persians, Indians, Native Americans, Aboriginals, and Huguenots, to Pacific Islanders, people have been pushed into volcanoes, drowned in lakes, thrown in fires, burned at the stake, buried in pits or walls, crucified, hanged, fed to hungry animals, sliced into pieces, or eaten for a ritual meal. The Great Wall of China is believed to have thousands of people entombed within it. Perhaps setting a world record, rivaling anything the Romans ever attempted, the Aztecs were reported to have killed close to eighty thousand sacrificial victims in a single ceremony.[18]

Victims have been sacrificed in the name of love, for the greater good of the community, to promote commerce or prosperity, as punishment, to sanctify a war, create a distraction, and of course as pure public entertainment. Emperors, kings, dictators, and rulers have used human sacrifices to satisfy their own lust for blood or because they believed they were only feeding the interest of their subjects. Such proceedings are almost always ritualized and undertaken in the name of some religious mission that has been sanctified by the gods, Satan, or some other deity.

SACRIFICES CONTINUE

Even today there remain cultural rituals of sacrifice and blood sports that feed the long-evolved instinctual attraction to violence and killing. Along the predominantly Hindu southern border of Nepal, over two hundred thousand animals—goats, chickens, water buffalo, pigeons—were sacrificed in a single day to honor the goddess Gadhimai, who apparently requires this sort of bloodletting in order to deliver continued prosperity.

As disturbing as animal sacrifices might be in this day and age, there are also reports of continued human killings in the name of a deity. One journalist and self-avowed voodoo practitioner followed news reports of such incidents during the previous decade.[19] A brief sample of incidents is beyond comprehension in terms of what some demented people will do in the name of their religious beliefs:

- 1999, Malaysia: A group of men beheaded a visiting American tourist, believing that it would improve their chances of winning the lottery.
- 2001, London: A five-year-old boy was found in the Thames River with his head cut off, the victim of an African "Juju" ritual.
- 2004, Lima, Peru: A baby was dismembered and surrounded by jugs of blood as an offering to an ancient Inca god.
- 2006, India: A sorcerer advised her "patient" that she must sacrifice a child in order to cure her nightmares. The woman and her sons kidnapped a seven-year-old boy and cut him into pieces.
- 2007, Papua New Guinea: Police units had to be sent into a remote area of the country in order to stop a rash of beheadings designed as ritual sacrifices.
- 2010, Uganda: In a disturbing trend, the number of ritual sacrifices has been steadily rising to more than two dozen cases each year. The problem is becoming alarming enough that two thousand Ugandan police are now being trained in how to recognize and arrest suspects who conduct these grisly ceremonies.[20]

And one last example that is much closer to home—California, actually. In 1995, three teenagers lured a fifteen-year-old girl into a field in order to offer a virgin to Satan. They had been allegedly inspired by a death metal song, "Alter of Sacrifice," that contained the lyrics, "Spilling the pure virgin blood." After the three boys stabbed their victim to death, they raped her corpse.[21]

What most of these horrifying events have in common, as would be the case for most sacrifices, is greed. It is not just about taking a life, or watching the killing for pure entertainment, but also about some benefit to oneself or others. There is a belief that by offering such a precious gift to the Supreme Being, the favor will be reciprocated. It is not just about the process of violence, but its desired outcome.

There has even been talk of starting a "human sacrifice channel" on cable to appeal to those who are interested in seeing ritualized slaughter for their nightly entertainment. The prospect was taken up by the US Supreme Court. Justice Antonin Scalia, a passionate hunter, thought that however distasteful this might be, it was protected by the First Amendment.[22] So, perhaps coming soon to a TV near you: *Executions and Human Sacrifices*.

A bit extreme, I admit. But there is a theory that most of us still practice a remnant of ritual sacrifice with respect to circumcision, wherein males have a piece of their reproductive organ, the foreskin of the penis, excised to avoid having to cut up a whole person.[23]

Human sacrifices are based on superstition and religious beliefs, using magic to please the gods in such a way that they will reward this commitment of taking a human life, the most valuable of all commodities. Remarking on the resurgence of interest in sacrificial rituals, particularly within Tantric sects in India that worship Kali, the goddess of destruction, one expert summarized: "They say Kali looks after those who look after her; bringing riches to the poor, revenge to the oppressed, and fertility to the childless—if she's paid with blood."[24]

There are literally millions of people who still subscribe to the beliefs that ritual public killings will prevent disasters and ensure good fortune. One South American shaman who was interviewed for a research project on sacrificial rituals believed with certainty that because sacrifices had been curtailed in recent years, that was one reason why there had been an increase in earthquakes and tsunamis.[25] She pined for the days when it had been so easy to take an orphan and kill the child to please the spirits.

St. Augustine described in his *Confessions* the disappointment and horror he felt when one of his prize students, a budding religious and legal scholar, was dragged to the gladiatorial games by friends and became caught up in the violent bloodlust: "Because along with the sight of blood he drank down a deep draught of inhumanity. He did not turn away, he continued to look, reveling in the wild frenzy without even realizing it, feasting his eyes on that damnable fight and making himself drunk on bloody sensuality."[26]

It was the works of writers like Augustine and the rise of Christianity that were partially responsible for a new consciousness about valuing human life. In the fourth century CE, Emperor Constantine finally attempted to reduce if not abolish gladiatorial events and human sacrifices, finding them both inhumane and a waste of manpower that was needed for more productive pursuits—like keeping the empire from falling apart. Eventually, the practice slowly died out of its own accord, although there persisted for another century the public slaughter of wild animals for public entertainment (which continues to this day in many parts of the world).

BUYING VOTES WITH SPECTACLES OF VIOLENCE

Whether killing people for sport in the arena, or doing so for a more private audience to please the spirits, there is some form of audience participation in the violence. In the case of gladiatorial combat, the spectators enjoyed the spectacle vicariously, just as in our contemporary versions of football, rugby, boxing, ultimate fighting, wrestling, and other contact sports. Certainly there is a component to appreciating the artistry and agility of the combatants, but also a form of fantasy participation in which members of the audience imagine themselves catching the touchdown pass or knocking out an opponent. Gladiators in all sports act as surrogates, in one sense designed to reduce violence in the world outside the stadium by providing ritualized enactments.

As I have mentioned, the gladiatorial games were originally designed not so much for public entertainment as much as they were a grand display of sacrifice to the gods. It was only over time that they evolved as a form of bribery by politicians to win favor with their constituencies. This was a time in Rome when riots and insurrection were common. The city of one million people had been host to civil war for decades, struggling to adapt to the new republic in which citizens voted for representation. And the most common way to win votes was to buy them by providing free food and entertainment—the more violent, the better. It was in 150 BCE, historian Rupert Matthews observed, that the emphasis changed from a religious ceremony to pure entertainment for public consumption.[27]

One ambitious politician, by the name of Julius Caesar, rose to power largely as the result of putting together the most spectacular display of entertainment violence ever seen in Rome—or anywhere else in the world. He recruited and trained hundreds of gladiators with remarkable skill, adorned them in solid silver armor, and then set them against each other to the thrill of the packed stadium. He forced two senators to fight each other to death. He imported giraffes to be slaughtered; Europeans had never seen such animals in this part of the world. He staged mock naval battles after building a lake for the spectacle. He spent a fortune reenacting famous battles in which opposing sides fought until their opponents were all killed.

The crowds loved the shows so much that they made little protest when Caesar declared himself dictator-for-life. Unfortunately, this life term lasted a mere two years before he was assassinated. Nevertheless, the lesson learned was one that was followed by Caesar's successors: If you want to grab and keep power, or merely earn public adulation, the most effective way to do so is to satisfy constituents' lust for blood.

Once the public grew tired of the same old violence for sport, the rulers had to construct new and more inventive ways to keep the masses satisfied. As the values in Rome changed over time, eventually outlawing killing in the arena, the next logical step was to bring the violence outside the walls to earn public support. Starting a war is perhaps the most flamboyant and dramatic way to do this. Throughout history, kings, queens, emperors, dictators, prime ministers, and presidents have launched attacks against real or imagined enemies in order to gain or hold popularity. Patriotism trumps criticism in any kind of military victory, as Presidents Bush I and II discovered with their Middle Eastern campaigns, just as other leaders have done before them. Nothing occupies public attention more than an old-fashioned war with daily news reports of battles and death counts, video footage of the action, and administration officials presenting the best possible spin on the results.

It may well seem that the extreme bloodshed of Roman, Greek, and Aztec times is beyond anything we could ever imagine. Yet the shift we have made in our own culture, from the Coliseum to the television, movie, or computer screen, testifies to the continued interest in entertainment violence in a different context. What we watch in the movie *Gladiator*, the television drama *Spartacus*, or the predator documentaries is pretty much the same melodrama that was observed live centuries ago. The structure of the entertainment is still basically the same even if we have invented a simulated way to satisfy this lust for blood.

Chapter 3

True Crime

At the ripe age of twenty, Franz Kafka already felt his life was over. He felt awkward, uncertain, despairing, and love-struck toward a woman who seemed unattainable. Yet it was only books that saved him, first as a voracious reader and then as the visionary writer of classics like *The Trial* and *Metamorphosis*, dark and disturbing stories that reflected his own inner pain (and eventually tuberculosis). "I think we ought to read only the kinds of books that wound and stab us," he observed. "If the book we are reading doesn't wake us up with a blow on the head, then what are we reading it for?"[1] Kafka felt strongly that a book should affect the reader like a disaster, a suicide, or the death of a loved one.

Kafka's idea was that the purpose of entertainment media like literature or drama was to wake up "the frozen sea inside us." Its most ambitious goal was to serve the public desire to be shocked, aroused, and disturbed. Although he was speaking primarily about the realm of fiction, there is so much more power embedded in true-life stories, especially those that are in any way related to violence or death.

LITERATURE EXPLORES THE DARK SIDE

As long as there has been storytelling, there has been violent entertainment to engage the audience and keep them interested in the narrative. Homer's

Iliad contains plenty of murder, battles, and mass executions. Chaucer's *Canterbury Tales* has its share of assaults and death. The epic poem *Beowulf* has plenty of blood and killing. The same is true of Dante's *Inferno*. Shakespeare's *Hamlet* and *Macbeth* are loaded with murder and suicide. The Old Testament contains numerous episodes of murder, patricide, genocide, suicide, and human sacrifice, just as the New Testament is filled with ritual torture, riots, and public executions.

There has always been a strong market for true-crime stories, whether presented in newspapers, comics, cartoons, films, books, or television. Some of the greatest American writers of the nineteenth century—Edgar Allan Poe, Nathaniel Hawthorne, Herman Melville—all made a living from this enterprise. The best-selling writers of today specialize in horror (e.g., Stephen King, Dean Koontz, and Peter Straub), crime (e.g., Mary Higgins Clark, James Ellroy, Michael Connelly, and John Grisham), serial killing (e.g., James Patterson, Thomas Harris, and Chelsea Cain), and terrorism (e.g., Tom Clancy and Vince Flynn). Their popularity attests to the widespread interest in what Kafka described as being wounded and stabbed. I count myself among those who enjoy such perverse pleasures.

Nathaniel Hawthorne's son would have been disappointed in me, as he was in his own father, calling the elder Hawthorne's interest in true crime "pathetic." "However pathetic it may have been," literature professor and crime writer Harold Schechter observed, "it certainly reflected the tastes of his countrymen, who possessed an unappeasable appetite for true-life stories of horrible murders and ghastly accidents—a taste that the popular press was only too happy to feed."[2] Even classics like Jane Austen's novels have been "zombieized" with *Sense and Sensibility and Sea Monsters* and *Pride and Prejudice and Zombies: The Classic Regency Romance Now*

Zombies are everywhere! They are not only featured in dozens of different films but they even inhabit the adaptation of Jane Austen's classic novel in the form of *Pride and Prejudice and Zombies*. The popularity of zombies in film and fiction has led a number of scholars to speculate that they represent rampant materialism, "America devouring itself," existential "uproarious meditation on the nature of death," or a "symbol of racial oppression."[3] Yet in all their many forms and manifestations, they aren't just an immersion in horror and gore but "the only movies that give much thought to the physicality of death."[4]

with Ultraviolent Mayhem. The latter opens with: "It is a truth universally acknowledged that a zombie in possession of brains must be in want of more brains."[5] The books have become so popular that now the author has worked his way into biography with *Abraham Lincoln: Vampire Hunter.*[6]

It was during the eighteenth century, the Age of Reason, that beliefs in supernatural phenomena were attacked aggressively. Interestingly, one device for doing so was to convert horror, as well as unexplained mysteries and fears, into literature. The first identified gothic horror tale, *Castle of Otranto*, was written in 1764, although it took another half century before the genre of horror fiction and true crime really caught on.

The first true-crime sensation occurred in the middle of the eighteenth century in England with the publication of a pamphlet describing a brutal crime, *The Murder in the Red Barn.* There was such public interest in the crime that over ten million copies sold, exceeding the population at the time! The scene of the crime, the red barn, also became a famous tourist attraction with thousands of people visiting before it was eventually destroyed.

In the late nineteenth century, a notorious murder took place in Massachusetts that has held the public's interest ever since: the alleged murder by Lizzie Borden of her parents. There have been hundreds of articles written about the crime, as well as books, movies, plays, even a ballet and an opera! Yet what was most noteworthy about the immediate aftermath was the

Established in 1845, the *National Police Gazette* was among the first lurid tabloids that specialized in stories of violence including murders, executions, assaults, and crimes of passion. Dozens of new magazines, like *True Police Cases*, *True Crime*, *Master Detective*, *Lady Killers*, *Women in Crime*, and *Confessions of a Private Dick*, entered the market during the following decades to feed the public interest in violent crime. Photo courtesy of the Library of Congress.

CAUGHT IN THE SHAFTING.

MISS SABINA GOUDETTE WHIRLED AROUND AND HORRIBLY MANGLED IN THE NORTH GROSVENOR COTTON MILLS, NEAR PUTNAM, CONN.

publication of books that presented details of the violence in the most vivid and lurid prose. "There was blood everywhere," wrote one such author, "on the flowered carpet, on the wall over the sofa, and even splattered on the picture hanging from the wall. Andrew's head was bent slightly to the right, but his face was unrecognizable as human. There were eleven distinct cuts across the forehead between the ears and above the mouth, slicing the flesh into a grotesque, seething patchwork. Fresh blood still seeped from the wounds. One eye had been cut in half and dangled from its socket. The nose had been severed, lopped loose from the upper jaw."[7]

More than a century after the murder, there is still a huge interest in this brutal, unsolved ax murder. Rising interest in more explicit true-crime stories coincided with these two famous murders. The *National Police Gazette*, for instance, was launched to specially address the public interest in violence. The editors didn't even pretend to be a news source for anything other than grisly accidents, murders, and other crimes. The *Gazette* featured stories of suicide (a man crucifies himself!), torture (at the hands of bloodthirsty savage Indians), violent accidents (a woman mangled in a cotton gin), and all kinds of brutal death, illustrated with gruesome drawings.

Literature is filled with stories about the dark side of human nature—the "other," Mr. Hyde, the Id, the Shadow. The original edition of *Grimm's Fairy Tales* was grim indeed. Of course Hansel and Gretel is a story about cannibalism, Little Red Riding Hood about rape and murder, but one of the first tales the Grimms produced, "How the Children Played Butcher with Each Other," takes brutality and violence to a whole new level, one that is difficult to fathom for an audience of children (which is why the story was deleted from the second edition).

The story is about two brothers who are playing outside together when they watch a pig being slaughtered with a knife slashed across the animal's throat and the blood gushing out. One brother invites the other to play butcher with him and so takes the knife and cuts his younger brother's throat, just as he witnessed a few minutes earlier. The mother, who was upstairs bathing her infant child, looked out the window and saw with horror what happened. She rushed outside, grabbed the bloody knife from her dead son's neck, and then stabbed her murderous son in a fit of anger. As if this isn't horrifying enough, the mother goes back into the house to discover that her infant drowned in the bathtub while she was gone. The mother then hangs herself in grief, after which the father returns home and dies suddenly after discovering his family gone.

I'm not sure what exactly the moral of this story should be. Perhaps it is one of the first warnings about allowing children to watch acts of violence because they may be inclined to imitate them. But if that is the case, then why read this story to children who might do exactly that?

In a scholarly annotation of classic fairy tales, Maria Tatar found a "complex duality" in the stories, "an ability to extract pleasure from pain."[8] She is referring, of course, to the bloodcurdling violence that so permeates plotlines. She cites "The Juniper Tree" as one example in which a stepmother cuts off the head of her stepson and then serves it in a stew to his father. She finally ends up crushed to death under a big rock. Since children tend to laugh hilariously at such narratives, Tatar believes that they serve a crucial function to help them come to terms with fears and anxieties they don't yet understand.[9] Most of the best stories don't have neat endings but leave it to the listener/reader to resolve things as an exercise in reflective thought.

Harold Schechter makes the point that even the most classic and revered American literature is filled with explicit violence. "Incest, rape, cannibalism, torture, homicide in all its myriad forms (matri-, patri-, regi-, infanti-, etc.)—the classics are packed with this stuff."[10] Edgar Allan Poe is just one example of a writer who filled his stories with gruesome details of horror and bloodlust. The operating philosophy that he believed most contributed to his popularity was to make certain that his narratives contained "the ludicrous heightened into the grotesque; the fearful colored into the horrible; the singular wrought into the strange."[11] Now *that* is a

Edgar Allan Poe became one of the first best-selling horror writers, a forerunner to Stephen King and Dean Koontz. His stories, such as "The Tell-Tale Heart" and "The Pit and the Pendulum," became classics that were eventually made into recordings and films.

recipe for success, and certainly a reason for the newfound interest of rewriting Jane Austen novels and including zombies or sea monsters.

During Poe and Austen's era, a new theater opened in Paris, the Grand Guignol, which was the first devoted entirely to the presentation of the most graphic and depraved violence that could be conceived at the time. The plan was to cross every imaginable taboo and so thoroughly shock the audience into a stupor that they would never recover from the experience. Writing about the debut of the first gory play, one critic commented: "Now, watching live realistic and gory enactments of mutilation, rape, torture, and murder, each spectator could play out his fantasies of victimization and retribution."[12] It is interesting that he recognized that identification with characters takes place on both sides of the violence equation, that is, audiences put themselves in the place of both killer *and* victim.

Even more gruesome than today's most violent splatter films, with their advanced special effects, the plays featured "gushing blood by the potful"[13] with the sole aim of making people sick. The productions proved so popular and successful that the formula was imitated by other theaters around the world.

TRUE CRIME IS EVEN BETTER THAN THE MADE-UP STUFF

"Live from News One," the sonorous voice breaks into your regularly scheduled program to present the latest carnage on the highway. A jerky camera shows an aerial view of a vacant highway. You can hear the rotor of a helicopter in the background, making it difficult to hear the voice-over, but the image is clear: A lone man standing next to his car screaming something at the gods, or maybe speaking to himself or the audience.

A number of years ago, a man who felt despondent over the way he was treated by his health insurance company decided to take his own life—on live television—for the entertainment of the masses. Thousands of viewers watched in fascinated horror as the man spread out a banner proclaiming, "Live Free, Love Safe or Die!" Then he proceeded to set himself on fire and, while running across the blocked-off freeway, blew his head off with a shotgun, also killing his dog in the collateral damage.

This news story, broadcast on most of the major stations in Los Angeles, commanded a sizeable viewership, just as you would imagine. A news director commented, "Usually the ratings shoot sky-high, and the viewers use their remote controls and zap from station to station. They watch them."[14] Such knowledge was borne from experience in which not

Truman Capote is credited with writing one of the first successful true-crime books, written in a style that not only described the violence and murders in vivid details but also got inside the killers' heads. The appeal of such books is not only to provide entertainment but also to teach readers about the circumstances that may lead to murder so that they might better protect themselves against a similar fate.

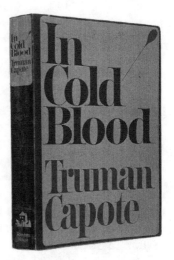

too many years earlier in Los Angeles, the O. J. Simpson murder case commanded such attention that even though there was a genocide going on in Rwanda at the time in which one million people were killed in a single month, the media didn't consider it newsworthy compared to the allure of a celebrity murder trial.[15]

There is a reason why the world—and your community—seems like such a violent and dangerous place. Roughly 15 to 20 percent of all news content in the media features violent crime; it is also the single most frequently reported topic on television.[16] Furthermore, there is a marked desensitization that develops among viewers in which it takes progressively more graphic and detailed stories to keep people interested. Over time we hardly notice the murder and mayhem. It takes a truly extraordinary act of violence, a story vividly told, in order to hold viewer attention. It is novelty that makes the difference, especially when it involves some killer on the rampage.

The genre of true-crime books is among the most consistent sellers in any publisher's list. Whereas crimes of revenge and impulse murder, or political shenanigans, do have their share of the market, there is nothing that comes close to serial killer books—"the more gruesome and grotesque, the better," in the words of one editor.[17] Although there have been true-crime comics and pamphlets around since the days of Jack the Ripper, it wasn't until Truman Capote's *In Cold Blood* was published in the 1960s that the public discovered a new guilty pleasure.

Capote's book is not nearly bloody and lurid enough to meet today's standards, yet it was groundbreaking at the time to have such a distinguished writer take on the subject of a senseless murder. Rather than merely describing the details of the attempted robbery that went wildly wrong, ending up in mass murder, Capote went deep into the killers' minds to unravel what led them to commit such acts. The book was an immediate sensation that launched thousands of imitations (including one that I wrote).

A number of years ago I collaborated with a student of mine to write a story about his forays into the world of serial killers. He was a precocious lad of eighteen, a freshman in college, when he first expressed an interest in studying the inner world of professional predators. Jason came up with the rather audacious plan that he would craft an assignment for a class into an excuse to write several infamous serial killers who were then imprisoned on death row. Ever since he had been a young boy, Jason had been fascinated by killers, reading their biographies and carefully following tales of their exploits in the media.

Jason was a bright boy and also very creative. He came up with a plan that he would carefully research the optimal bait by which to attract the attention of a particular killer. In the case of Charles Manson (responsible for the "Helter Skelter" killings), he literally spoke his language, writing to him in a jibberish syntax that Manson seemed to understand. With Jeffrey Dahmer (the cannibal) he mimicked the killer's childhood history, writing to him about a fictitious past that would sound familiar. With John Wayne Gacy (the Clown Killer), Jason realized he had a physical resemblance to Gacy's victims and so presented himself as sexually confused and malleable. Jason discovered that Richard Ramirez (the California Night Stalker) was attracted to Asian women, so he claimed to head a satanic cult composed of beautiful Asian models who worshipped Ramirez. Henry Lee Lucas (killer of two hundred) fancied himself as an artist, so Jason claimed to be an art dealer who wanted to represent him. To make a very long story short, Jason managed to insinuate himself into the lives of a half dozen serial killers, earning their trust, encouraging them to share secrets, and in the case of Gacy, stimulating an obsession and infatuation.

As Jason's projects escalated from letter writing to more personal contact, Jason began visiting some of these killers, Gacy most of all. Whereas Jason believed he was manipulating these killers, demonstrating his superior intellect, it turned out that Gacy was actually planning to rape and murder him as his "last victim" (hence the title of our book).[18] It was during their last visit together, a few weeks before Gacy's scheduled execution, that Gacy managed to hold a pen to Jason's carotid artery, masturbating as he whispered that he was going to kill Jason at the moment

Jason Moss, collaborator with the author on a true-crime book that told the story of his exploits trying to manipulate and earn the trust of a half dozen famous serial killers. Ultimately, the book's title, *The Last Victim*, foreshadowed Jason's eventual tragic end.

of his ejaculation. Jason's life was spared only because a lawyer happened to be walking by the cell and interrupted the attempted murder.

Jason eventually recovered some semblance of his composure, resumed his studies in earnest, and we ended up writing this book together, which eventually became a bestseller and was made into a Hollywood movie. Jason was able to use the money from the book to attend law school, and we lost touch with each other for several years thereafter. Meanwhile, there was incredible interest in this project. Web sites and blogs were launched to celebrate or criticize what Jason had done as audacious or immoral. Women pestered him as groupies. Fame and fortune resulted because of the incredible interest in this inner world of serial killers. And I must admit that I was dumbfounded.

Why was there such overwhelming interest in this subject? Why are people so intrigued with these killers who think nothing of taking another life? There are legions of books published each year that glorify and celebrate their exploits, delving deeply into their violent crimes and psychopathic disregard for human life. There is even a coffee table photographic book that presents the likenesses of famous killers like Jesse James, the Dalton Brothers, and Bonnie and Clyde, as well as those who are bit more obscure.[19]

NEW DEVELOPMENTS

In spite of widespread belief that serial killers are both clever and brilliant in the mold of Hannibal Lecter from *The Silence of the Lambs*, they are

Jeffrey Kottler and Jason Moss working on the book *The Last Victim*. This was a title that had been selected to describe the way that Jason had suffered psychologically as a result of getting too close to killers like John Wayne Gacy, Charles Manson, Jeffrey Dahmer, Henry Lee Lucas, and Richard Ramirez. Little did he know that the toxic effects would continue to fester to the point that Jason's own suffering became intolerable. It is difficult to immerse oneself in the world of murder and violence without feeling some negative effects, especially with regard to increased mistrust of others, disturbing dreams and images, and sometimes greater hostility.

often neither particularly bright nor attractive—in fact, what I learned from interviewing several is that they are fairly stupid and unimaginative, not at all like the scheming operators you see in the movies.

What is the attraction that people have to the whole genre of true crime, reading about the most horrific examples of inhumanity and brutality? What is the appeal of this lust for blood—at a safe distance?

I must confess that I have been thinking about these questions for the past decade since the book was first published, still mulling over the reasons why violence is such a riveting subject to explore. I could still find few answers that really made sense or captured the essence of what appeared to be going on.

I lost interest in true crime and the subject of serial killers immediately after the book was completed. In fact, I have never been that interested in this genre but rather was intrigued by the brilliance and capability of Jason. We tried to keep in touch after Jason left for law school, but eventually our only contact involved brief e-mails or conversations about selling the movie rights. As a newly minted lawyer, Jason was driving our agent crazy with detailed revisions and objections to every paragraph on contracts. Finally, after one relinquished the movie rights that he locked up for years, the book became available again and was purchased by Clark Peterson, the producer of *Monster*, which won an Academy Award for Charlize Theron as best actress.

Jason was ecstatic about the possibility that the movie about him would finally be made: the book would finally come to the big screen. Everything was finally falling into place. It was May in 2006 when Jason called me to check in and talk about new developments.

NOT THE END OF THE STORY

Just two weeks later, on June 6, 2006, Jason was in an especially good mood. For the previous weeks he had been severely depressed and erratic in his behavior. He would become angry at the slightest provocation. He spent most of his days in bed, using an assortment of drugs and watching movies. Yet on this particular day he woke up with more energy than he had a long time.[20]

Jason asked his wife to make a deposit at the bank, an errand that seemed unnecessary given the small amount of the check. She was also struck by how unusual it was that he would trust her with anything related to money: Jason controlled almost every aspect of their lives. It was while standing in line that she examined the check and noticed that the date was absent. She found this particularly strange because Jason was so meticulous about everything he did. She shrugged. Maybe it was the drugs he had been taking that distracted him.

She looked around the bank and caught a glimpse of the date: 6/6/06. There was something about those numbers that seemed ominous, their association with Satan. Lately, Jason had become more and more engrossed in satanic cults, an interest that began during his "collaboration" with serial killer Richard Ramirez. Suddenly, she felt this incredibly strong impulse that something was very wrong. Without another thought she raced back to her car and headed home.

Jason's wife walked into the house and noticed a large bottle of Jack Daniels sitting on the kitchen counter, half emptied in the time she'd been gone. Jason never drank alcohol, so this made her pulse race even more. She called out to him but received no response.

She walked upstairs, feeling increasingly anxious. Jason always had the television going, but now the house was eerily quiet. She walked into the bedroom, then peered in the bathroom, where she found her husband "dead of a self-inflicted gunshot wound," in the words of the coroner. He was sitting on the floor, propped up against the bathtub. What struck her most was that it was the first time she could ever remember that he looked at peace—all the tension in his face was gone.

THE LAST VICTIM AFTER ALL

Our book was supposed to have a happy ending. John Wayne Gacy was executed for his crimes. Jason was a hero, a media sensation, a big hit on the talk show circuit. He hit the jackpot in terms of the attention he so craved and the money that would finance his education. He proved to his parents, and the rest of the world, that through sheer force of will, he really could do almost anything he wanted.

As I mentioned, I lost touch with Jason for many years after he left home to go to law school at the University of Michigan. At that time he had been absolutely giddy with the possibilities for the future and ready to move on to new and better things. I had understood from the beginning of our relationship that Jason trusted nobody, including me: people existed in his world to serve him. In some ways I felt considerable relief that he had moved on. I experienced my own traumatic stress delving into the secret world of serial killers, not to mention that I found it exhausting managing my time with Jason, who could be quite demanding.

Over the next few years we would occasionally correspond or chat briefly, but it wasn't until I got involved in the screenplay for the movie that I learned what had happened in Jason's life. Nothing could have prepared me for what had transformed him from the precocious boy I had once known into the terrified and raging man he had become. Yes, I know: readers of the book, colleagues, friends, others who knew Jason (if anyone could really know him), all claim to have seen the earliest signs of his darkness and depravity. Maybe I was blind to Jason's faults because I genuinely liked him so much and because I was so invested in trying to help him.

I know it was hard for Jason competing with others as an undergraduate student, always needing to be the best in every class, but it was even more difficult for him to adjust to being one brilliant student among so many at a top law school. He studied hard, isolating himself as much as possible to focus on the single-minded goal to excel as he had always done. It didn't take him long to figure out that he would never make money or attain the fame he so desperately sought through a career in law enforcement. He loved the idea of getting close to criminals, the more violent the better, gaining their trust and learning their secrets. He felt an affinity for those without a conscience, often wondering what stopped himself from acting out his most violent impulses. He knew he was smarter than anyone he'd ever met and he could easily outwit anyone who tried to catch him, especially with his new-found knowledge of the law. But Jason also wanted respectability and to be admired. He had been most impressed with John Wayne Gacy above all others because of Gacy's success as a pillar in the community.

During the summer internships, Jason returned home to Las Vegas, where he worked in the public defender's office to get trial experience. He also enjoyed hearing the stories of the criminals he represented; this was even better than reading about them. He realized that the best and brightest among his class were preparing themselves to make bucket loads of money in the corporate world. While he couldn't imagine himself working under those restraints, he now realized that his persuasive powers could be best put to use in the competitive field of litigation. And there was no better place to gain experience in the courtroom than with the indigent.

For a second summer Jason worked for the public defender's office in Las Vegas, putting his competitive talents to work, convincing his employers that he was indispensable. It must have come as quite a blow to graduate from law school and not be offered a permanent position. In fact, it was a disappointment from which he never recovered.

During the time I learned about what had happened to Jason in these intervening years, and was writing this account, I received an e-mail that reads as follows:

> I just recently heard about what happened with Jason Moss. I knew him as a law student here at UM. He was nice to me at first, then changed into an awful person who treated me like dirt, which ended our relationship. We dated briefly, he was sweet, kind and then like Jekyll/Hyde, he would change. I tried to talk to him about getting help. I sensed he was deeply troubled and felt bad for him, but he would turn and accuse me of horrible things.

I tracked down this woman, who, even after all these years, still felt troubled by her brief romantic relationship with Jason.

"It was a Friday when I first heard from him," she recalled. They had been corresponding via the Internet for some weeks and then he called. "I was starting to get sick—the flu or something so I didn't feel well. After we talked for an hour, he convinced me to come over to his apartment. I still don't know how he did that, but he could convince anyone to do anything."

She couldn't understand how sometimes Jason could be so attentive and caring, and then at other times he could be so cruel. "He would say awful mean things, trying to humiliate and hurt me. He twisted everything I said and turned it around. It was scary. Yet he had this power over me. Finally, it was my friends who convinced me to stay away from him."

There must have been others who were early victims of Jason's wrath during this period when he started to change. He was always someone who was so convinced of his own specialness that he lacked the capacity to care much about how others reacted. One of our editors commented to me when he learned about recent events: "I think we all knew that Jason was aberrant in some way—existing somewhere in the margins. Obviously, he was way too invested in a self-image of a person who can control people and events around him. When he started to realize he actually had less and less control over himself, it all started to unravel. If you'll recall, a lot of the editing process was about cloaking his egomania that kept leaking through the lines. I doubt you'll ever have a collaborative challenge to match that one."

His future wife was totally taken with this charismatic young man with so many plans for the future. He was a strange one, no doubt about that, but he had reasonable explanations for everything, including why they saw the movie *Hannibal* on their first date (it was for research about the predators he intended to represent).

Jason felt the need to dominate and control his wife's life totally so he could trust her. He was so tired of being alone, so exhausted trying to manage his perfect outside image, and increasingly afraid of his own impulses. Nightmares disrupted his sleep, reenactments of killings he had studied or conversations he'd had with Gacy, Ramirez, Manson, or Dahmer about their own grisly work. His moods started to fluctuate from those in which he felt boundless energy to times of despair.

After moving back to Las Vegas and taking the law bar exam, Jason experienced the major disappointment of his life in not being offered a job with the public defender's office. He believed this was just another case of people feeling threatened by his brilliance and superior skills. He was right about one thing: many of his colleagues *did* feel threatened by Jason, even if they couldn't articulate why.

Now in his late twenties, Jason was starting to struggle with depressions that were lasting longer and longer. Besides his wife, there was nobody else in his world he would dare trust, certainly not a therapist. He felt all therapists were quacks. Instead, he convinced a doctor to supply him with a succession of antidepressants based on his self-(mis)diagnosis. He tried a half dozen different medications, coupled with a variety of recreational drugs that he began experimenting with—methamphetamines and cocaine when he was down, Valium and Xanax when he felt anxious or manic. Sometimes during an episode he might take as many as a half dozen tranquilizers, coupled with as many sleeping pills, and still find himself so jittery he would have to drive around at night.

Jason settled for going to work with a prestigious law firm in Las Vegas, but he quickly became disgruntled with being a worker instead of a star. He was frustrated at the way the partners ran their operation, continually disappointed that people did not listen to him or meet his expectations, and envious that the partners were raking in all the big money. He was smarter than everyone else, bragging that he would never lose a case: Why didn't people realize this?

Jason was sure he could do better on his own and so opened his own practice, which would give him the opportunities, freedom, and recognition that he so yearned for. On his business card he advertised himself as a "Specialist in Murder, Assault, and other Violent Crimes." Most of the clients he defended were drug dealers, drunk drivers, and child molesters.

Jason loved hearing his clients' stories under the veil of confidentiality, licensed to ask the most personal and pointed questions about what they did and why they did it. He wanted to know how they felt when they committed their crimes. What did it feel like to hurt people? How did they live with themselves afterward? What mistakes had they made? Jason was still a student, still learning from those who had been caught. If he ever decided to act out his own impulses, he would never be so stupid as these idiots who couldn't control themselves and couldn't plan properly.

Meanwhile, Jason was still a haunted man. He frequently had nightmares fueled not only by his past adventures with serial killers but also by his continued indulgence in the world of satanism and perversity. He ordered transcripts from the trial of Jeffrey Dahmer, including the most grisly photographs of the victims who had been cannibalized. He bought magazines that featured explicit gore. And he continued to self-medicate with any drugs he could get hold of, or convince doctors to supply.

During the day there was little respite as he continued to struggle in his work, moving to four different small firms in the next few months. Eventually word got out around town that he was unreliable, mercurial, hostile, and perhaps dangerous. He began taking out his frustrations on his wife, then become remorseful and begging for another chance. He tried to shock her and earn her pity with any stunt he could think of. He cut himself several times in front of her, slashing his arm; another time he made a snowflake design on his belly with cuts of the knife.

She wanted to leave but felt responsible for Jason, knowing that she was the only person in the world who he now trusted even a little bit. Yet Jason's behavior became more disturbed. Finally, she escaped to save herself. She moved back in with her family and tried to put together the pieces of her life. This wasn't easy with Jason calling her eight to ten times each day saying that literally he couldn't live without her, that he needed her, that he couldn't survive on his own. After months of badgering he claimed he had entered therapy and was prepared to begin marriage counseling if she returned. He was a changed man.

In spite of the warnings and pleadings of her family, she returned to Jason. She was a nurse, used to taking care of patients, and her husband was her greatest failure; she believed she could save him. Besides, she'd never met anyone who was so interesting. She liked him being dependent on her and liked being dependent on him.

During the months that she moved back home, Jason had certainly changed, but into something she no longer recognized. He had gambled a lot of money. He bought guns—a 9-millimeter Beretta, an AK-47, and an AR-15 semi-automatic machine gun. This was in addition to his extensive knife collection. He claimed that they were all for protection.

Looking back on the whole tragic episode, she wished she could have done something different. Yet in second-guessing herself, she remembered how impossible it was to make Jason do anything he didn't want to do. He would not seek help from a therapist. He wouldn't ever admit he had a problem. Involuntary hospitalization was never an option because Jason was so good at fooling people; he could be perfectly charming when the situation called for it. As I mentioned, I had spoken to him just a few weeks before his death and he had sounded totally upbeat, just like Jason, filled with all kinds of plans and schemes. Our last conversation ended with a promise that we would stay in touch and even plan another book together.

She finally came to the conclusion that Jason had killed himself not only to put himself out of his misery, but also to save her. He knew that his violence was escalating, fueled by his depression, sense of helplessness, and drugs. It was just a matter of time before he started killing people, her first of all. Jason was finally his own last victim, destroyed by the obsessions with serial killers and the dark worlds they inhabited.

SERIAL KILLER CELEBRITIES

If you feel any sympathy for Jason's tragic end, that is often the writer's purpose in constructing a book, article, or screenplay. If you don't like the character, or at least feel some connection or understanding of his plight, then you won't care what happens to him or her. For example, Hannibal Lecter is among the most brutal sociopaths ever portrayed in fiction (or reality). Taking a life for him was as easy as preparing a meal (which often was the case). Yet the reader of Thomas Harris's books, or viewer of the Hannibal films, actually ends up hoping he will escape capture and survive to kill again.

It is also often the case that the writer of true-crime screenplays or books becomes attached and overinvolved with his subject, actually sympathetic to his plight and an advocate on his behalf. Norman Mailer wrote a biography of murderer Gary Gilmore, *The Executioner's Song*, and ended up fighting on Gilmore's behalf. In the case of Truman Capote, after spending so much time with his subjects, he counted the killers among his friends, escorted them to their execution, and wept in grief for days afterward.[21]

In his scholarly treatise on serial killer celebrities, David Schmid writes critically and disparagingly about Jason's journey, describing it as "the most egregious example of second-order celebrity of true-crime writers" and an obvious attempt "to exploit Gacy's fame for his own pecuniary benefit."[22] My initial reaction after reading this was defensive: How can you say that about someone you don't know, that you just met through a book? I felt a loyalty and commitment to Jason, no matter how wounded he might have been. It was my job to tell his story so that he did come across as someone deserving of understanding. And although Schmid is certainly correct in that Jason was motivated by the prospect of fame and fortune, he really did (in the beginning) have an academic interest in the subject of developing alternative ways to elicit information from professional liars. That Jason was exploitive, even unethical, in the ways he lied, manipulated, and tried to control the killers is certainly true. But . . . (here it comes) Jason really had hoped that this experience would qualify him for admission to a good law school and a career in law enforcement. He was definitely self-serving, but he also had a deep concern for making a positive difference, making his mark in a constructive way.

Since I was out of touch with him for years preceding his suicide, I really don't know where and how things went awry. Did he always have within him the potential to go one way or the other? I have heard other police and law enforcement officers admit that if they hadn't joined the force they might very well have become criminals themselves. It wasn't the crime that attracted them but the violence, drama, action, and excitement of living on the edge, the adrenaline rush that comes from carrying a gun and having authority to command attention and compliance.

Jason's story is an extreme example of someone attracted to true crime who was literally driven mad by the obsession. For most of us, reading about murder provides both a form of alluring entertainment, as well as a kind of education about worst-case scenarios that might somehow prevent us from becoming victims ourselves. Reading (or viewing) accounts of mayhem and murder offers lessons about how to avoid becoming a victim.

Each of us is a complex composite of calculation and impulsivity, selfishness and altruism, reason and emotion, transparency and secrecy, compassion and exploitation. Each of us has the capacity for violence, madness, immorality, and self-destructiveness, yet it is the rare individual who acts on these impulses. Likewise, although there are notable cases of

This image of someone screaming in agony represents the demons that reside in every one of us, whether they haunt us in fantasies, dreams, or disturbing thoughts and anxious feelings. Exploring true crime and violence vicariously can not only provide a safe outlet for pent-up aggression and feed curiosity about the forbidden, but it can help us to come to terms with the dark side of human nature. It is through acknowledgment of such impulses, as well as discussion of them in honest and open ways, that it is often possible to live a more peaceful, compassionate life. Whereas some people are traumatized by exposure to violence, loss, and abuse, others report "post-traumatic growth" and greater resilience as a result of the meaning they find or create from the experience.23 Image © Konstantynov, 2009. Used under license of Shutterstock.com.

"divine madness," extraordinary creative geniuses like writers Ernest Hemingway, Virginia Woolf, and Sylvia Plath, actors like Judy Garland, Marilyn Monroe, and Heath Ledger, or artists like Mark Rothko and Vincent van Gogh, the vast majority of us are able to *enhance* our lives as a result of investigating the dark and forbidden aspects of existence.24 Although there is much attention and publicity related to those soldiers returning from war who are suffering from post-traumatic stress, or others experiencing trauma as a result of exposure to crime, disaster, terrorism, violence, or abuse, there are also those who are made stronger by such experiences. Such "post-traumatic growth" occurs when people are able to learn from their own (or others') misery. They find ways to create meaning from the suffering they experienced and report feeling more alive and engaged with life after facing near-death episodes or loss.25 This is true as well for volunteers and professional helpers who experience vicarious trauma as a result of being so close to the misery of others.26 It so happens that many people become more resilient after facing hardships and life-threatening challenges.[27] While speculative, it may also be entirely possible that we seek to fortify ourselves against future adversity by building immunity through progressive exposure to fear-inducing stimuli such as true crime or other entertainment violence.

During these journeys into the dark side of human nature, there are opportunities to explore and come to terms with the hurtful aspects of ourselves, whether directed inward or toward others. That is one reason why it is so important to acknowledge the disturbing feelings evoked by forays into vicarious crime and violence. There are feelings of arousal and curiosity, also accompanied by shame and guilt. For some, a very small minority, fascination with crime and murder can indeed create a tumult of anxiety leading, in some cases, to violent or self-destructive behavior. For most of us, however, it is through such explorations that we experience and come to terms with our most forbidden desires. We are able to find "relatively" benign outlets to cleanse ourselves of aggression and learn to live with aspects of our humanity that can only be controlled through greater awareness, ownership, and acceptance of the consequences of such behavior.

Chapter 4
Sports Fans

It's a Friday night in Los Angeles. There's plenty going on in the city—poetry readings, comedy club routines, concerts, a Lakers basketball game, hundreds of high school football games, but here I am standing in a snaking line of hundreds of people winding through a parking lot. We are at a golf course clubhouse, but clearly this is no sport of gentlemen and kings. Besides myself and a friend, there is nobody over twenty-five years old. I can hear hip-hop music blaring from inside.

As the line inches forward and we approach the entrance, I see two ambulances parked in front, flanked by emergency personnel. Standing in front of them are six huge security guards dressed in identical black suits. Most have shaved heads and an assortment of tattoos that can be seen creeping out of their collars. They are frisking people as they walk through the entrance.

Once inside I see a huge ballroom crammed with people milling around, drinking beer and eating heaping plates of nachos. I am surprised by how many women are here, both as dates and in pairs.

The room is arranged with concentric circles of chairs surrounding a stage located in the middle, the fighting ring encased as a cage. It looks like a mini-playground, a hexagon surrounded by thick black wire fencing.

Cage fighting, mixed martial arts, or ultimate fighting, is the latest incarnation of gladiators locked in combat, although it resembles the no-holds-barred version that was first invented in ancient Greece and Rome: fighters are allowed—even encouraged—to beat one another into oblivion using hands, feet, elbows, knees, almost anything except a blunt instrument. By comparison, boxing is for wimps with its cushioned gloves and elaborate rules. Of course cage fighting has rules too, but they include things like you're not allowed to spit your mouth guard at your opponent or insert your finger into any orifice. Other than that, pretty much anything else goes.

Sitting on my right is Flynn, an ex-college wrestler and wrestling coach, who is here to watch some of his friends fight. He's been in this world of wrestling and fighting for most of his life, although you'd never guess it from his easygoing, soft-spoken presence. "You seem like such a peaceful kind of guy," I commented to him while we waited for the fights to begin.

"I am," Flynn laughed. "But watch me when the fight starts."

I asked Flynn how he got into this sort of thing since I know he sometimes manages and trains fighters.

"I wrestled since I was eight years old. I've always been drawn to ultimate fighting as an extension of wrestling. It was the culture I grew up in. Guys would come over to my house after school and we'd watch the fights on TV and then go outside and stage our own fights on the trampoline."

"So," I asked him, "what is it about this sort of entertainment that appeals to so many people?" I gesture around the room at all the couples on date night, single girls, and everyone else who paid as much as a hundred dollars per ticket.

"As a fan, this sort of thing appeals to the deepest part of us—at our most primitive and raw element. I don't even see it as violent but as a sport, a competition, a test of skill." Flynn looked thoughtful for a moment, so I waited.

"No," he added. "That's not really true. If I'm really honest the fights are really boring if someone doesn't get hurt."

Flynn explained to me that the fighters only make a few hundred dollars. On top of that they are expected to sell at least thirty tickets to friends in order to be included in the event.

"So," I couldn't help but ask, "why the heck do they subject themselves to this kind of punishment, being locked in a cage with someone else who intends to do them serious harm?"

"It's the girls," Flynn says casually.

"The girls?"

"Yeah. Look around you." Flynn points to two different pairs of rather attractive young women sitting in the row in front of us. They are wearing short skirts and tops that display major cleavage. "The girls love the fighters. They're lining up to meet them after the fight."

It occurs to me this is not unlike the phenomena that occurred with gladiators in ancient Rome who had their own share of groupies and love interests. Even the daughters of senators and emperors fell in love with their favorite warriors. Women would wear combs in their hair, carved in a likeness of their hero's symbol or in the shape of a sword and dipped in their blood.

FIGHTING IN A CAGE

It was in ancient Greece and Rome that battles between individual fighters in the ring were first presented for public entertainment. To add to the appeal of the fights, as well as to celebrate the aesthetic beauty of the human body, the Greeks would arrange wrestling and boxing tournaments in the nude, with oiled bodies on display. The Romans were considerably more inhibited with respect to sexual matters—with the noted exception of Caligula's orgies—so their boxing tournaments featured fighters in their underwear, similar to the gladiator garments without the armor.

Unlike ultimate fighting described earlier, and more similar to modern-day boxing, the fighters were not permitted to grapple or kick each other, but only to use their fists to pummel each other. The difference, however, is that there was no time limit and the fight only ended when one of the fighters surrendered or was beaten unconscious.

Given the increasing popularity of ultimate fighting among all age groups, rules have slowly been implemented to protect fighters from becoming so brutally hurt that they are disabled or killed. But anything short of that is wildly appreciated by fans.

Trey is an executive for a liquor and beer distributor, one of the largest wholesalers in the country. "The bars are swarming whenever the cage fighting is on. Standing room only. People plan their weekends around it. They all know the fighters and follow them whenever they're on. The bars love it. As a marketing person, these are the most loyal consumers. They drink themselves into oblivion while screaming for their favorite fighter. The bars charge ten dollars and require each patron to buy at least two drinks, so they make a fortune. And then as soon as the fights end, the bars empty out."

"How do you explain this phenomenon?" I asked him.

"No clue. But who cares? It's fun!"

I kept asking this question over and over, often getting the same answer. People didn't seem to care much about why they enjoyed the violence; most preferred not to think about it at all because it might ruin their fun.

Mixed martial arts, or "cage fighting," is illegal in many states because of its brutality and no-holds-barred brawls. Yet it is the fastest-growing sport in the United States and a billion-dollar industry that is described as a "lifestyle" rather than just another spectator sport.[1] Photo courtesy of US Army.

I looked around the venue during the first few fights, more curious about the crowd's behavior than the fighters themselves. I was just so surprised to find so many women in attendance, most of whom were enjoying themselves immensely, ogling the oiled bodies of the men, screaming their hearts out for their heroes.

It struck me that this was a clear example of evolution at work. Women in their prime mating years are unconsciously attracted to successful warriors who, in the good old days, would have been the ones who enjoyed the greatest status and access to meat and resources. These are the alpha males in this culture and, whether the women realize it or not, they are drawn to guys who display ultimate masculine dominance qualities.

Sitting on my left is a woman a bit older than the norm, perhaps in her thirties. She is with her boyfriend and she keeps asking him if they can leave yet. Every time a fight begins, she averts her head and covers her eyes, sometimes daring a peek between her fingers. It doesn't look at all like she is lusting after the guys in the ring, but rather is here to accompany her friend who is avidly watching the show.

Speaking of the fights themselves, the first one lasted exactly twelve seconds. The two guys walked through the door of the cage, faced each other in a boxing stance, and then the horn sounded and the action began. The guy in the white bike shorts immediately launched a kick at his opponent in black, baggy nylons. Baggy pants ducked underneath it and delivered a forearm to the guy's head, knocking him to his knees, after which he collapsed on the floor.

The girl on my left missed the whole thing, for which she seemed grateful. Trey, on my right, explained the fight was over, that bike shorts had a cut above his eye.

And so it went, three-minute rounds for the amateurs and five-minute rounds for the pros, each fight usually ending after a few minutes of grappling. Then one of them is thrown to the mat, after which his face is pounded into the ground until he gives up. The survivor raises his hands in the air, pounds his chest, and then the crowd roars. Me too.

Actually, as brutal as the display of violence might be, it was strangely interesting to watch. I wasn't willing to admit that I'd go again, but Trey had no compunctions about enjoying the drama in the cage and wanting more.

"You know, that last fight?" he asked me. "When I was watching I could feel my heart pounding, kind of like my blood was boiling. It's like it was me in there. Pretty awesome, huh?"

I was prepared to feel scorn for this whole ridiculous display of staged violence. I was appalled at the very idea that people would pay to watch guys in a cage trying their best to hurt one another. So I was surprised to find myself admiring the level of skill that was demonstrated. Besides the usual fisticuffs, the fighters use all kinds of spins, kicks, grapple holds, and maneuvers they borrowed from kickboxing, judo, wrestling, karate, and every other fighting discipline. They also have a kind of dignity in their performances. After each fight, the combatants hug one another in what appears to be genuine respect. I don't see evidence of pouting or even residual aggression. Even the losers are gracious in defeat. The fighters are exhausted, of course, and relieved they survived with their bodies reasonably intact, but they also seem remarkably calm and proud of themselves.

The audience, as well, was remarkably well behaved. There are more than a thousand young people crowded in a room reeking of violence and alcohol. Yet they are more controlled than the bleachers at any baseball game.

I look around the room and everyone is having a wonderful time. The beer is flowing. The music is pulsing. The fighters who have finished their battles are congratulated by their friends and fans. Even the couple next to me seems to be enjoying themselves (although the woman is resting her head on her boyfriend's shoulder and just seems to be enjoying being with him). What am doing here? I wonder. Although I doubt I will be returning to a fight again, I leave understanding its definite appeal. And I know I'm not the only one.

You would think that a victim of spousal abuse would have a hard time watching people pummeling one another half to death. On the contrary, one woman I interviewed loves watching mixed martial arts on pay-per-view even though she is on a very tight budget after divorcing her abusive husband. "The truth is that I *love* violence on television or the big screen or scheduled fights even though I know it doesn't make sense, given my history. But I think it's interesting that the few times I actually went to see a fight in person, it was too much for me and I had to leave."

She finds the difference astonishing in that when she watches a fight at home and can yell and scream her heart out, she totally enjoys the show. She can give vent to her forbidden impulses and feelings that might otherwise elicit shame when others are around.

"Not only can I not stand seeing fighters in the ring but I actually have zero tolerance for any sort of fights between people I know. In these situations I plead with people to stop arguing or fighting and do everything I can to stop it. It just makes me sick. And I have to do something."

She is describing the way a view-screen, whether on a television, computer, or in a movie theater, acts as a filter, making acts of violence more easily digestible. As long as she is watching strangers fighting during a staged event, in the comfort and solitude of her living room, she can enjoy the spectacle. Yet once she is physically present, surrounded by other witnesses—even if they, too, are having a good time and validating the legitimacy of the arousal—she finds the experience way too real and reminiscent of the physical abuse she suffered firsthand.

This woman's complex and differential reactions to watching violence as painful or pleasurable echoes what many people feel yet are unable to explain. How is it that you can watch some examples of simulated or staged brutality in a play, movie, or TV show, yet find others so abhorrent that you feel sick to your stomach? It is not only a matter of degree, that is, how explicit the depictions might be, but also your prior associations with events that may resemble what is being acted out. Each of us has different tolerances, varied interpretations, and quite personal reactions to the same violent entertainment. That is one reason there is so much variety of stimuli available, appealing to any consumer's preferences and tastes. The same people who adore playing *Doom* or *Manhunt* on their computers may not tolerate watching reports about war or murder on the news. I interviewed some people who refuse to watch any movie or television show that displays violence, yet they are glued to CNN and Fox News for hours each day following the latest atrocity, act of genocide, terrorism, or murder. I spoke with others who can't handle reading about or watching acts of inhumanity committed around the world, yet they live for watching hockey and football games.

EXCITEMENT IN REAL TIME

Human beings have an innate drive to play, a phenomenon that can easily be observed in the young of all animal species—running, wrestling, chasing, stalking. Spectator sports serve the purpose of satisfying vicarious play, especially violent forms that could be most dangerous to citizens in less than peak physical condition. Professional sports teams thus represent identified communities, complete with symbolic totem names such as those found in the National Football League: Detroit *Lions*, Chicago *Bears*, Carolina *Panthers*, St. Louis *Rams*, Philadelphia *Eagles*. Some team names are even more descriptive of the potential violence they can bring to the game, such as the Tampa Bay *Buccaneers*, Minnesota *Vikings*, and Oakland *Raiders*.

One sports photographer who spends a lot of time monitoring games had some interesting observations about the ways that fans identify with their teams. He observed the ways people tend to project their frustrations and anger toward the so-called bad guys, who are demonized as the enemy. Football players, locked in ritual combat, become archetypal heroes or villains, complete with princesses (cheerleaders) waiting breathlessly on the sidelines. They perform in sacred temples, called stadiums, named after sponsored "gods" (corporations). Throughout the staged events the spectators shout prayers ("Please God, let them score!") and communal chants ("Kill 'em!"). They wear costumes (jerseys, T-shirts, hats) that mirror their designated champions on the field. Even more interesting, in American culture the games are scheduled as a kind of secular worship that take place on Sunday afternoons after church. "The postmodern players of televised sports do not fight to the death as Roman gladiators did. But they do become sacrificial victims and sacred objects in their violent struggle to achieve victorious scores, noble statistics, and immortal identities."[2]

Theater critic Mark Pizzato likens the contemporary NFL to Aztec and Roman spectacles.[3] The gladiators are godlike figures with celebrity status, riches, and fame. They represent emperors (owners) and perform in coliseums. They fight furiously to "penetrate" one another's defenses, "slice" through the line, throw "bombs," "cut deep" into the enemy. They attempt to "draw blood," to invade and capture territory, and score "fatal blows." The arenas are treated as battlefields in which each team tries to "destroy" the other. And just like in ancient times, spectators are separated by class differences (general seating, box seats, luxury boxes). Perhaps taking this symbolic stuff a bit too far, the author also views the football, the primary performance prop, as a severed head.

Sports represent far more than catharsis or mere entertainment. Violent sports, in particular, reflect our larger cultural fabric that includes an appreciation for aesthetic grace, suspenseful competition, and brutal aggression. "In all its varieties," explains sociologist Norbert Elias, "sport is always a controlled battle in an imaginary setting."[4] It doesn't matter whether the opponent is another team, a single adversary, a mountain, the sea, or a large animal in nature, whether it takes place in football, tennis, or shuffleboard, it is a "spectacle of mock combat." The ideal sport, then, is one that provides maximum violence with minimized injuries. Rules are constructed to keep excitement at its peak but still protect the valuable assets of players. Penalties against "unsportsmanlike conduct" or "roughing the kicker" in football are installed to keep things violent but within manageable restraints.

To add to the thrill, increasing the appeal of violent sports over any other form of entertainment, is that the action is unscripted. The teams might rehearse their plays over and over, but the outcome remains unpredictable. Anyone might get injured. Even a hopeless team might steal an occasional victory.

The true irony of spectator sports of almost all varieties is that although they are designed to keep the public entertained, most fans are doomed to frustration, at least if satisfaction is determined to a large part by identifying with a winner. Commentator Matt Taibbi observed that although people watch sports to escape the doldrums of their ordinary lives, 99 percent of the time they are left with "agonizing memories of crushing defeats." Taibbi cites the reality that if there are two or three dozen teams competing for a championship, the odds of your favorite winning are pretty remote. He finds it more than a little amusing that although men ridicule women for buying "girlie" magazines like *Vogue, Cosmopolitan,* and *Marie Claire,* imagining themselves as tall, statuesque models in the most fashionable wardrobe, male sports fans have an even more desperate experience of humiliation and self-abasement. All the while that men shake their heads in wonder at the ways that women spend their time, "those same men spend 340 nights a year following, with racing pulses and gritted teeth, sports teams doomed to disappoint them in 98 percent of the cases."[5]

There is indeed a sadomasochistic connection between spectators and their favorite teams and players. Fans place wagers on games in order to increase their personal investment and commitment to the outcome. They revel in the suffering and wounds inflicted on their opponents yet also feel a kind of masochistic pleasure while losing, as if the bleeding on the field reflects the shared loss of their money and identity. There is a kind of tragic catharsis in defeat, similar to the appeal of a heartbreaking film (e.g., *Brokeback Mountain, Braveheart,* or *Titanic*) or play (e.g., *Romeo and Juliet, West Side Story,* or *Phantom of the Opera*).

Clearly the attraction of watching any sport, whether violent or relatively benign, such as dance, talent, or game shows on television, is not directly related to picking the winner, however desirable that might be. It is the physical conflict in the case of football, rugby, boxing, and similar combative contests, or the psychological damage inflicted during reality shows, that audiences find most appealing.

MAXIMIZING VIOLENCE AS SPORTS ENTERTAINMENT

Jamie Levine is the only Extreme Fighting Champion to ever retire undefeated, with thirty consecutive wins. Commenting on the appeal of his sport, as well as others such as hockey, football, or car wrecks, he observed: "You don't go to a rodeo to watch a guy stay on a bull for eight seconds. You want to see the guy thrown off and stomped."[6]

Al "Chico" Evans, a professional heavyweight boxer, who was interviewed for this book, was asked why he thinks fans are so interested in watching violent fights. I don't think he'd given the subject much thought because the question seemed so obvious to him. "People come to watch me in the ring to let out their own anxiety and fear. They're watching something that they know they can't do themselves. They depend on me to do it for them. They probably wish they could be doing it, but they can't. They'd love to punch someone. They like to see blood, pain, and hurt. Most of all they like to see someone knocked out." He laughed. "I prefer it to be the other guy."

Unfortunately for Evans, that wasn't quite the case since he lost more fights than he won. Nevertheless, he was philosophical about that since he'd done his best—he'd actually gotten in the ring, which is something that most people would never do.

"I think people like the realness of someone being hurt. It's not like TV at all. It's not like a movie that they know is fake. They want to watch something real, something they can smell and feel. But they don't care about me. The only one who cares about me is the doctor when I get hit. There could be someone lifeless on the ground and the crowd is just there yelling and laughing."

Many of the most popular spectator sports—hockey, football, rugby, boxing, wrestling, ultimate fighting—are designed as much around maximizing violence as demonstrating skill and artistry. Hard checking in hockey, rough hits in football, and aggressive play are cheered by the audience even when they have little to do with the outcome of the game or match. In a study of how the context of such sports affects the mood of

Studies have been structured in which hockey fans were asked to rate their enjoyment of the experience. Surprisingly, the single-best predictor wasn't who won or lost, how competitive the game was, or how skillfully the players performed, but rather the number of penalty minutes accrued, which signified maximum violence. The researchers concluded it wasn't just suspense that leads to arousal during games, but the roughest possible play (alcohol consumption only intensifies the effects).[7] Photo courtesy of the *Edmonton Journal*.

viewers, the researchers found that both men and women fans prefer violent over nonviolent displays, especially when they are "unscripted," to build suspense rather than the kind of scripted violence in pro wrestling or roller derby.[8] Even nonfans enjoyed the kind of spontaneous eruptions of violence that occur during a hockey game fight or a vicious tackle.

Boxing, wrestling, and mixed martial arts specialize in providing the most violence compressed into the briefest periods of time—two- or three-minute rounds. One woman, Morgan, recalled watching fights as a kid with her family and described it as a bonding experience. "I've always been a fan of boxing," she said. "As a child my family would rally around the television for the big Mike Tyson pay-per-view events. My father followed boxing for the majority of his life and would share stories about the great Mohammed Ali 'rumble in the jungle' fights, or Roberto Duran and Sugar Ray Leonard. It's become a family event everyone has come to enjoy."

Since those early days, Morgan has now become a huge fan of cage fighting, which she finds ten times more exciting because of the increased level of violence displayed. "I could never do this sort of thing myself, but I love watching the recklessness and unpredictability of what happens in the cage or the ring. I enjoy watching a competitor go out in the ring incredibly focused and put everything on the line for their opportunity to be great. Is he calm and collected, or rattled? Is he going to look the competitor in the eye, or was the fight lost at the stare down? Watching someone enter the ring and almost scientifically pick apart the opponent is impressive, as is a great knock-down, drag-out fight. Anything can happen at anytime in that ring. There can be a lucky punch. It's just so exciting to watch it in real time."

When watching violent sports like boxing, or especially a complex spectacle like football, there is far more at work than meets the eye. Football players, wearing coats of armor, march out into the stadium to trumpets blaring and screaming crowds. Cheerleaders, wearing skirts so short they intend for their underwear to be displayed, dance and gyrate themselves into a frenzy, cheering for the alpha males on the field. And for those of us who are watching—we are playing our own roles in the affair, mostly as it relates to gender socialization, in which males are taught to watch violence unflinchingly and females are taught to worship those who are most stoic and courageous in the face of bloodshed. Across cultures, whether in the South Pacific, Africa, Asia, or among Native American tribes, young males are taught to suffer mutilation and commit violence while females are the primary audience.[9]

Tolerating and learning to enjoy violence is a rite of passage for adolescent boys. This is especially the case within traditional hunter-gatherer cultures but can still be seen operating in our schools today. So-called horseplay and playground fights are simply part of the gender socialization in which young animals of all species learn the rituals and skills of hunting and self-protection.

A classic interaction demonstrating these socialized gender roles is described by a journalist for *Seventeen* who interviewed kids waiting in line to see a sequel to *A Nightmare on Elm Street*. One adolescent girl talked about why she was waiting to get into the theater: "They're fun to watch. You go with your friends and try to get scared and everything. And you can just be rowdy. You can get all rowdy with boys and jump into their laps, and they can comfort you."[10] She went on to say that she likes it when the boys try to comfort her, acting brave and in control, when she knows deep down inside they are as terrified as she is. But it is a ritualized script they are playing out, one that has been repeated for generations.

One role of violent sports and media is thus to serve as a "convenient testing ground for the display of appropriate emotional reactions to situations posing grave danger."[11] In other words, males learn that they are supposed to pretend to be fearless and calm when confronted with displays of violence in sports or horror in film. Young women also have roles they are learning to play as cheerleaders.

FROM HUMANS TO ANIMALS

Throughout the ages animals have been subjected to torture for the amusement of their masters. I mentioned in a previous chapter that during Roman times thousands of exotic species imported from Africa and elsewhere were killed in a single day, with the carnage piled so high it would take hours to remove all the bodies for disposal.

Cruelty to animals is now outlawed in most jurisdictions, but its use as entertainment in fighting arenas is still very much alive and well. Dog fighting, for instance, still remains a popular sport in many parts of the country. Puppies are trained to maim and kill from birth, often dragged behind cars or forced to walk around carrying heavy chains in order to toughen them up and build strength. Dozens, or even hundreds of dogs, are held in captivity by trainers, often in small cages for days without food. There are tens of thousands of fighting dogs all around the country, hidden away on farms and in barns, being prepared for mortal combat in a gambling enterprise that sometimes nets $100,000 prize money for the winning owner. Although it is illegal to *stage* fights, it is perfectly acceptable in some states to *own* fighting dogs or *attend* the fights.[12]

As abhorrent as this practice might be, authorities are at a loss as to how to break up the dog fighting rings. What happens after they bust a trainer and take custody of his hundreds of animals? The dogs have been trained to viciously maul other animals or even attack without provocation. Who would take them as pets? If they can't be rehabilitated, which most of them cannot, they are "put to sleep," a euphemism for euthanasia. That is why large-scale crackdowns are so rare and why the practice continues.[13]

You wouldn't believe all the animals that are thrown into arenas to fight to the death for human entertainment. You are already familiar with bullfights, dogfights, and cockfights. However, there are also all kinds of other creatures that are forced into combat for entertainment—fighting fish or canaries, even crickets and spiders are "trained" to engage in combat for an audience. Then there are all the other ways that humans use and abuse animals for pleasure—hunting foxes, elephants, lions, wolves, and bears, none of which are actually used as food sources very often.

It is cockfighting that remains a thriving entertainment industry today in the United States, a practice that began with the first settlers. In case you have never had the experience of such a spectacle, roosters are bred and trained as fighters. Razor blades are attached to their legs. They are thrown into a ring in front of a huge audience that bets furiously on the outcome, and then the cocks do their level best to maim and kill each other in a vicious knife fight.

There is huge money to be made from such enterprises, given the high demand for blood sports. A congressman from a county in Louisiana, Elbert Lee Guillory, who voted against making the sport illegal, commented, "The cockfighting industry in St. Landry County is a $12 million industry, in a place where there are very few industries and it's very difficult for people to make a living here. We eat billions of chickens every day. What we're talking about is putting the interest of chickens over the interests of people."[14] Of course he's leaving out the part that these animals are actually being tortured for public entertainment rather than being sacrificed for food.

Ernest Hemingway, a writer who greatly admired bullfighting as a display of courage, was also amazed at the ways the violence of the crowd would be stirred up by the spectacle of blood-letting. And if they were disappointed because the bullfighter was unable or unwilling to kill the animal, the crowd took things literally into their own hands, "swarming on him [the bull] . . . with knifes, daggers, butcher knives, and rocks . . . cutting up at him until he sways and goes down."[15]

In an article in *Sports Illustrated*, a number of professional athletes were asked if bullfighting even qualifies as a "sport."[16] Whereas some of the athletes found the practice merely a form of cruel butchery with an audience, basketball player Raja Bell compared it to being a quarterback in football: "Thousands of fans are screaming at you, and a 500-pound animal is trying to rip your head off." Denver Broncos linebacker John Mobley heartily agreed: "Have you seen the size of those bulls' nuts? You go up against anyone with nuts that big, it's a serious sport." Yet baseball pitcher Jeff Zimmerman reflected that the best way to answer this question

Cockfighting, although illegal, is popular in most countries around the world as a form of entertainment. Both combatants in this fight staged in a village in India suffered mortal wounds.

is to ask the bull, who would probably have a very different answer. Rich Garces, another pitcher, said that the ritual is more of a show rather than a sport since "people show up, but it's only to watch someone stab a bull or to see the bull kill a guy."

Whether watching animals or humans engaged in violent combat, there has long been an assumption that this would increase the likelihood of aggression in fans. There have been several well-publicized incidents in which unruly crowds started riots to celebrate a win or express rage after a loss. Hundreds of spectators have been injured or killed in the melee. One study sought to test this phenomenon by looking at the instances of physical or child abuse immediately following the broadcast of sporting events like hockey and football and found no noticeable increase in such behavior.[17]

One significant exception to the supposed cathartic effect of watching sports to drain off aggressive energy in fans is when a team wins a championship. When the Detroit Pistons won a basketball trophy in 1990, the riots that occurred afterward left eight people dead. Even the Canadians, ordinarily very peaceful citizens, got way out of control when the Montreal hockey team won the Stanley Cup: 170 people were injured.[18] There have been other well-publicized instances of overzealous fans taking things into their own hands because they so over-identified with the competition on the field. In 1964 there were three hundred spectators killed in a violent clash between Argentina and Peru, sort of a small-scale war between the countries—over a soccer game! Five years later, El Salvador and Honduras recalled their ambassadors after a game and declared a *real* war on each other. Riots in Britain resulted in four hundred injuries and forty deaths during a 1984 match. They actually finished the contest before they could remove the corpses. Throughout the rest of the world, on every con-

Spanish matador Israel Lancho is gored during a bullfight in Madrid. Whereas the fans watching are initially revolted by the violence, they are also totally riveted by the unexpected action. This photograph not only won an award for capturing this frozen moment of horror but also is a popular image in demand. AP photo.

tinent, there have been similar incidents in which hundreds of fans have been injured or killed as a result of their overinvolvement in the violence on the field.[19]

The stated purpose of such mock battles is to help citizens siphon off their own violent impulses, rather than to act them out, but it seems that sometimes things get quite out of control. That is one reason why sometimes watching violence isn't quite enough and people look for other means to express their aggressive urges.

VIRTUAL FIGHTING AND COMBAT

It is one thing to watch a sport and participate vicariously and quite another to join the action through simulations. Video and online games are a major source of entertainment, not only among adolescents but across the age range. Whether playing fantasy football, video golf, or any of the other sports that have been converted to virtual experiences, anyone can experience what it's like to compete like a professional athlete, warlord, gang leader, army general, or serial killer.

Whereas readers of suspense novels, audiences in movie theaters, or viewers of a violent story on the nightly news have absolutely no input on the outcome (whether the lost boy is found, the gang lord captured, the serial killer arrested, or the monster defeated), video game players do control what happens in the narrative they are *living*, albeit vicariously. Depending on their memory, perceptual acuity, cognitive processing, decision making, manual dexterity, and motor skills, they can determine what happens in the game by moving up levels of difficulty, achieving goals, and defeating enemies. They can actually measure their impact by the score attained.

The differences between passive (viewing, reading) and active (playing) entertainment are evident in a number of significant ways:

1. *Attention.* In a movie, television show, book, or sports event (especially baseball) you can easily let your mind wander without losing the main thread of what is happening (instant replays help too). In a video game, however, such a lapse will get you "killed."
2. *Mental maps.* In order to negotiate the world of a particular video game the player must use imagination to visualize the three-dimensional world in which the characters operate. This includes learning the geography, landmarks, transportation systems, weapons or tools available, as well as the personalities and traits of the characters.

3. *Predictions*. There is a kind of predictability and repetitious aspect of games in which players can count on certain rules. In the same way that children enjoy hearing the same stories read over and over, so, too, do players come to enjoy the suspense that is bounded between anticipated and predicted outcomes. They know if they open a box what will pop out, or if they take a particular path where it will lead.

4. *Managing arousal*. Take the pulse of a player during a heated game and it is likely to be almost as elevated as if the events were happening in real life. In order to function effectively the player must learn to manage arousal levels so as to maintain optimal functioning. This includes juggling multiple tasks, accessing memory, and planning strategy and future moves.

5. *Continuous reinforcement*. Throughout the game the player is continuously rewarded for making good choices and successful decisions. Points are accumulated as immediate feedback regarding what is working and what is not, allowing adjustments and increased performance.

6. *Personal agency*. Players are the ones who determine whether the experience is satisfying or not, depending on their motivation and skill.

7. *Social interaction*. Many games involve multiple players, on-site or in cyberspace. The interaction between players, working as teams or competitors, forges relationships and social communication.

8. *Self-esteem*. In today's culture, mastery of video games is considered an adolescent rite of passage. Just as children and adults attain a sense of confidence from their athletic, intellectual, and interpersonal abilities, they also bolster self-esteem through performances in games.[20]

In a review of the hottest and most popular video games released, there is an obvious predominant theme that resonates throughout the best sellers. *MAGs* (which stands for "massive action game") allow hundreds of simultaneous players to attack and kill one another. *Bioshock* provides opportunities to kill zombie-like spiders, *Battlefield: Bad Company* to blow up tanks and soldiers, *Dante's Inferno* to wreck havoc in hell, *Just Cause* to kill militants and drug lords, *Red Dead Redemption* to start a bloody revolution, *Super Street Fighter* to enjoy gang fights, or *Mobster* to lead a crime syndicate. The latest edition of *God of War* promises to "up the quality of carnage." In the words of the developer, "If this game puts a smile on the player's face, I want them to feel a little guilty, then feel good about what they just did." And what the players do is "unleash blood-spurting whup-ass."[21]

One young man explained that the games for him were really about the way he could identify with the characters and experience an alternative reality when he no longer felt like a spectator.

> I just think it's kind of cool to pretend you've got superpowers or some kind of special skill, even if it's blowing shit up. I just marvel at what I can do and not feel the least guilty about it afterwards. Don't get me wrong—I don't really get that excited from the killing. I actually think it's pretty funny. But it's not about the killing but just getting to the next level. Sometimes the action is so surreal you just feel in awe of the visuals and the sounds and how badass they make the fighting scenes. It's like in action movies too where splatters of blood shoot out everywhere. It's the same thing with ultimate fighting if there's no knockdown—it's just boring. But it's really, like, how you connect with the characters and can feel yourself inside them.

This is the guy's version of the experience, but when he convinced his girlfriend to play one of the war games, she couldn't believe how fun it was for different reasons. "I got to be a scuba diver and ride a snowmobile and fire a rocket launcher, all in the span of a few minutes. It's like I got to totally escape from reality and have a ball. Who wouldn't like that?"

In different ways, and using gendered language, each of them describes the intense thrill that comes from actually *entering* the competition rather than just watching on the sidelines. Depending on your imagination and ability to suspend reality, it is entirely possible to become the characters in the games, to imagine you are the one scoring the touchdown, saving the universe, or destroying a pack of raging werewolves.

Somewhere close to three-quarters of video games are violent in nature, with the usual plot of some armed conflict.[22] There are at least a dozen reasons for their overwhelming popularity, especially among boys and men:

1. Socialization in the male gender role as warrior/hunter
2. The need for excitement and intense suspense
3. Engagement in a variety of emotional arousal experiences, including joy, pride, disappointment, frustration, anger, fear, and disgust
4. Development of problem solving and dexterity skills
5. Social interaction with others who share interests

6. Identification with various characters and their traits (courage, ruthlessness, poise under pressure, intelligence, superhuman strength, resilience, etc.)
7. The expression of aggression
8. Testing of skills in competition
9. An antidote for boredom
10. A feeling of competence in moving up levels
11. Exercise in power and control
12. The pure aesthetic pleasure obtained from destruction (it's fun to knock things down or blow them up!)[23]

Journalist Chris Baker field-tested the latest version of *Grand Theft Auto* and was left disturbed and unnerved afterward, not specifically because of the violence as much as how easily he was seduced by the game. "Shoot an innocent bystander, and you see his face contort in agony. He'll clutch at the wound and begin to stagger away, desperately seeking safety." After an initial hesitance and sense of guilt over the virtual mayhem he was creating, he decided to make himself invulnerable, loaded up ammo for his rocket launcher, and started destroying everything in sight. "Then I try to rack up a body count that would make Attila the Hun jealous." In conclusion, he admits he felt totally hooked by the complexity of the virtual world and the challenges it presents. It's "not an orgy of death. It's a living, breathing place—and when you're forced to kill, it's nothing to celebrate."[24]

Another game reviewer had a different reaction when trying out the new editions of *Modern Warfare* and *Left4Dead*. Awarding each game a perfect "A" for their realistic portrayal of violence and "harrowing journey into darkness," the author concluded that on a more complex level the games are about "adapting to mental and moral disorientation" in figuring out when, and under what circumstances, it is okay to take a human life. Yet, ultimately, video games like these are about maximum mayhem described as "safe, insane catharsis for the stress of living in an unsafe, equally insane *Modern Warfare* world."[25] In theory, anyway, the idea is that perpetuating mayhem in the fantasy world of games prevents people from acting out this behavior in the real world. While there is some evidence that this may be true with most people, there are also individuals who are so activated and aroused by the simulated killing that they feel an intense desire to take things to the next level of reality.

If these moral dilemmas are an intrinsic part of this game, then that isn't the case with *God of War*, which is described as "visceral, violent,

One of the most violent video games on the market, *Manhunt 2* presents players with the scenario that they are psychotic killers whose job is to hack up as many victims as possible in order to earn points.

bloody, gore-soaked, no-holds-barred-over-the-top fighting feat that has you chopping off limbs and heads on your way to mythological glory." According to the developers, the goal is no less than to "make the player feel brutal, letting their inner beast free and just going nuts."[26]

And if that strikes you as rather extreme, how about the game that is so ultraviolent that it has been banned in a half dozen countries? *Manhunt 2* revolves around a main character who is a psychotic killer, confined to a mental institution. He escapes and goes on a berserk murder spree: "You simply go around killing people in extraordinarily violent ways."[27]

In a review of the effects that violent video games like *Mortal Kombat* and *Doom* have on aggression, most researchers expected (and predicted) that there would be powerful connections. Almost all studies hypothesized that people (mostly young men) who are the most avid players would also have a tendency to be more aggressive and violent than those who are not attracted to this recreational outlet. In truth, the results are inconsistent and the lasting effects are minimal. Even more surprising is that players who spend more time in the violent gaming world are actually *less* aggressive.[28] In some cases participation actually appears to help people work off their frustrations and anger and reduce potential toward acting out violence. Of course there are also notable and dramatic exceptions, such as the case of the school shooter who dressed the part of a character in the game and then went to work with his weapons on innocent victims.

It is so difficult to generalize from these studies because the kinds of games investigated are so different, just as are the reasons why people play them. Interviews with frequent players generate a whole host of stated reasons:

- "I don't know. I just get bored or something. I was spending way too much time vegging out on the couch watching TV. I like game shows and cooking shows mostly, although I'm also hooked on *Dancing with the Stars*. [Laughs] At least now that I'm playing *Halo* or *Doom* my fingers are getting some exercise." [Laughs]
- "My friends and me, we just kind of like to hang out and stuff, you know? It's all social. Sometimes we'll play online or we go to each other's houses and see who can kick some ass."
- "I just get to work out some of my frustrations, you know? I get so much crap all day from my boss that it gives me a kick to play when he's not around. I picture it's him that I'm killing and, you know, it feels good. It relaxes me."
- "It's weird because I can't stand violence but, for some reason, the game totally hooked me. It was just so fun to be a character in the game and start shooting people and stuff even though I'd never even think of doing a thing like that. But it's not real. And that's what makes it so fun."
- "I think playing provides an outlet for any stress, anger, annoyance, or whatever is on your mind. You get to test yourself against others who are trying to counteract everything you're doing. I also like that I can have a completely different personality in the game, do anything I want, and *there's no consequences*. That's freedom that most people only dream about."

In these few disclosures we see highlighted the motives that involve dealing with boredom, social interaction, dealing with stress, taking on different roles, enjoying competition, and working through aggression. In addition, players talk a lot about the problem solving involved in the games as they move up to higher levels, challenging them to test their skills. And for others, playing represents pure escapist fantasy.

One gamer, a self-described "adrenaline junkie," wrote in an online chat room:

> It's an "I love it—I hate it" thing for me. I get cranked up. It's like my survival is on the line. I feel a little surge of fear as I creep up to the next corner and peep around, knowing I may get my guts blown out. But if I'm fast enough, if my survival instincts are quick enough, I may get lucky and blow the bad guy away. It's kill or be killed.

This was written not by some bored adolescent, but by a businessman who finds the stimulation he feels from playing a boost to his deal-making prowess. He finds strength and resources in the games, a sense of empowerment that carries over into other areas of his life.

It is often the case that it isn't so much the violence in video games that attracts the players as the sensory stimulation that comes from loud noises, bright colors, fast movement, and realistic simulations. It is like you enter that world and are actually experiencing all the excitement of being in a street gang, or on patrol on the Western Front, or repelling an alien invasion. What could be more fun than that?

Then there are all the things that players learn from video games. I'm not just talking about the increased eye-hand coordination and dexterity, but the problem solving inherent in the games. As a player moves up levels, there are mysteries to be solved, puzzles to be decoded, sequences of movement that must be memorized, strategies to be created and implemented, and constant vigilance. It is funny how kids (and adults) who seem to have the attention span of gnats when it comes to studying or completing work, can spend hours, if not whole evenings, in front of the screen with complete concentration and rapt attention.

Among the thousands of studies undertaken in the last decades to determine the effects of video game violence on subsequent aggressive behavior, especially among children, there was assumed to be a causal relationship in which children (and adults) who play fantasy games online are

Doom was one of the initial first-person shooter games that was credited with helping to launch super-violent computer entertainment. It combines science fiction, satanic imagery, horror, and plenty of opportunities to kill using pistols, rocket launchers, and shotguns—and chainsaws for close-up work.

more likely to end up taking to arms in the real world as a mass murderer or turn to a life of crime to up the thrill ante. While the actual results are more mixed and complicated than originally thought (and hoped), there are contextual factors at work. It turns out that there is little definitive evidence to support one position or the other, and there are conflicting claims that vicarious violent entertainment reduces aggression in some and increases it in others. Depending on why someone is playing in the first place, what needs are being met, and what else is going on in the person's life, these games, like the sports entertainment described earlier, can have a number of different meanings. Watching sports or playing games that feature violence up the ante, so to speak, of the stakes involved. Events or simulations feel more exciting when there is the possibility that someone could get hurt.

Contests and competitions were originally invented as ways to provide *simulated* combat that would actually prevent more serious casualties. There is some degree of violence, whether actual or symbolic, in almost all such contests. Even the games of chess, checkers, or backgammon are all about engaging in a war in which the object is to destroy or capture the others person's soldiers. Likewise, football and many other competitive sports involve defeating opponents by using physical strength and athleticism. For those among us who are not blessed with such attributes, watching such contests for entertainment provides an outlet. For others, video or computer versions of the games provide an alternative venue for the experiences in which players feel more actively involved.

Many children and adult game players don't really care about the violence at all but rather enjoy other facets of the experience. They enjoy losing themselves in a concentrated task that requires all their attention. They enjoy the social interactions that take place playing with friends or opponents. Many report that it feels good to have some control over the outcome of the game, depending on their skill with a joystick, since their lives outside the game may feel more random or powerless.

There is an identification process that takes place when cheering for any team or competitor to defeat an opponent. For a little while it feels like *you* are the one who is inhabiting the body of the graceful and powerful athlete on the field, the one who can do things that you can only dream about doing. This is true for any sport, just as it is for a designated persona when you take on the role of a video game character. You are fearless and courageous. You have superpowers, or at least additional abilities you weren't born with. For a few minutes or hours, it is *you* who can battle with exceptional skill and grace. This is the ultimate fantasy for most people who yearn to be the "alpha" male or female, the dominant member of the tribe. Throughout history, until recent times, the main qualification for such a position is the willingness and ability to display brutal violence to keep others in their place. It is no wonder, then, that most of us find pleasure in watching athletic contests that allow us to imagine ourselves fighting for such dominance.

Chapter 5
Zombies, Vampires, Monsters

D ramatic theater was invented in ancient Greece primarily as a form of ritual blood sacrifice for the audience. The first plays depicted characters, both human and animal, whose main function was to appease the gods through their death. The audience, acting as a chorus, participated in the ritual through their screams. Such enactments were designed to replace actual blood sacrifices that had taken place earlier in history.

The messages implicit in the earliest Greek dramas are the negative consequences of taking an evil path. These messages continue to be present in contemporary plays, films, and fictional stories. In most violent children's programming, for instance, the plots are structured in such a way for kids to see their fears expressed and vanquished in the form of monsters and demons destroyed. Whether in cartoons, comic books, video games, or movies, children follow the same mythological story that has been told since the beginning of human history. There is evil in the world. There are monsters that live among us. Some are easily recognizable by their appearance, but others look just like you and me. They are Satan and Darth Vader and Dracula and Freddy Krueger and Hannibal Lecter and the Predator and the Wicked Witch. Hiding under the covers will not make them go away. These villains must be challenged with violence equal to that which they bring to the battle.

SCREAMING YOUR HEAD OFF WITH A GRIN ON YOUR FACE

"I've been described as the ultimate 'girly girl,'" Pam says with a laugh. You can tell she's proud of her femininity, hair perfectly coifed, slender body wrapped in designer clothes. She is by no means wealthy or privileged; she is actually from a struggling immigrant family, the first among her relatives to ever attend college. She works hard to earn a living and feels entitled to reward herself for the sacrifices she's made along the way.

"My favorite pastime is shopping," Pam says, again with that infectious laugh. "I love anything that involves makeup. I have so many purses I can hardly count them. And shoes," she says, pointing at her Jimmy Choo pumps, "don't get me started. Got these on sale for half off."

There is a pause in the conversation and I wait, literally, for the other shoe to drop.

"Okay, here goes," Pam says with a deep breath. "Most people are pretty shocked to find out how much I *love* horror movies. I'm not talking about a casual fan—I mean I really am obsessed with them. Ever since I was a kid I always preferred movies that scare the crap out of me. I love the real classics like *Halloween*, *A Nightmare on Elm Street*, and *The Shining*."

Pam waits for a reaction from me, and I can tell she's disappointed by my casual head nod. After all, I'm a therapist who is used to such confessions, plus I've been listening to hundreds of stories like this for years. It would take a lot more than this confession to get a noticeable reaction.

Encouraged by her sympathetic audience, Pam explained that she is always searching for that movie that will terrify her so much she can't sleep at night. After years of investment in the genre, it takes quite a lot to produce the effect she's looking for. "I think one reason for that is that I'm a skeptic about things. I don't believe in ghosts or the supernatural, so when I see that stuff I barely blink. I just can't imagine any of that stuff happening to me."

Pam's point is that the movies she most enjoys are the ones in which she can easily project herself into the story and imagine that she is the one in jeopardy. "It's easy to get sucked into the plot if I'm a part of it. But I love that I can't really get hurt—at least most of the time I remember that. The thought of being chased is absolutely terrifying, but if I am just watching it in a movie I know I will not die even though the character might. I guess what I'm saying is that it's fun to be scared when I know that I won't be hurt."

Pam is actually describing the same kind of thrill that is felt on a roller coaster. Part of you is screaming, "I hate this. I hate this. Let me out of here." Another part is screaming your head off with a huge grin on your face.

SPEAKING TO FEAR

In the movies *Saw* and *Hostel*, and their sequels, characters are systematically tortured in the most vivid, brutal ways possible. People are forced to cut off their own body parts. Naked women are hung up in meat lockers. Chained victims are subjected to all kinds of cutting instruments, blowtorches, and power tools. Blood and human viscera are literally scattered everywhere on screen. These franchises, and others like them, have generated billions of dollars in ticket sales from moviegoers. And, I shamefully admit, I'm one of them.

I can't actually watch the most explicit violence on screen. I avert my eyes at times, close my ears to the sounds of the more brutal screams, repeat a Tibetan mantra to myself, stare at the exit, and sometimes have to get up and leave to catch my breath. But I come back. In fact I find the films inventive, if not ingenious, in their plots—the very idea of seeing how far people will go out of avarice or self-interest, or how evil manifests itself in human behavior. I can't watch much of the violence itself (which is more than half of the films), but I do so enjoy the suspense.

I know I'm not alone in my ambivalence. Critic David Edelstein, a self-described "horror maven," has reached his limit of what he can tolerate in terms of the scenes of mutilation and "torture porn."[1] Others set the bar at a different level. One movie fan remarked, "It's all about excitement for me—the more, the better. I like the over-the-top stuff with maximum gore. It's kind of like seeing a car wreck that's just too good to pass by; you have to see what's there even though you know it's going to be horrible."

Directors like Eli Roth, George Romero, and Rob Zombie are known as members of the "splat pack," filmmakers who specialize in splatter films, those that feature gore and graphic violence as their *raison d'être*. Just to clarify the categories of the genre, in case you're a bit confused, "horror" movies are the old standbys that speak to fear. Usually these involve some supernatural force or monster—aliens, zombies, vampires, and the like. "Splatter" films, on the contrary, are all about the special effects, often related to the destruction of the body in particularly gruesome ways that leave limbs, guts, and fluids prominently displayed. "Slasher" films are a subset of the latter category since they have a single primary villain, usually a deviant serial killer who stalks (and it is all about the predation—the hunting of prey) his victims and then kills them with blunt or sharp instruments.[2]

As brilliant as Shakespeare's dialogue and complex plots are, even he was forced to add swordfights, graveyard scenes, murders, patricide, and

Torture scenes from the movie *Hostel* were extraordinarily gruesome and revolting. The film was designed to shock viewers beyond any explicit violence they'd ever seen before and was promoted with the promise: "The scariest American movie in a decade."

suicides to his plays in order to maintain audience attention. Likewise, there has been an escalation in the quantity and brutality of violence portrayed in media precisely because the audience demands new thrills. Films like *A Nightmare on Elm Street, The Texas Chainsaw Massacre,* or *Phantom of the Opera* were considered groundbreaking because they took the audience to places they had never seen before and experienced feelings of horror that upped the ante to new levels. The producers of the film *The House on Haunted Hill* actually made use of an incident in which one audience member was literally scared to death. This only added to the film's popularity in much the same way that a more recent film, *127 Hours,* advertised with pride how many audience members fainted when the protagonist cut off his own arm with a blunt knife.

MOVIES YOU WATCH THROUGH YOUR FINGERS

In the original screenplay for the groundbreaking and brutally violent film *Bonnie and Clyde,* the love-struck couple is enjoying a picnic and the fruits of their labor as bank robbers and killers. The ambush that soon unfolds is one of the most memorable visual spectacles of violence ever created. In excruciatingly slow motion, and meticulously choreographed by director Arthur Penn, the couple is riddled with machine gun bullets while they jerk around like puppets with epilepsy. The sequence is described by writers Robert Benton and David Newman:

> We see, alternately, the bodies of Clyde and Bonnie, twisting, shaking, horribly distorted; much of the action is in slow motion. Clyde is on the ground, his body arching and rolling from the impact of the bullets. Bonnie is still in her seat: her body jerking and swaying as the bullets thud relentlessly into her and the framework of the car.

This may have taken just a few seconds to read, but on screen the violent finale, the close-ups of bullets hitting flesh, the wounds opening up, the grimaces of agony, the death throes, all seem to last for several minutes. We watch horrified—and yet compelled—to continue viewing this orgy of execution that is presented as an artistic masterpiece. The film received ten Academy Award nominations and was even recognized by the National Catholic Office for Motion Pictures as the best movie of the year. In Penn's own explanation, he felt that the violence in the film was absolutely necessary to heighten its emotional impact. And he was probably right.

When asked what he was attempting to do in creating a movie as violent as *The Wild Bunch* in 1969, director Sam Peckinpah just shrugged, saying, "I was trying to show what the hell it's like to get shot." Well, he certainly succeeded if the measure was to create the most brutally violent film made at that time. The first scene in the film, which portends what is to follow, shows children playing in the dirt by feeding scorpions to thousands of voracious red ants. The opening gunfight that followed, lasting over twenty minutes, was just the beginning of a body count that reached 145 by the end of the story.

In spite of all the protests, hoopla, and controversy that swirled around the film's release, one critic called it the "most essential American film from the Sixties because it confronted point-blank the audience's fear and fascination with violence."[3]

In order to get a better grasp on this phenomenon, I met with movie producer Clark Peterson at his Hollywood home.[4] Peterson is best known for his movie *Monster* about serial killer Aileen Wuornos, who murdered seven men. Peterson began his career working on a number of other violent and horror films including *Scanners, Stranger in the House, Wishmaster, The Killing Ground,* and, most recently, *Dear Mr. Gacy*. He is currently working on a remake of *Scanners*, a groundbreaking film, which was the first of its kind to feature exploding heads.

Peterson's first big break was working with Roger Corman, who has made more "B movies" than probably anyone in Hollywood. In his prime Corman would produce up to a half dozen such films per year. He created *Little Shop of Horrors* in two days! Among some of his most well-known films were *The Pit and the Pendulum*, *The Raven*, and *Death Race 2000*, as well as some classics like *A Bucket of Blood* and *Attack of the Crab Monsters*.

"Roger gave me this script to read," Peterson recalls with a smile, "and my assignment was to go through the script and make sure there was an act of violence at least every eight pages. This was my initiation into the business as a young story editor."

I asked the producer about why he thinks that explicit violence, presented as creatively as possible, is so crucial to a film's success with the audience. "Violence has this universal appeal that transcends language, cultures, and borders," he told me. Indeed, Peterson's films are driven by the worldwide marketplace, so he feels it's crucial that they speak to people everywhere. "Whereas humor varies across cultures and doesn't translate well, everyone understands violence and can immediately relate to it. That's why films depend on it."

Knowing that violence sells, I asked him how he increases the tension when he shoots scenes. "There are all kinds of ways to use violence. You can use it as suspense in which the anticipation is where the action is. You can use it as a surprise attack, which is a powerful device. And then there's the emotional impact of violence, which we tried to focus on in *Monster*. Even in the very violent scenes we tried to focus on how it affected them. Finally, there's the actual violence itself that you find in slasher and splatter films."

Peterson confessed that although he's been involved in the gore, it's not something that appeals to him personally. He's aware that audiences get really turned on by the bloody stuff, but he likes it when the violence is more implied or subtle. "I've realized how much making successful movies means stimulating the audience by showing more—they've become desensitized to normal stuff. In a weird way part of making horror movies is to create new kinds of violence that have never been seen or imagined before."

Peterson has been involved in making the *Scanners* movies, in which the main narrative hook was related to people's heads exploding. Nobody had ever seen that before. "I remember the trailer for the film showed the lead up to the exploding head and then cut to a shot of the horrified audience. You could see how incredibly shocked they were. It was the number one movie at the box office when it was released."

Peterson went on to say: "Since then I've worked on sequels to it and now I'm working on a remake of the original. We literally sit around in a room—the producer, the director, the writers, and the studio—thinking about how we can outdo ourselves with new kinds of shock violence. We've already seen the guy's skin frying off his own body or his head exploding. How do we go beyond this to the next level? Sometimes I'm sitting there thinking, I went to college for this? I'm with all these smart people and this is what we're doing? But this is what the audience wants. They want to see stuff they've never seen before."

Peterson likens the job of making a new horror film to acting as a kind of personal coach for those in the audience who want to increase their excitement levels. "It's like exercising a muscle of your body. It just feels good to stimulate a part of you that's been inactive. When you're working out you have to keep lifting more weight to feel the benefits and the challenge. That's why we keep pushing the boundaries to do stuff that's never been done before to excite new parts of the psyche."

Hollywood directors are not misguided in their common knowledge that it requires higher doses of violent stimulation to evoke greater reactions in today's audiences. Whether in news coverage or entertainment, viewers become desensitized and blasé over time.[5] Just as the Roman emperors and Aztec priests discovered that they had to invent newer and more unusual forms of human destruction in order to keep the masses satisfied, so contemporary writers, as well as film and television producers, create more graphic, bizarre, and over-the-top depictions of tragedy and horror in order to make their mark.

THE CLASSICS

Whereas the writers and directors of new horror films are trying to push the boundaries of creativity, there are old standbys that never seem to become tiresome. I am talking about monsters, aliens, vampires, and zombies. The latter two seem to be everywhere these days: in books, on television, and in movies. Vampires you might well understand, muses critic Lev Grossman: "They're good-looking and sophisticated and well dressed. They're immortal. They even have castles."[6] He admits that it might be very cool to be a vampire, or even to sleep with one. But zombies? Who would ever want to sleep with one of those creatures? "They're hideous and mindless." They can barely walk straight, lurching around as they do with their arms outstretched for balance. They can barely carry on a decent conversation and can only think about one thing—devouring your brain. But, Grossman acknowledges, they do have their appeal in that they're tenacious, reliable, and humble. They are monsters of the people, so to speak, unlike vampires, who appear to be aristocratic and privileged blood-sucking parasites, like the investment bankers who brought down the economy.

Although science fiction horror remains popular, it is vampires and zombies who enjoy unprecedented popularity in all their manifestations. What both vampires and zombies share is immortality; they are members of the undead club. We are fascinated with them as much for their ability to cheat death as for their monstrous predation. They literally feast off the energy and spirit of the living, a perfect metaphor for anyone who seeks wealth, power, and status at the expense of others' misfortune. However disturbing their behavior, on some level we admire their sheer resilience to survive at all costs.

It is interesting to consider that the breakthrough in violent films occurred during the Great Depression when people were most desperate for ways to escape the hopelessness of their lives.[7] This was the golden age of horror, with the release of dozens of films featuring Dracula and Frankenstein as immortal characters who appeared over and over in various forms. Lon Chaney, Boris Karloff, Bela Lugosi, Peter Lorre, Vincent Price, Christopher Lee, and others became box office sensations, appearing in classics such as *Dracula* (1931), *Frankenstein* (1931), *The Mummy* (1932), *White Zombie* (1932), *Murders in the Rue Morgue* (1932), *Island*

Vampire lore that features blood-sucking predators who roam the night has permeated human culture for thousands of years. The Dracula myth, popularized by Bram Stoker in the gothic story, was based, in part, on a bloodthirsty Romanian count, Vlad Tepes, or Vlad the Impaler, who didn't actually drink the blood of his victims. The story of Dracula is now so popular that there are fan clubs and even a Dracula World Congress each year.[8]

of *Lost Souls* (1933), *The Black Cat* (1934), *Bride of Frankenstein* (1935), *Dracula's Daughter* (1936), *Revolt of the Zombies* (1936), and *Son of Frankenstein* (1939). *Dr. Jekyll and Mr. Hyde* even won a best acting Academy Award for Frederic March in 1932.

In addition to the various siblings, offspring, and spouses of monsters who earned their own feature films, it wasn't until twenty years later, in the 1950s, that science fiction films presented new opportunities to display dramatic mayhem. Although vampires, mummies, and zombies remained popular (e.g., *The Aztec Mummy, Curse of Frankenstein, Horror of Dracula, Revenge of Frankenstein*), once alien and mutant creatures were added to the mix, wholesale slaughter became the order of the day. There were gigantic mutant ants (*Them!*), spiders (*Tarantula*), birds (*The Giant Claw*), organic substances (*The Blob*), lizards (*Godzilla*), and of course alien invasions (e.g., *Invasion of the Body Snatchers, It Conquered the World, I Married a Monster from Outer Space, Invaders from Mars*).

It was during this same era that another form of entertainment violence was seducing a whole generation of children and teenagers (and adults): comic books. During the 1950s there were over 150 million comics sold each month![9] These included not only superheroes like Batman and Superman, but also the creepy characters of *Tales from the Crypt, Weird Mysteries, Tomb of Terror*. Blood was spilled on almost every page.

One psychiatrist claimed that violent comic books seduced children into lives of crime and depravity. He equated Superman with the Nazi ideal of Aryan perfection, claimed Batman and Robin were engaged in homo-erotic behavior, and declared that Wonder Woman was a lesbian; these were not the best models for youth.[10] Nevertheless, in spite of the critics, comics became a complement to the films of the time, showing gruesome crimes in vivid colors and simplistic prose, drawing readers into the fantasy world in which evil could often be defeated by heroes using brutal force.

The film *Tarantula* is one of a series of disaster/monster/horror films from the fifties that featured a giant, predatory spider that destroyed everything in its path. The moral of the story, and so many others like it, is that human beings experiment with nature at their peril. Many of these fictional killers, like Godzilla, have resulted from scientific experiments gone awry.

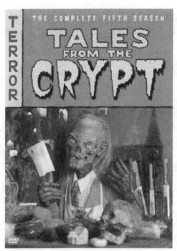

Tales from the Crypt comics were published during the 1950s, featuring terror and violence for adolescents with scantily clad, voluptuous women. Congress got involved to shut down the operation, although it made a comeback years later in a popular television series.

VIOLENCE AND ULTRAVIOLENCE: IT'S ALL ABOUT SHOCK VALUE

I have been speaking about media violence as if it is a single entity, but it can more accurately be described along a continuum. Picture television shows or movies you've seen that are action-packed or include a lot of dramatic tension. Think of the books you've read that have similar features. On one end of the scale are those that include "suggestive violence," meaning that it is implied but not actually viewed or described. There may be a gunshot or scream off screen or in the background, or a brief description or quick pan of the outcome (a shot is fired and then viewers see a lifeless body on the floor), or the whole tragic end is left to your imagination.

The next level on the continuum is "mild or narrative violence," the kind that is crucial to the plot and presented in a relatively "tasteful" manner, meaning that there is no serious blood spatter or prolonged bludgeoning. Any abuse or killing is an integral part of the plot. Perhaps a woman is subjected to physical and emotional abuse that is important to display so that the audience can later appreciate the depth of her courage and resilience to recover from her wounds and lead a cause for restorative justice.

Next on the list is "graphic and explicit" violence, the standard fare at the multiplex that contains a significant body count, multiple spectacular explosions, and often the fate of the whole human race at stake if our hero does not slay enough invading aliens, zombies, vampires, monsters, scheming masterminds, or invading hordes. Although highly realistic, with special effects budgets that often exceed the actors' salaries, there is almost a comical quality to the carnage and destruction. Even with all the imploded bodies, severed limbs, slow-motion death throes, it is like being on a roller coaster that is exciting and entertaining, but on some level you know it isn't real and that eventually you can get off the ride even if you feel a little dizzy and nauseous.

Finally, on the ultimate end of the continuum is "ultraviolence," also known as "violence porn." Plot is irrelevant. If there is a story at all, it becomes lost in all the carnage that is lovingly portrayed with almost an artistic obsession to getting the details of gore right. In these films, the only goal is to provide the most lurid and grotesque (I'm searching for relatively neutral words) descriptions or images one can devise. Heads explode with brain matter splattered everywhere. Viscera are opened with all kinds of sharp implements of destruction—samurai swords, power drills, double-sided axes, soldering irons—you name it and it has been used somewhere. Shock is the primary objective, and if it can make you sick, then the writer counts it a success.

STRUCTURES WITHIN THE GENRE: CHALLENGING ASSUMPTIONS OF REALITY

Hollywood directors, writers, and producers are mostly at a loss to explain the appeal of their violent films; all they know is that they are guaranteed to score at the box office. Producer Clark Peterson just shrugs when the question is posed. He finds it intriguing, from a marketing perspective, that the primary audience for violent films seems to match the dominant victims, that is, young women tend to frequent slasher films in which their counterparts are the ones who are slaughtered; teenagers prefer films like *Scream* in which their age group is the target of killers; young men go to see war movies in which people who look like them are the ones who are killed. Peterson wonders if his newest film, which features a serial killer who preyed on gay men (John Wayne Gacy), would have special appeal within the gay community. This is certainly not logical speculation, but he notices that this phenomenon appears to hold true.

For her doctoral research on the structure of horror films, Isabel Pinedo first laid out the typical narrative of the classics of the 1930s like *Frankenstein* and *Dracula* or *The Thing* and *Invasion of the Body Snatchers* of the 1950s.

Scene I: A monster or alien enters and goes on a rampage.

Scene II: The male hero tries to stop the mad scientist or supernatural force but is repeatedly defeated.

Scene III: The good hero finally conquers evil through comparable brutal force and restores order.[11]

What Pinedo calls the "postmodern" version in recent times has a very different structure. Films like *Halloween*, *Henry: Portrait of a Serial Killer*, *Scream*, and *A Nightmare on Elm Street* begin essentially the same way as the classics but with considerably more brutal and explicit violence during the rampage. And in the end, the villain or monster escapes confinement or destruction (for a sequel!). More to the point, the male expert fighting these monsters is never as effective as the "ordinary victim," often a sexualized woman who is subjected to repeated violence before she neutralizes the threat. In *Alien*, for example, Sigourney Weaver runs around in her sheer underwear, succeeding in the battle against the attacking creature where the macho men have failed. You will also notice that in contemporary versions of horror, the monsters are often not external threats from other planets or supernatural forces but rather threats from within—seemingly ordinary people who live among us. The films violate usual boundaries and expectations and rarely offer definitive closure. And they are all about eliciting fear, but in a way quite different from their predecessors.

Pinedo finds the violence in most films not to be gratuitous but actually crucial to their purpose. The more the natural order of things is disrupted by the killer who breaks all the rules (as well as the filmmaker), the more our assumptions about reality are challenged. Of course, that's a fancy way of endorsing the power of shock value to violate established boundaries. Whatever you think is really going on—in the movie, book, or television show, as well as your own life—is only an illusion. Surprises await.

Rationality, logic, and brute force, the gods of maleness, usually don't work to defeat the monster. It takes the female quality of intuition to devise an indirect and illogical solution to the problem, one fueled by the very emotions that women are—at least in a traditional sense—not permitted to express. They also get to do some "whup-ass" and express their own violence—as is the case for the lead character in the television series *Buffy the Vampire Slayer* when she drives a stake into the predatory creature, or The Bride (Uma Thurman) hunting down her attempted murderer (David Carradine) in *Kill Bill*. For many viewers (especially women), "the horror film is an exquisite exercise in coping with the terrors of everyday life."[12]

DEATH BY PROXY

Cultural critic David Schmid suggests that, however paradoxical it might appear at first, studying death as up close as possible (but not *too* close) helps us to deal with anxieties about our own annihilation. Existentialist philosophers of the last century noted that preoccupation with our own fears of death is a major life occupation, one that creates tremendous terror, but also, ultimately, motivates us to live each moment with great appreciation and satisfaction. In a sense, we feel more alive during those times when we are most fearful: "We experience death by proxy," writes Schmid.[13] That explains why people deliberately jump off cliffs or out of airplanes, why they race cars, climb mountains, or take other life-threatening risks. And if you can do so, vicariously, without having to actually put your life in jeopardy, so much the better. In fact, watching a scary show, a horror movie, or reading a terrifying thriller allows you to experience death—both as a killer and a victim—in controlled, self-moderated doses. If things become too intense, or you become *too* frightened, you can always close your eyes, put the book down, or even turn off the sound.

There is clearly an identification process going on when watching any media violence, but the interesting question is who, exactly, we are identifying with—the killer or the victim? It isn't actually an either/or question since there are two different processes involved. When identifying with the killer, that is, pretending that you are stalking a victim right alongside (or inside) the predator, you are merely indulging in programming from ten million years of evolution in which it was your primary job to kill efficiently, whether that included animals for food or enemies who infringed on your territory. There is guilt and shame associated with these forbidden feelings, and these are reasons some people find identification with the killer if not enjoyable, then at least satisfying on some level. Apologize all you want for these impulses, but deep down inside we are all capable of savagery no matter how thick we wear the veneer of civilization.

Personally, I can't figure out who I'm identifying with during violent movies or in books, but I don't think it's the killer. Oh, don't get me wrong—I occasionally have very violent fantasies of strangling someone who annoys me (loud talkers on cell phones come to mind). More seriously, and difficult to confess, I have also entertained fantasies of wishing adversaries dead. I didn't imagine I could ever do the deed myself, but I wondered, just for a little while, how difficult it would be to find some Mafioso enforcer to break a leg or two to teach someone a lesson. I lived with this frustration for a few years in which I felt abused in a work setting and was witness to far more destructive behavior among colleagues. I felt powerless to do anything. I felt unable to protect myself from harm to the extent I would have preferred. And more than ever before, I *so* enjoyed violent movies and books in which I did imagine myself as the one doing some serious damage—not to an innocent victim but to my nemesis. It felt good, in fact better than I'd like to admit, imagining myself dishing out revenge in the most brutal way possible. In that sense, I suppose I was identifying with the victims but in such a way that I was fighting back. I actually believe this coping mechanism allowed me to function far longer in this work setting than I could have otherwise (which maybe wasn't a good thing at all).

Beyond any identification process, any good film sucks you into the experience so that you lose yourself. Some time ago, a psychologist used the word *flow* to describe the perfect balance between boredom and anxiety.[14] That model fits nicely with the different ways that people typically respond to this genre of entertainment. Some people are totally bored by these movies, find them contrived, predictable, and stupid. On the other end of the continuum are those who absolutely freak out by watching violence—it is sensory overload and they have so little tolerance for the horror experience that they consider it unendurably painful. Then, somewhere in the middle, are thrill seekers who love the stimulation of being scared half to death—but with a degree of control. One such fan who really enjoys scary movies, but whose husband falls into the overanxious group, describes her system for solitary pleasure. First she carefully chooses a movie that is scary, but not *too* scary. "Before turning on the TV, I carefully lock all the doors, especially the one to the basement."[15] Everyone knows that if a monster is going to get you, surely it will come from the basement. And now if there is some kind of creepy noise she hears, she knows it is only a tree branch rather than someone coming to get her.

EDUCATION AND SELF-PROTECTION

In addition to providing safe opportunities to explore the forbidden and feeding our curiosity, there is also strong interest in making sense of creatures that are like-us-but-not-like-us. Almost all of us have the capacity to kill in certain circumstances, whether for survival or to protect loved ones against harm. It is even possible to understand killing for greed or financial gain in which someone murders in order to obtain advantageous resources. Yet it is difficult to fathom killing for the pure pleasure that the act affords. There are certain people who are born without the capacity to feel empathy for others. They are missing whatever psychological capacity permits humans to feel compassion, guilt, remorse, or concern for others. From the earliest age, they begin to experiment by torturing animals, and then their violence escalates and they turn toward human victims. They enjoy watching others in pain, especially if they are the ones inflicting it. By almost all definitions, they are insane, outside the realm of anything we would consider normal. They are monsters, but ones who look just like us and live within our midst.

Consider prototypical serial killers like Jeffrey Dahmer, the Unabomber, the Son of Sam, other mass murderers, or even a seemingly emerging market of killer—school shooters. They are "outsiders" or "loners," clearly strange dudes who almost everyone could easily identify as lacking adequate social skills. But what about killers like Ted Bundy and John Wayne Gacy, who were very charming, socially skilled, seductive, and even successful, operating quite comfortably in plain view? They could have been your neighbors, coworkers, or even your friends (okay, maybe not friends). Even more disturbing is to consider who else is out there in the world, in *your* world—is there a budding psychopath working himself up toward a killing spree somewhere nearby?

There is a belief, most likely an illusion, that somehow you might protect yourself against being a victim if you can in some way learn to recognize the signs and symptoms of a predator on the hunt. Hundreds of biographies, documentaries, and films have been made about these characters as retrospective case studies of how they grew to be who they were. Yet in spite of all the authorities and experts talking about what went wrong, how they became so demented, and analyzing their cases, the fact remains that it is still mostly a mystery.

Nevertheless, it is one of the most natural instincts for humans to be curious about violence and murder, as well as how and why it occurs. In spite of protestations to the contrary, 90 percent of people admit that on occasion they have fantasized about killing someone; among those who have been interviewed about their homicidal urges, many estimate that they were close to 60 percent (or higher) certain that they were about to act on their impulses.[16]

An eighteen-year-old female bookstore employee was alarmingly honest about such feelings: "A part of me wants to kill other people, but I don't want to fry. It makes me feel good to watch others suffer. I think all the time about killing others, but I'm afraid of getting caught. I have always wished that everyone could be allowed to kill just one person. The only thing I wouldn't like about it is that I could be that one person."

It is confessions such as this that help explain the universal popularity of violence as entertainment. Such media serve the simultaneous functions of allowing us to explore fascinating territory, yet also vent forbidden thoughts and feelings that might otherwise fester. A look at the evolution of dramatic enactments offers other useful ideas to explain the appeal.

A GLIMPSE BACK INTO HISTORY

From the time that visual and auditory media were first invented in the late nineteenth century, violence was a predominant focus of entertainment. Thomas Edison, inventor of the phonograph, lightbulb, and other technological marvels, was himself fascinated with murders and lurid crimes. One of his first phonograph recordings included someone reading the confessions of H. H. Holmes, America's first "official" serial killer. William Randolph Hearst paid Holmes a fortune for the syndication rights to his story—and made a substantial profit from the enterprise. This was just the beginning of a whole new industry to feed the public lust for blood.[17]

One of Edison's first kinetoscopes (a predecessor of the film projector) featured the re-created execution of Mary, Queen of Scots. Long before the Internet provided instant access to videos of homicide scenes, corpses, or executions, Edison was producing his own versions of the macabre. Speaking of which, there is a Web site called Ogrish.com that specializes in displaying ultraviolence in the form of previously filmed beheadings, executions, homicides, and body parts.[18]

The slasher genre began in the 1960s with films like *Blood Feast* and *Two Thousand Maniacs!*, which created the formula of having beautiful women terrorized by violent lunatics. In a review of the most popular hits, all the violent acts committed, averaging fifty per film, were cataloged, including: 32 percent beatings, 21 percent stabbings, and 18 percent shootings, with the balance made up of your everyday bludgeoning, burning, poisoning, beheading, strangling, sawing, electrocuting, hanging, and dismembering. And, oh, yes—verbal abuse thrown in about 1 percent of the time.[19]

You might be surprised to find out that women are *not* the primary victims in these films—more innocent men are killed. So where would we get the impression that the films are all about torturing and slaying half-naked women? The researchers found that the reason had to do with the excessive screen time allotted to showing women screaming and expressing fear. Apparently *this* is the visual image that people pay to see. Women are channeling their own fears into the character, and men are being tested to watch the brutality without blinking.

Again, one of the supreme ironies of slasher/splatter movies, those that feature brutal torture and ultra-explicit violence, is that audiences for these films are often composed of young women, akin to the ones who are being stalked in the films. In other words, people watch films in which *they* are the identified victims. Diablo Cody, screenwriter of the comedy *Juno*, but also of the extremely violent *Jennifer's Body*, admits her guilty pleasure. She wrote the screenplay for the film because "I knew about the female horror audience and am a fan myself. . . . I was absolutely mesmerized by the horror section at the local video store."[20]

Darcy, a store manager in her late twenties, admits that she becomes emotionally and even sexually aroused by violent horror movies. "A lot of times I don't even realize how excited I am until after it's over and I feel drained. It's just the whole idea of being excited that leads up to the suspense. There are movies when they show a really graphic scene and when that happens I like to rewind it and watch it again. It makes me feel bad in kind of good way. It makes me want to touch myself."

In the typical slasher movies, attractive, young virginal women are chased by virile, crazy guys who stalk, torture, rape, and kill them in the most lurid, disgusting ways imaginable. Knives, saws, axes, blowtorches, power drills, and any other killing tool you can image are employed in progressively more creative and explicit imagery. Whereas you might imagine that the primary audience for these flicks would be testosterone-driven men who want to see their own violent, forbidden fantasies acted out on the screen, you would be wrong. Ticket buyers for gruesome films are frequently women, sometimes as much as 65 percent of the audience. Brad Fuller, the producer of the films *Texas Chainsaw Massacre* and *Friday the 13th*, complained about his biggest marketing challenge for future horror movies: "For us, the issue now is that it's harder for us to get young men into the theater than women."[21] This observation is echoed by the founder of FEARnet, a video-on-demand channel that features torture porn in which young women are subjected to unspeakable acts of violence. When he did focus groups to define his potential market, he was shocked to discover that interest in the new enterprise was primarily driven by women.

In an article exploring this phenomenon, entertainment reporter Christine Spines offered several explanations including the surge of excitement that takes place during the heightened tension, and, surprisingly, what women interpret as an empowering message of the films—after all, the women fight back against the knife-wielding monsters, and at least one usually prevails through her ingenuity and perseverance. Horror movie producer Susan Downy explains: "Horror films tap into the most primal fears. And when we put a woman through this mythological journey and have her come out at the end kicking ass, the guys get their eye candy they want and the girls get the sense of 'I can face my demon.'"[22]

There is another force operating as well. Horror and splatter films often attract dates in which the women have an excuse to cuddle and have a reason to hold on to the guy who is doing his level best to appear in control. Men are actually being tested during the viewings, expected to show minimal fear and absolute control, even though inside they may be as terrified as little girls.

PAYING TO LOSE CONTROL

Quentin Tarantino has written and directed some of the bloodiest and most violent mainstream films of the past decades, including *Reservoir Dogs*, *Pulp Fiction*, *Kill Bill*, and *Inglourious Basterds*. Yet he is unapologetic about the brutal scenes he creates and displays: "I'm *trying* to be disturbing," he admits.[23] Tarantino *wants* to get under your skin, to haunt you with his realism that makes everything on the screen come alive. For Tarantino, his violence is about aesthetics. "Saying you don't like violence in movies is like saying you don't like dance sequences in movies."[24] According to him, violence is as much a part of life as anything else that is portrayed in fictional narratives, and his job is to present the viewing experience as powerfully and viscerally as possible.

Sam Peckinpah, who laid the groundwork for the violence in cinema of his generation, heartily agrees with Tarantino. In his films *Wild Bunch* and *Straw Dogs*, the public outcry only fed greater interest. Audiences appeared to clamor for the privilege of paying money to be horrified. Peckinpah claimed his films were actually antiviolent since they portray human behavior at its most base, primitive, and awful. "And yet there's a certain response that you get from it, an excitement, because we're all violent people, we have violence within us."[25]

As previously mentioned, there is also a control element to the experience of viewing such films. You have the power at almost any moment to moderate the level of arousal you are feeling. If you become too terrified by what is happening on the screen, you always have the option to remind yourself that *it is only a movie*. Look at your watch. Close your eyes.

Sneak a peek at your phone. Stretch. Reorient yourself. Repeat the mantra: "It's only a movie. It's not real. It's not happening *to me*."

If, on the other hand, you are feeling bored and disengaged from the film and want to ratchet up the excitement, then you can pretend that it *is* real. Jump in with both feet. Imagine that it's you who is running, hiding, or fighting. What would *you* do in this predicament?

This happened to me recently while attending a horrifying and disturbing movie about the end of the world as we know it. I think at one point I started to shut down because I was so freaked out. I kept looking at my watch and yawning. I started thinking about the set design and the camera angles, admiring the acting, wondering about how the special effects were designed. I was in perfect control—or so I thought at the time. But with an hour left to go, feeling restless and bored, I thought, "What the hell," and slipped back into the narrative without my seatbelt attached. The film became so real for me that when the lights came back on, I was still *there*. I couldn't stop crying and couldn't even explain to my son why I was so upset.

The film was *The Road*, based on Cormac McCarthy's story about a father's legacy to his son in a post-apocalyptic world. I couldn't stop thinking about what I would do in such circumstances, what I would do to survive and protect my own family against marauding killers. And I couldn't stop crying because, for me, even a week later, the movie hadn't yet ended; I was still living it.

Did I get my money's worth from an entertainment experience that still haunts me and invades my dreams and fantasies? You betcha. But I also lost control and I'm still paying for it.

ENJOYING DISASTERS—WHEN THEY HAPPEN TO OTHER PEOPLE

The genre of disaster films has been a major Hollywood staple since the 1930s. People love to see some spectacular but terrible catastrophe befall the human race, hopefully with a major body count. The template for such plots is predictable. We meet the unsuspecting characters who look just like us (or like we prefer to see ourselves)—attractive, moral, kind, but troubled in some way. There are always a few villain types who display a level of selfishness that we just know is going to play out in the story when they try to steal the lifeboat/food supply/escape vehicle for themselves and leave everyone else stranded. There are bound to be amazing special effects. And there will be survivors who earned that right as a function of their compatibility with audience identification.

The list of categories within the disaster film genre is virtually endless. You have your basic avalanches and earthquakes, along with meteor strikes, volcanic eruptions, floods, tsunamis, and the occasional rogue wave. Global warming has spawned another whole list of possible disasters including floods, tornados, and fires. Monsters, aliens, vampires, and zombies are huge hits, as are any kind of epidemic. In fact, there are no fewer than sixty different movies about rampant diseases that nearly wipe out the human race. Finally, there are human-made disasters—blackouts; nuclear accidents; computer crashes; chemical explosions; airplane, train, truck, or car crashes; plus the spectacles of submarines, ships, or spaceships in jeopardy. When I said there was an endless list, I mean that practically every month there is a new disaster film released, another experience designed to make us feel better about having survived when the lights come back on.

Consider that the highest-grossing movie for over a decade, *Titanic*, was essentially a disaster movie. Although a substantial appeal of the film is the romance and storyline, there is also a curiosity about who survives and who dies, and why. As with all disasters, whether earthquakes, burning buildings, sinking ships, or terrorist attacks, we wonder why some people lived and others perished. Was it luck? Or rather, was there some particular skill or preparation that allowed some people to escape? The World Trade Center attacks have been studied over and over to determine how it was that some survivors managed to elude the fate of others.

Yet it is far more than curiosity that motivates audiences to consume violent entertainment with such an avid appetite. Scary, violent movies, full of monsters, zombies, aliens, vampires, or plain old mortal serial killers, exist, in the words of horror maven Wes Craven, to "break through the audience's complacency." By this he means that it is necessary to break rules, transcend boundaries, and catch people off guard and vulnerable. He cites this media as the equivalent of our modern mythology, with Freddy Krueger as the Minotaur of ancient Greece, and the themes explored relate to conquering fear.[26]

Zombies, vampires, monsters, and other terrors on the screen, in video games, or in books are clearly not real, and (most) viewers know and understand the difference. That is precisely the appeal of these media. There is a game being played between the writers and the audience, one in which the object is to catch consumers off guard, to shock them in ways that are unexpected. The entertainer's job, argues media critic Walter Kendrick, is to stun the audience in the most imaginative ways possible.[27] This becomes progressively more difficult as viewers/readers develop greater sophistication and experience with the media. If the object is to make people feel strong emotions, then it takes more potent doses to elicit the desired reactions.

Among the possible ways to evoke strong emotion, anything to do with death is a surefire device. As viewers and readers and game players become desensitized over time, it takes even greater creativity to catch people off guard. The cleverest films and books examine the horror of death in such a way that "dying is rendered safe; it is turned into a celebration of being permanently alive, forever immune to decay."[28] Zombies and vampires are perhaps the best vehicles for doing so.

Even better is when a horror film or book manages to insert some type of social commentary or political criticism. Feminism has invaded the contemporary slasher films in which women are no longer portrayed as helpless victims. They may still be half-naked sex objects, but they are also empowered to defeat the monsters through their superior intuition, skill, and guile. Popular shows on television like *True Blood* have a strong subtext addressing issues of racism and homophobia (the vampires have been oppressed and are subject to discrimination and restricted rights). The science fiction film *District 9* was only thinly disguised as a story about apartheid in South Africa.

Any moral issues that are embedded in violent media are offset by other considerations that make us question the priorities of our culture in which killers have been so glorified. In the next chapter we examine this phenomenon in which legions of fans have become attracted to killers for purposes that transcend mere entertainment and reveal far deeper and darker motivations.

Chapter 6

Serial Killer Groupies: Attraction to Predators

W hereas the attraction to violence and fascination with murder are both commonplace and relatively benign, there are those who live vicariously through serial killers, even worship them. They are intrigued with the power and control that such murderers wield; on some level they feel curiosity and envy but also some semblance of a conscience. Instead of acting on their own impulses, they sublimate this lust for blood by studying brutal crimes with obsessive focus. They read biographies of the killers, watch documentaries and films about their evil ways, scrutinize their methods as well as what led to their eventual capture. Some fans join clubs that celebrate killers' exploits, and they purchase souvenirs including computer screen-savers and calendars just as they would of any rock star or film celebrity.

Serial killer and cannibal Jeffrey Dahmer was featured several times on the covers of national magazines such as *People.* Another celebrity serial killer, John Wayne Gacy, bragged that he had received over 27,000 letters from fans. "Some weeks I get more than 50 people writing to me, all wanting to know things about me. They write because I'm famous."[1]

Gacy, murderer of at least thirty-three boys, became one of the most famous people in America during the 1980s, although he also had to compete for attention with the likes of Richard Ramirez, Jeffrey Dahmer, Ted Bundy, and Charles Manson. It was a golden era for serial killers—and their fans.

In his book on the ways that serial killers have become celebrities in

There are Web sites like *Serial Killer Central* that sell T-shirts, souvenirs, and *murderabilia* from famous killers. You can purchase a drawing by Richard (the Night Stalker) Ramirez, or a painting by John Wayne Gacy, for thousands of dollars. You can own a lock of Charles Manson's hair or a brick from Jeffrey Dahmer's apartment for close to the same amount. You can collect serial killer trading cards or purchase a calendar featuring the "Killer Hall of Fame" to post on your bedroom wall.

our culture, David Schmid finds it utterly perplexing that nobody has investigated why they have been treated as folk heroes and celebrities, worshipped by fans, and viewed as objects of envy, admiration, fascination, and lust.[2] He cites the cases of the first publicized serial killers in Britain and America, Jack the Ripper and H. H. Holmes, respectively, who not only became world famous but still enjoy tremendous notoriety. Even 125 years after the Ripper operated throughout London, he remains a big attraction at wax museums and as a tourist destination for a walking tour. In the 1880s when he was killing, enterprising businessmen would charge people a toll to visit the streets where victims were found. He is treated as a kind of Robin Hood figure, his killing glossed over because of admiration that he was never caught or even positively identified.[3]

THE APPEAL OF SERIAL KILLERS

Throughout history, there has long been a morbid interest—and glorification—of outlaws and killers who operated outside any conventional morality or legal system. In the mold of Robin Hood, Jesse James, Bonnie and Clyde, Billy the Kid, all cold-blooded killers, they captured public attention and adulation precisely because of their complete disregard for the consequences of their behavior. Our fascination with killers is rooted, in part, in the secret admiration of their daring. After investigating dozens of cases involving famous pirates, bank robbers, anarchists, serial killers, and unscrupulous scoundrels and murderers, Laurent Marechaux concludes that they actually deserve our admiration: "Too cowardly or reasonable to follow in their footsteps, we are left standing on the shore, secretly sharing their thirst for rebellion."[4]

There are actually several very good reasons why serial killers attract such public interest. First of all, they are *rare* in the killing business with perhaps only a few hundred operating at any one time around the world. Second, they often kill randomly, choosing victims based on opportunities presented—this makes *anyone* a potential victim, even if the odds of ever running into one are about the same as getting struck by lightning. Third, they are *prolific*, meaning that they kill lots of people over a period of many years rather than in a single, impulsive act. Finally, their behavior appears *inexplicable* and without apparent motive: they don't act out of greed, jealousy, passion, revenge, or exploitation (the usual reasons) but rather in order to live out their perverse fantasies.[5]

One of the most popular tourist destinations in London is the "Jack the Ripper Tour," in which visitors have the opportunity to visit the grisly locations of all the serial killer's mutilations.

Serial killers have been given virtual hero status in movies and television in which the audience roots for them to succeed on some level. Freddy Krueger (*A Nightmare on Elm Street*), Mickey Knox (*Natural Born Killers*), Michael Myers (*Halloween*), Leatherface (*The Texas Chainsaw Massacre*), Jason Voorhees (*Friday the 13th*), and more recently, Dexter Morgan (*Dexter*) and Sweeney Todd (aka Johnny Depp) in *The Demon Barber of Fleet Street*, are all examples of fictional killers who have become the main protagonists of the stories. This has become only a little less true with real-life killers who have a considerable fan base.

Dexter is one of the most popular and critically acclaimed shows on cable television, featuring a serial killer who is the hero. He dispatches his victims with creative relish, speaking at length about the "Dark Passenger" that inhabits his psyche and drives him to stalk his victims and torture them while tied down to a table. Yet he is a "good" serial killer, if not a man with a conscience then at least with his own moral compass that directs him to kill only other bad guys. Nevertheless, we can't help but cheer him on in his lust for blood. As with Patricia Highsmith's Tom Ripley novels, "There is a transference at work in *Dexter*, an unlikely and guilty pleasure in identifying with the practical problems of a killer. The truth is that if Dexter is caught, all the fun ends."[6]

In a thesis analyzing how sympathy is developed for a character like Dexter, it is surmised that it is basically the result of working outside of the audience's expectations for the genre.[7] The storyline is so unfamiliar and novel to viewers, the very idea that a serial killer could be a sympathetic hero opens new possibilities for generating alternative forms of identification. There is something altogether satisfying about pretending you are the serial killer, but one with a noble mission. While you are imagining yourself as the protagonist, you get to kill people, but only those who deserve it (other serial killers). In a sense, Dexter is doing us all a service.

CURIOUS SELF-PROTECTION

America has had a love affair with serial killers and mass murderers, documented by an insatiable appetite for films on the subject, hundreds of them telling the gruesome stories of homicide in the most graphic way possible. From the early classics like *Psycho* (1960), *Bonnie and Clyde* (1967), *Boston Strangler* (1968), and *In Cold Blood* (1968), the golden era of the nineties with *Henry: Portrait of a Serial Killer* (1990), *American Psycho* (1991), *Silence of the Lambs* (1991), *Kalifornia* (1991), *Natural Born*

Although killers are so often glorified on the screen, they bear little resemblance to their appearance and behavior in real life. Arthur Penn's film about the exploits of Bonnie and Clyde presents them as misunderstood tragic heroes, star-crossed lovers, who were victims of their life circumstances and just tried to make the best of things. In truth Clyde Barrow was a sadistic serial killer with a death toll exceeding fifteen, mostly innocent victims. He liked to torture animals and was described in newspapers as "a snake-eyed murderer." In contrast to their portrayal in the film, the couple was actually "physically offensive," smelled terrible most of the time, and were not really in love.[8]

Killers (1994), *Se7en* (1995), to more recent classics like *From Hell* (2001), *Monster* (2003), *Zodiac* (2007), and *Riverman* (2010), such films consistently attract large audiences (and often critical acclaim).

Echoing the fascination that so many people have for serial killers, horror writer Stephen King kept scrapbooks on murderers like Charlie Starkweather for much of his life. When asked why he has this morbid interest, he explained: "Well, it was never like, 'Yeah, go Charlie, kill some more.' It was more like, 'Charlie, if I ever see anyone like you, I'll be able to get the hell away.'"[9]

This theme of curious self-protection is one that is frequently mentioned by the majority of people who spend inordinate amounts of time studying the behavior and crimes of serial murderers. Yet in some cases, the interest is actually created by the media as a way to increase customer interest. In a study of news reports in the *New York Times* about three different serial killers from different times—the Son of Sam (David Berkowitz), the California Night Stalker (Richard Ramirez), and the Boston Strangler (Albert DeSalvo), I found that this one prestigious source (hardly the *National Enquirer*), representative of other media, didn't so much report news but rather *created* a market for a relatively minor series of incidents (compared to all the other carnage, war, and violence taking place on the planet).[10] Each of these serial killers, and dozens of others that are familiar, were elevated to star status, celebrities who enjoyed fame and notoriety that exceeded that of scientists, writers, politicians, and other professionals who were doing groundbreaking work.

There is indeed a direct relationship between stories in the news about serial killers and a significant increase in readership or viewership. The *New York Times* published 148 different stories about David Berkowitz, the Son of Sam.[11] In order for stories to be successful (meaning there will be an interest for more on the subject), the main character has to be sympathetic in some way. Whether describing a serial killer or a mass murderer, most news stories describe the killer as a "loner," someone of "humble origins," someone who was "misunderstood" or "bullied." In the quest to make sense of horrific acts of violence, one consistent storyline is that the killer's behavior was inevitable given the abuse or neglect he suffered as a child. There is sometimes a kind of perverse admiration for a criminal who manages to elude authorities for years and still continues his murder spree.

As mentioned, the irony is that serial killing is so rare that it actually represents less than 1 percent of homicides, yet one might very well get the impression from the media that there are legions of these predators operating at a "breakneck" pace.[12] It is difficult to blame newspapers, magazines, books, Web sites, and television for publicizing the exploits of serial murderers since these publications are only feeding public interest with the message: "People are being brutally murdered. We don't know who is doing this, but he is still on a rampage. Watch out!" Who wouldn't want to protect against such an apparent and impending dangerous threat?

KILLERS AS SUPERSTARS

Whereas the behavior of serial killers, mass murderers, and school shooters might seem inexplicable in that they are not motivated by financial gain or any particular advantage, they do attain a tremendous amount of power and actually achieve their most desired goal, which is increased status. Most such killers are from the lower economic stratum and feel some need to redress ways that they have been ignored, marginalized, or otherwise relegated to the bottom of the power hierarchy. They feel powerless and frustrated and seek some revenge against those in power or those who represent such authorities. Charles Manson is a classic case of this:

his mass murder of Sharon Tate and others was intended to attack the rich and famous. Similarly, school shooters have often been bullied or isolated and wish to fight back against this perceived oppression. Interestingly, most of the killers succeed in their goal: they *do* become famous celebrities who attain a perverted status. Famous writers want to interview them. Movie producers want to make films about their life stories. FBI agents and interrogators want to pick their brains. Women propose marriage. Fan clubs and Web sites are launched to celebrate their grisly deeds. They receive all the attention they ever dreamed about. "Serial killers, through extensive news coverage, become superstars as big as the movie action hero, home run hitter and pop star."[13]

Serial killers are bestowed with nicknames that proclaim their superstar status—the Clown Killer, Night Stalker, Boston Strangler, Jack the Ripper, Lonely Hearts Killer, Milwaukee Monster, Coed Killer, Candyman, Freeway Killer, Angel of Death, Unabomber, Campus Killer. People study the characteristics or appearance of the victims to see if they "qualify" as potential bait.

Henry Lee Lucas killed hundreds of people. He used knives, guns, a car, and his bare hands. He worked alone sometimes. Other times he worked with a partner. He killed children. He killed adults and old people. He even created a "family" that he hoped would help him in his murder spree. His "wife," by the way, was nine years old when he first began

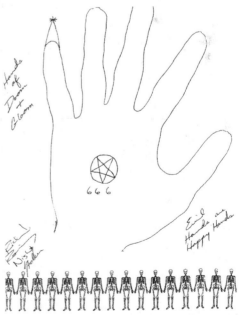

Serial killer Richard "California Night Stalker" Ramirez fancied himself an artist, creating and selling drawings and self-portraits. This drawing of his own hand contains satanic symbols, inscriptions saying "Hands of Doom and Gloom" and "Evil Hands are Happy Hands," and features skeletons holding hands along the bottom. Drawing sent to Jason Moss as a gift. Moss gave the drawing to the author.

training her, and she was thirteen when they began living together. She didn't survive their relationship. Like most of his victims, he had sex with her corpse. Sometimes he was fond of eating his victims, although he found the taste "gamey." Most of all, he loved the attention from the public. He thrived on the notoriety, having lived in obscurity as a drifter all his life. In fact, he did everything he could to make himself the most famous man alive, confessing to crimes he didn't commit and leading police on treasure hunts for dead bodies.[14]

Whereas it is easy to blame the media for publicizing the exploits of killers and to lament the moral decline of our culture because of the sensational stories, there isn't a definitive link between cause and effect: the violence portrayed in the media has not been definitely shown to lead to anything specific in outcome. It turns out that the impact is far more subtle and complex—there are certain people who are more susceptible than others. Some people are horrified and disturbed, some aroused, some desensitized and indifferent (not a good thing either).[15]

Against their will, women are drawn to men who have power, even if these guys are not particularly attractive. This can be demonstrated through wealth, intelligence, access to resources, positions of authority in the community, and physical prowess. As to the latter, which today is manifested in sports figures, it was traditionally demonstrated through effectiveness in dominance and violence. Essentially, the most attractive mates were those who were most skilled as killers. These were the Genghis Khans, the Alexander the Greats, the Ivan the Terribles, and even Ted Bundy and Richard Ramirez, serial killers who enjoyed the attention and aggressive seductions of thousands of women who sent letters of admiration, money, pornographic photos of themselves, even marriage proposals.

Tired of restraint, rules, boundaries, and moral codes, these killers obey no laws except their own. They hold nothing sacred except their own lust for blood. And if that's not enough, they don't even have a guilty conscience! They are admired for this ruthlessness and audacity. For some, they become folk heroes and objects of infatuation.

This infatuation is all the more remarkable when you consider that Bundy used to repeatedly have sex with his victims, after they were already dead, or that Ramirez indiscriminately raped any woman he could find before he killed her.

I'D MARRY A SERIAL KILLER

Ninety percent of the letters that Richard Ramirez receives on death row are from women, even though he already married one of his fans in a ceremony that was held at the prison. One of the jurors who convicted him became a devoted fan after the trial and tried to work for his release. When we interviewed his wife, Doreen, a number of years ago, she described herself as "a good Catholic girl and a virgin." She had just married the Night Stalker and, twelve years later, she was still married to him. "He's kind, he's funny, he's charming," she gushed, "I think he's really a great person. He's my best friend; he's my buddy."[16]

Doreen was ostracized by her family, ridiculed by the media, an object of both fascination and pity. Nobody understood how she could fall so madly in love with a man whose life ambition had always been to be known as the most famous killer the world had ever known. She admitted it's a lonely life since she settles for a brief conversation and a kiss on the cheek. Yet she remains his conduit to the outside world, the person who passes messages back and forth, who runs his "business" of self-promotion.

The partnership between Doreen and Ramirez is especially incongruent given her innocent and sheltered demeanor. In various media interviews, she has admitted that he is a little scary at first, but once you get used to him, he can be quite kind, funny, and charming.[17] Like many other women who are so drawn to incarcerated killers, she enjoys the control she feels over the relationship.[18]

Even among murderers with only one or two victims to their credit, there is still a large fan base. After Scott Peterson was sentenced for mur-

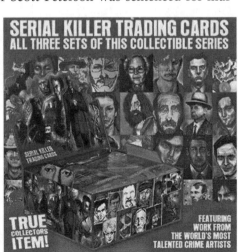

Serial killers enjoy so much fame and notoriety that there are actually trading cards featuring their images and "accomplishments."

dering his wife and unborn child, he received a marriage proposal from his next perspective mate within an hour of his arrival at San Quentin Penitentiary. On his first day in prison he received over thirty phone calls from admiring women who wanted to write to him or visit him. And he is hardly alone in having passionate suitors, considering there are an average of ten wedding ceremonies performed each month at the California prison.[19]

Killer groupies are essentially no different than those who follow rock stars or athletes, observes criminologist Jack Levin.[20] Yet these women have a much better chance of getting a response from inmates since these men have little to do all day but respond to correspondence. Whatever fantasy relationship they imagine can actually be enacted in a limited way.

When Jason Moss was continuing his studies of serial killers that I described in our book, he decided to escalate his relationship with Ramirez after John Wayne Gacy was executed. After studying Ramirez's weaknesses, Jason learned that the killer had a special interest in young Asian women. He then concocted a scheme to present himself as head of a satanic cult of Asian women who worshipped the Night Stalker. He sent photos of gorgeous Asian models and said they were among the followers. Eventually Ramirez trusted Jason enough to "deputize" him as his lieutenant and make contact with other serial killers around the country. Among the things that Jason learned was that many of the incarcerated serial killers around the country were in contact with one another through intermediaries to compare notes on their interrogators and swap information that might be useful in their defense. Ramirez also found it hilarious, and wildly entertaining, that gorgeous women would come to visit him in prison, sit opposite him, and begin masturbating between spread legs without any underwear. When asked why they would do such a thing, Jason reported that the women admitted they found it extremely exciting to titillate a caged animal who had such a successful murderous track record. As they touched themselves, they felt tremendous power and control without the risk of danger.[21]

There are a number of other motives suggested for those who are drawn to serial killers as objects of infatuation.[22] Some of the women have rescue fantasies that they will somehow save these hopeless cases, either by helping them find redemption or by leading them to follow the right and moral path. As mentioned earlier, some women are afraid of intimate, committed relationships in which they would surrender control, so what better context for a romance than one in which you know your man is locked in a cell every night? Whatever he did previously, it is hard for him to get in much trouble when he is literally being watched twenty-four hours a day. It is thus possible to have the perfect boyfriend who waits all week long for a visit and then feels extremely grateful for the attention. Moreover, unless the prisoner is getting it on with a cellmate, the woman can feel reasonably assured that their relationship will be exclusive. Of course what she doesn't know is that her lover is also corresponding with dozens of other women at the same time.

There is a tremendous sense of drama and excitement in being associated with a notorious and infamous boyfriend. Serial killer groupies bask in the glory. They feel important because they are connected to someone else who receives so much attention. They become celebrities in their own right, invitees on talk shows, and interviewees for articles about this strange phenomenon, which really isn't all that strange after all when you consider all the payoffs. Women who previously felt marginalized now feel like they are the center of the universe. In addition, they have none of the normal tensions and responsibilities associated with negotiating problems and dealing with household issues, especially with a man prone to extreme violence: if things reach the point of an argument, they can just hang up the phone or walk away until the guy begs forgiveness. They don't have to consummate sex either.

Keep in mind that many of these women are not hopeless "losers" but rather attractive professionals with positions, security, and sometimes families. They just like the idea of being with a man who has so much testosterone-charged aggression, quite unlike the civilized, passive guys they must deal with at work. This is not unlike what happens among apes and chimpanzees when females are drawn to the males who display the most propensity toward violence.[23]

CELEBRATING OUTLAWS AND REBELS

However strange and inexplicable it might seem that groupies and fan clubs vie for the attention of convicted serial murderers, in some ways even celebrating their brutal crimes, such behavior represents the kind of celebrity worship that has become so common in our culture—and perhaps has always served a need. Those who attain such status are often rock stars and Hollywood actors, the most accomplished artists, but just as often there are those who exemplify physical attributes that are used for displays of violence. Whereas sports figures might perform in stadiums for public entertainment, serial killers treat the world as their stage. They sometimes commit wanton acts of brutality as much for the attention it brings as any internal satisfaction from the killing itself. And we all participate in this "collaboration," whether our interest is the result of manipulation by the media constantly bombarding us with violent stories, or whether they are just doing their jobs of satisfying the demand.

There is a secret thrill often reported by those who enjoy following the exploits of murderers. The killers are seen as rebels and nihilists who don't obey the laws and morality that apply to the rest of us. They feel a compulsion and thrill to hold someone else's life in their hands, to manipulate and control others by force, a feeling that many of us might entertain but would never act out because of a sense of conscience and concern for the welfare of others. We might be sickened by their behavior, and especially the consequences of harming others, but there is also a perverse fascination that they have the gumption to do whatever they want without concern for what anyone else thinks or feels. There are times when each of us wishes we could lash out at others who we believe have done us harm, who are in our way, or who simply have something we desire.

More than only enjoying the thrill of taking human lives, serial killers also revel in the attention they receive. They are envied by their brethren who commit "lesser" crimes. They receive unparalleled publicity in the media. They have truly become superstars, with devoted clubs and groupies, because they stand out from the crowd. Like pirates (Blackbeard), rebels (Robin Hood), bandits (Jesse James), gunslingers (Billy the Kid), gangsters (Al Capone), revolutionaries (Pancho Villa), and outlaws (Butch Cassidy) throughout history, wanton killers are often romanticized as defying the status quo and world order. They live by their own rules and do whatever they want. On some level it is hard not to admire such bravado even as we may feel repelled by the evil nature of their violent acts.

"They deserve our recognition," writes journalist Laurent Marechaux in his book on outlaws in history. "Without them, the maps of this world would be less colorful, our taxes and rights would be less human . . . and our eternal quest for a better world would be nothing but an outmoded fancy."[24] While taking things a bit far, this statement captures the ongoing interest that people have always had for those who live outside the boundaries that apply to everyone else.

Chapter 7

Moving Violations and Other Eyewitness Curiosities

Y ou are driving down the freeway, making excellent time, when all of a sudden traffic slows to a crawl, then a complete standstill. You decide that it must be an accident ahead since it isn't rush hour and the weather is perfectly clear. Over the course of the next half hour you inch along, stopping and starting, looking for the flashing lights of the emergency vehicles that signal you have finally arrived at the choke point. But wait—traffic starts to speed up ahead with no blockage in sight.

You glance across the median and there, on the other side of the road, are two cars that have been involved in a terrible crash. One is tipped halfway over, and, even with the brief glimpse, you can see the legs of a body trapped underneath. Everyone in front of you is staring as well, which explains the jam-up. There is actually nothing that is obstructing the flow of traffic except the insatiable curiosity of gawkers who can't resist the temptation to check out the accident.

It is difficult to think of watching car accidents, or viewing a crime scene, as a form of entertainment, but indeed there are few incidents in life that attract more attention. It may seem morbid, or even morose, that such a guilty pleasure is so captivating, but there are actually some very good reasons for this intense interest. If watching violence on television and at the movies is alluring, or reading about it in books or magazines, then actually seeing the real thing is utterly irresistible. This isn't just about satisfying one's bloodlust but rather curiosity about what happened and why. As we've discussed in other contexts, there is actually considerable adaptive value studying how people get hurt so as to perhaps avoid a similar fate. And there are few experiences in life more exciting—and transformative—than feeling like you survived a close call.

THE IRRESISTIBLE APPEAL OF CAR CRASHES

We were driving from Kathmandu to Beshisahar, Nepal, the trailhead for a trek to a remote village to award scholarships to girls at risk for being sold into sex slavery. This is part of a project I began ten years ago with our first girl, now supporting over 140 children in a dozen schools in the most remote parts of the country.[1] It was an important cause but one that required spending hours on the chaotic, rutted roads of the country.

It was approaching dusk and we'd been on the road for five hours, averaging about twenty miles per hour on the cratered, gravel highway that was the main artery in the country from Tibet to India. There had been a general strike called by the Maoists, so the road was far less crowded than usual. Drivers were now trying to make up time by taking crazy risks trying to pass one another.

We finally came to a complete stop without any movement for several minutes, then an hour. I crawled out of the van and made my way to the front of the lineup. There was a green truck, festooned with colorful paintings and a nameplate, "Road King," tipped over on its side. There had been a collision with a car, and its front end was crushed. There were hundreds of people standing around in the dark, talking animatedly, eating snacks, enjoying the entertainment. By the size of the crowd, it seemed like it was the most interesting thing that had happened in this village in months. People were pointing and discussing the accident, offering their opinions about who was at fault. My Nepali language skills aren't very good, but I understood a lot from their gestures. Apparently the motorists had been playing "chicken" to see which one would back down first and allow the other to pass. It was clear both had lost the contest.

Judging by the relatively few dwellings in the vicinity, spectators had come from miles around to observe the carnage and discuss the incident. There was a policeman on the scene, armed with a rifle, but he was totally swallowed by the crowed, unable to establish any order—it seemed the people were having too much fun.

After another hour delay, our van was finally able to squeeze through a narrow opening between the two vehicles. Nobody was making any attempt to move the wrecks, and traffic was still backed up for miles in both directions, the highway virtually closed. Yet there was a festival in progress. As I looked out the back window I could see that people had brought their dinners for picnics on the side of the road. This road accident seemed to be the absolute entertainment highlight of the year, although those accustomed to daily highway travel are used to such spectacles.

David Cronenberg won a Cannes Film Festival prize for his movie *Crash*, in which a couple become addicted to the thrill of surviving car crashes. In the film, members of a special club re-create famous accidents like that of James Dean and become erotically aroused by the destruction. The couple, played by Holly Hunter and James Spader, first meet when they literally crash into each other. Hunter's character's husband is killed in the crash. Yet the survivors both feel excited by the near-death experience and begin chasing more accidents to re-create the adrenaline rush they felt the first time.

Car crashes seem to have particular appeal to us as spectators because of the definite likelihood that such incidents could lead to our own demise. Practically every month we have a close call in which our lives could have been ended by some errant driver, or as a result of our own mistakes. And it is no wonder, considering that what may seem like a simple act that you take for granted as reasonably mindless actually requires processing 1,320 pieces of information every single minute, scanning for hazards, adjusting speed, anticipating future obstacles, and changing lanes. Driving requires over 1,500 distinct skills to navigate and propel the machine.[2]

Among all the fears that people have about dying, the odds are far greater that you will die in a car (1 in 83) than by murder (1 in 210), than in an airplane (1 in 5,000), than by a terrorist attack (1 in 1,300), than by lightning strike (1 in 80,000), or by an asteroid hitting the earth (1 in 200,000).[3] Poor General George Patton survived World War II only to die in a car accident, just after the war ended. A similar fate befell T. E. Lawrence (Lawrence of Arabia), but on a motorcycle.

The reality of the increased risk might partially explain the increased fascination that people have when celebrities die in car crashes because it could so easily happen to *you*. Footage of Princess Diana's deadly wreck in a Paris tunnel was replayed so often that it seemed like we were actually at the scene. One of the very first celebrity deaths by car accident was the dancer Isadora Duncan, who had the distinction of actually strangling to death when her scarf got caught in the rear wheel of her Bugatti. Actress Jayne Mansfield's death in a car accident also made headline news for some time because of the gruesome rumors of how her head became separated from her voluptuous body. Such incidents have the double appeal of a violent death coupled with the fall of someone well known and perhaps beloved. They

Students watch the drama of a simulated drunk driving crash in the parking lot of a high school. Photo by Sam Gangwer. Courtesy of the *Orange County Register.*

may have been rich and famous, privileged in all kinds of ways, yet they couldn't escape the fate that you have thus far managed to avoid.

The appeal of a car crash is so compelling to some that gawkers will stand by and watch the show rather than do anything to help. When a truck driver crashed outside of Sydney, Australia, "crash vampires" stood around the wreck, "watching as if it were a half-price matinee."[4] While the driver lay on the road dying, spectators stood around gossiping and making jokes. Nobody offered him any comfort. Emergency personnel who finally arrived on the scene complained that there were so many spectators watching that they had to forcibly push people out of the way so they could deliver care.

Sallie, one avid spectator of tragedies, uses police scanners and Web sites in order to find out where ambulances and fire trucks are dispatched to the scenes of disasters or accidents. She spends between five and six hours per day on her laptop monitoring developments and then hops in her car and follows the emergency vehicle when things look promising. She admits that she doesn't so much like blood and guts, it's just that she is so darn curious. Because she feels bored by staged violence in the media, she much prefers the real thing: "On the scanner I heard that a car burst into flames when it hit a tree. They were talking about bodies lying in the road," Sallie said with excitement, remembering this highlight of her week. "When I heard that I knew it was gory. So that's when I grabbed my dog and said, 'Let's go.'"[5]

Sallie is not without compassion for the victims. Once her curiosity is satisfied, she prays for them and hopes they won't die. Then she goes home and waits for the next tragedy to unfold. It would be difficult for Sallie, or anyone else, to admit it, but one of the appeals of viewing such a violent incident is that it happened to someone else.

NOTHING ATTRACTS A CROWD LIKE A GOOD DISASTER

"If it bleeds, it leads," goes the maxim of the news business. People just *love* a good disaster, and the media capitalizes on this interest by feeding avid viewers twenty-four hours of coverage. It could be a murder trial like O. J. Simpson's, a terrorist attack, a shipwreck, or some natural holocaust caused by earthquake, flood, tornado, hurricane, or fire. Some of the most popular sites on the Internet involve disasters—Titanic (forty million hits), Hurricane Katrina (ten million), San Francisco Earthquake (five million). Google "9/11" and there are a whopping two billion hits! And the single biggest tourist spot in Dallas, Texas, is the plaza where President Kennedy was killed nearly fifty years ago.[6]

Disasters are so popular as entertainment that people at the turn of the twentieth century would attend staged train wrecks. The first of these events premiered near Columbus, Ohio, in 1896 and attracted thirty thousand spectators. Others were promoted in Chattanooga and Columbus, in which spectators paid a dollar for box seats and fifty cents for general admission (kids cost twenty-five cents). Even today promoters stage car crashes for audience amusement—and sometimes insurance fraud. One of the Discovery Channel's most popular shows is *Destroyed in Seconds*. Film clips are shown featuring "Awesome explosions, spectacular crashes, and lots of crazy wipeouts!"

And if you think staged car or train crashes are an outlandish form of entertainment, consider that Julius Caesar arranged a full-scale naval battle in 46 BCE in order to win public popularity. First he created an artificial lake as a stage, one thousand times larger than any Cirque du Soleil extravaganza in Las Vegas. He conscripted more than three thousand men to fight aboard a dozen different ships in order to reenact a famous Egyptian battle. It was such a huge hit that after Caesar's assassination, his nephew Augustus outdid his uncle by loading five thousand condemned prisoners aboard ships and required them to fight to the death. Years later, another emperor, Claudius, upped the ante further by adding twenty thousand prisoners to the cast of a naval engagement, making sure they rammed one another's ships and then slaughtered one another to the delight of hundreds of thousands of spectators who lined the banks of the lake.[7]

Whereas nobody since has come close to topping the sheer inventiveness of Roman spectacles of violence, we can still see the remnants of the attraction every time traffic slows on the freeway to catch a glimpse of a wreck. With the advent of technology, there are also opportunities to watch televised police chases in real time or review the most exciting, horrific crashes on the Internet.[8]

GAWKERS AND RUBBERNECKERS

Rubbernecking was originally a term that referred to tourists in New York and elsewhere who always seem to be straining their necks to take in the sights. Over time it has come to mean exaggerated or morbid curiosity. That's fine if you are walking along a sidewalk and see something that strikes your interest, but when you are driving a car, such inquisitiveness leads a person to slow down and gawk, creating backups and accidents. Remarkably, 60 percent of the total congestion on urban freeways in the United States occurs as a result of rubbernecking, that is, curious onlookers slowing down on the *other* side of the road to check out an accident.[9] In addition, 13 percent of the traffic slowdown immediately after a crash is the result of gawkers *on the other side of the road* who have no blockage whatsoever.[10] There is a double motive operating here. First, drivers have a morbid curiosity about what happened to cause the accident and wish to see a glimpse of the result. But to add to the chaos, people also don't want to miss out on what others are looking at for fear they will be put at some disadvantage.[11]

With advances in technology, there is now a new phenomenon in which onlookers not only want to eyeball the accident scene but they want to take a photo of it with their phones to show their friends. Traffic cops call this "digi-necking."[12] The accumulative result is that, after fatigue, the leading cause of distraction-related car accidents is actually trying to look at other crashes![13]

I asked a police officer who works traffic accidents what meaning he ascribes to this behavior. At first, he just shook his head in disgust, but then he admitted that he actually understands what's going on. "I just think that people have this craving for safe forms of stimulation, any excitement that allows them to feel something but doesn't directly put them into the path of danger."

Law enforcement and highway engineers are concerned enough about the problem with gawkers that they've been experimenting with installing giant screens at accident scenes to block the view from onlookers. The manufacture of these devices, similar to the privacy curtains in an emergency room, are designed to shield mangled bodies from passing motorists who insist on stopping to catch a glimpse of death in real life. A company representative for the screens commented: "Most drivers have a natural compulsion to look at others people's misery and dangerous situations are frequently the consequence."[14]

Similar to Sallie's experience, evolutionary theorists believe this behavior makes perfect sense. The mood of bystanders is lifted when a potential rival is eliminated (one less competitor for limited resources). No matter how poorly you are doing in your life, or how dissatisfied you are with the way things are going at home, at work, or with respect to your health and life situation, it feels good to see someone in worse shape.[15] There's nothing worse than being dead.

Morbid curiosity about accidents and disasters also acts as a state of preparedness. In one sense it is a perfectly reasonable way to anticipate trouble and better predict satisfactory outcomes. As an avid bike rider, I know each spot along my usual route where someone has been hit previously. Should I forget, there are even memorial markers with flowers and signs as reminders. And each time I pass those places, I take extra special care to protect myself against potential trouble.

A BRIEF HISTORY OF PUBLIC EXECUTIONS AS A SPECTATOR SPORT

In the context of reality-based mayhem as entertainment, there is nothing more graphic than actually watching the death of someone, especially a convicted criminal condemned by the courts, who (it is believed) deserves to sacrifice his life for the greater good of the community. Public executions have thus held a prominent place in human history throughout time. They are intended to act as a deterrent against similar violations, but they have also served (and still do in some areas of the world) as public amusement.

Executions have been staged in many cultures and eras as "spectacles of suffering," according to historian Pieter Spierenburg, who collected examples of some of the most gruesome public executions that were designed for audience enjoyment.[16] In the tradition of Scottish freedom fighter William Wallace (reenacted in the movie *Braveheart*), who was beaten, tortured, castrated, disemboweled, drawn and quartered, and then decapitated, victims during the seventeenth and eighteenth centuries were subjected to multiple forms of torture before their deaths, all designed to draw out the "performance" as long as possible. During one Portuguese death festival in which twenty-one offenders were burned at the stake, there were estimated to be over twenty thousand delighted spectators. In another such event in Britain, about the same number turned out to watch the burning of a murderess. Double that number of witnesses, over forty-five thousand people, turned out to watch two English robbers be hanged. America was no different a century later, with record-setting audiences traveling two days' ride on horseback just to watch a hanging. In a description of one such gathering, "Vendors did a brisk business in lemonade, peanuts, and confections, fathers hoisted their children onto their shoulders to give the little ones a better view, and women, young and old, chatted gaily."[17]

We ordinarily think about entertainment sport as the viewing of competition that is based on skill, either between combatants or teams. Yet watching people die by hanging, beheading, shooting, poisoning, stabbing, bludgeoning, stoning, flogging, drowning, burning, electrocution, suffocation, crucifixion, or strangulation has always been around for audience consumption. Whether it was mass slayings during the gladiatorial games, burning at the stake during the witch trials, the guillotine during the French Revolution, or lynch mobs in the American South, these rituals became social occasions in which hundreds, sometimes thousands, of spectators would show up for the death ritual. Whereas we supposedly have civilized ourselves beyond such blood sport, law enforcement personnel wonder whether this is really the case.

As we've seen, Roman emperors were by far the most imaginative when it came to staging executions for public enjoyment. Today it is usually the crime of murder that earns the offender a trip to the gallows, chopping block, gas chamber, electric chair, or lethal injection chamber. During Roman times they expanded the possible offenses to include a flexible definition of treason, tax evasion, fraud, or even just disagreeing or annoying the emperor.[18]

The Romans had in mind crime deterrence as a factor in the executions they initiated, but far more than that, they recognized the pure entertainment value of killing convicted criminals in progressively more bizarre and creative ways. After all, the public grew bored with mere beheadings, strangulations, and stabbings, which didn't seem nearly horrific enough to provide the desired object lesson. Throwing Christians to the lions represented an "advancement" of sorts in terms of eliciting enthusiastic audience response, but even that ended far too quickly to suit the organizers. That is why they invented progressively more brutal and novel forms of execution to entertain audiences for hours on end.

Emperor Nero fancied himself a creative genius, writing plays that featured actual executions as a climax. In one of his dramas, the last scene included covering an actor in tar and setting him on fire as he was hustled on stage, screaming in agony. As the variety and quantity of executions continued to multiply at an astronomical pace, eventually there developed a public backlash that was influenced by several factors. After seven hun-

Capital punishment has always been part of human culture, portrayed on cave walls as well as described in the Bible and the Koran. It has often been designed as a deterrent not only to prevent crime but also as a form of public entertainment. Whereas the majority of countries have eliminated the death penalty, China leads the world with an estimated 5,000 executions each year, followed by Iran (388), Iraq (120), Saudi Arabia (69), and then the United States (52 executions per year).[19] Image © ppl, 2009. Used under license of Shutterstock.com.

dred years of popularity, the Coliseum and its satellites throughout the Roman Empire were shut down within a single generation.

Certainly the rise of Christianity played an important role, as did the fall of the empire, but also a number of philosophers like Seneca and Plutarch became public critics of the brutality. Later, Christian writers such as St. Augustine added to the outspoken criticism by not only objecting to the violence against victims but also the effects on the audience, who allow themselves to become seduced by the violence, which fed their worst instincts.

As recently as the seventeenth and eighteenth centuries, many European cities and towns frequently erected scaffolds in the main square where convicted criminals were hanged, sometimes dozens at a time. In one particularly gruesome public execution, the attempted assassin of Louis XV was made an example for anyone else who was unhappy with Louis's leadership. The prisoner was led to a specially constructed stage that provided maximum visibility for the crowd. First he was skinned alive with a pair of hot pliers, then parts of his body were carefully and strategically set on fire with burning oil or molten lead. Then each limb was attached to one of four horses, and he was slowly pulled apart, after which his pieces were burned into ashes. The crowd went wild with delight, perhaps realizing that this would be the last Frenchman to ever be drawn and quartered.[20]

Although this represented a "greatest hits" of torture technology of the era, humans became even more inventive in later years, experimenting more with burning oil, the rack, the wheel, hammers, stakes, garrotes, and other means of killing. In Portugal during the seventeenth century (well into the Age of Enlightenment), sometimes dozens of people were executed at the same time in a carnival-like atmosphere, attracting tens of thousands of spectators. One British hanging, a century later, was witnessed by more than forty thousand people. When Charles Dickens attended one such execution, he was appalled by the way the crowd behaved: "Nothing but ribaldry, debauchery, levity, drunkenness, and flaunting vice in fifty other shapes." Fights and riots were not unusual during such hanging festivals. Sometimes spectators were killed.

During the French Revolution when the guillotine was the preferred mode of public execution, there was tremendous interest among the crowd. People held dinner parties following an afternoon's entertainment. Guests wore guillotine earrings and other jewelry to the affairs. These were social events and sanctioned entertainment for the masses, designed to satisfy the almost universal interest in watching someone die. The priest who accompanied Louis XVI on the way to the monarch's execution described the celebratory crowd's reactions in which they "became seized with violence" and "dragged him under the axe of the guillotine." Once a guard held up the severed head, the crowd screamed with joy and threw their hats in the air.[21]

Witnesses to these events describe feelings that parallel those of contemporary movie audiences who watch death and mayhem on the screen with both fascination and revulsion. A part of us wants to look away, to flee, and yet another forbidden voice whispers, "You know you want to see it. Go ahead. Don't be afraid." The reality throughout the ages is that indeed there has been nothing more alluring as entertainment than watching someone die before your eyes. Part of the attraction is the pure novelty of the experience in that this is a rare occurrence, especially with a subject that is so frightening and inevitable as death. Another facet, at least as capital punishment was originally conceived, is that it represents fair justice, an eye for an eye. There is a feeling of closure for the family members and friends of the victim in that they are allowed to watch the perpetrator of the crime receive a "just reward" for the heinous act. There is also a certain amount of relief felt that the criminal of an especially terrible crime will never be able to inflict such harm again on others. "I saw what I wanted to see. I'm glad," reported the relative of a victim whose murderer was executed at San Quentin Prison. "He was awful. He deserved to die."[22]

On a more personal level, however, people are just downright curious about what it is like to watch someone die, a stranger best of all, and a stranger who deserves to die is the most attractive of all to audiences. When one murderer on death row in Texas was told he was allowed to invite five witnesses to his execution, he held an auction for the right to watch him die. Two bidders paid more than a thousand dollars for the privilege.[23]

When people are forced to watch executions because it is part of their jobs, such as journalists or prison personnel, the experience is disturbing enough that witnesses exhibit dissociative symptoms in which they experience detachment from others in the room and feel emotions blunted.[24] This makes sense that audience reactions would be strongly influenced and affected by the social and physical environment. Beheadings that took place in France during the Revolution, or lynchings in the American South, were community events that were staged as much for audience entertainment as punishment. Yet nowadays in American executions, the witnesses sit in a sterile, quiet room in which the audience is mostly silent and respectful, literally holding their collective breaths until the prisoner is pronounced dead.

Regardless of the setting and era, witnesses have always played an active role in the execution rituals, giving legitimacy to the proceedings. Until the nineteenth century, audiences attending hangings or beheadings often had the power to pardon the accused, or at the very least, to show their disdain or admiration for the way the condemned person met his fate. Audiences have also influenced the execution process by involving victims or the relatives as witnesses; this has led to more painless and supposedly humane forms of death (lethal injection versus being drawn and quartered, crucified, or burned alive).[25] Second, public viewings are designed to bring closure to the lingering effects of a horrendous crime. According to sociologist Annulla Linders, that is one reason why mass murderers like Timothy McVeigh have sparked increased interest to have more public executions—and why there is such demand to view them on the Internet.[26]

THE EXECUTION FACTORY

John Boyer was the first man legally executed in Wyoming Territory in 1870. He was half French, half Sioux Indian, and in a fit of anger he killed the men who had raped his mother and sister. He was sentenced to die by hanging for his revengeful acts. Just before they dropped the trap door, he screamed out his last words: "Look at me! I no cry. I no woman; I man. I die brave."

The crowd went wild, delighted by the show.

A few years later, hangings became so popular as entertainment that crowds would show up at the local jails every evening trying to catch a glimpse of the condemned prisoner or hear a report about his mental condition. Historian Larry Brown, who has studied the execution rituals of this era, described all the elaborate rituals that were instituted as part of the drama that was enacted for public consumption.[27] First there was the slow and meticulous building of the gallows over a period of several days, inviting curious onlookers to study the structure as it neared completion, building anticipation for the main event. There was a careful selection of the rope, tying of the special "hangman's knot," lubricating the noose so it would slide smoothly, positioning the knot in such a way that it would (hopefully) break the prisoner's neck—otherwise it could take several minutes for him to strangle to death. Throughout all of these tasks, hecklers in the crowd would yell out encouragement, ridicule, or scorn. The condemned man would be invited to address the crowd, and visible disappointment would be evident should he decline this last speech to confess his crimes or protest his innocence. After the hanging was over, spectators would view the corpse swinging underneath the platform and then fight for pieces of the rope as souvenirs.

In addition to state-sanctioned official executions of convicted criminals, there were over five thousand lynchings in the United States during a fifty-year period, beginning in the 1880s.[28] These were public murders in which mobs of citizens, some as many as fifteen thousand strong, would grab someone (usually a black man) they felt deserved swift and immediate punishment. This was a kind of entertainment violence practiced in the South in which the crowd could also be part of the "performance."

It is interesting that once state-sanctioned executions were initiated in the early twentieth century, lynchings all but ceased.[29] The government stepped in to legitimize what mobs were doing anyway to exact punishment for real (murder, theft, assault) or imagined (insulting a white person, using foul language) crimes.

One of the first documented lynchings in the South occurred in 1899. A black man had killed his white employer in self-defense. As an example to other "uppity" blacks, a Georgia mob composed of two thousand witnesses and participants stripped the accused man of his clothes, cut off his ears, fingers, and penis, skinned his face, stabbed him, doused him in oil,

One of the last documented lynchings of an African American in the United States (1925), a public spectacle that was intended not only for punishment but also as entertainment for the audience, which often numbered in the hundreds. Such events were also planned as an object lesson to teach people of color their place in society, one in which they should not attempt to challenge the will and power of the white majority. Courtesy of Library of Congress.

then burned him alive. Then the crowd worked themselves into a frenzy fighting over his body parts as souvenirs.[30] When several members of the crowd were later interviewed by police about the incident, they bragged that it was the most fun they'd had in a long time and felt no need to hide their participation.[31]

People watching executions, even witnesses today who represent families of victims who were murdered, are looking for some sort of satisfaction. It is more than just an eye for an eye, a tooth for a tooth; they want justice in the form of visible evidence that the accused feels remorse and regret for the heinous acts. Alas, most spectators are disappointed by the relative lack of emotional response from the condemned and the marked lack of drama in the event.

I interviewed Michael, an official who represented the most productive execution factory in the Western world, the Texas Department of Corrections. He had witnessed hundreds of executions by lethal injection and he can only recall three or four prisoners who displayed any real emotion at the impending moment of their death. "Of those I have seen cry on the gurney," Michael recalled, "I think their tears flowed partly from the sudden realization that they were really going to die. No more stays. No more cheating death. All of those had served many years on death row and had escaped scheduled dates several times because of stays and appeals. But now they knew there would be no more postponements."

Michael remembered quite vividly the execution that stands out among the rest precisely because there was such a strong emotional response. "One, I remember, was even somewhat cocky about it all and carried a certain smirk. But now here he was, flat on his back and tied down, completely helpless, seconds away from death, and he was no longer smirking. His father was watching the whole thing and they were both crying. The guy was terrified."

What Michael didn't say directly, but implied, was that the witnesses loved this particular "show," as painful as it was to watch. The family members got what they had hoped for, which was some sort of acknowledgment that the murderer felt remorse and was truly suffering, just as they were in agony. Indeed what people are often looking for, hoping for, when watching people put to death is not dignity and self-control but rather someone begging for mercy and falling apart. It is in such emotional displays that witnesses feel relief in the public confession that legitimizes the execution, as well as provides entertainment in the form of a real drama.

CRIME SCENE BEHAVIOR

If observing someone else's sanctioned death is among the ultimate in close associations with death, the next best thing is to visit the scene of a violent crime. Such locations are also huge tourist destinations, such as the apartment building in New York John Lennon was shot in front of, the location in Dallas where John Kennedy was assassinated, the places in London where Jack the Ripper operated, and various death camps such as Auschwitz and Dachau of the Nazi era, or the killing fields of Cambodia. The visits take place, in some cases, to honor the dead or to understand better what happened and why, but also because of the morbid curiosity that people have toward extraordinary acts of violent death.

When Jack the Ripper began his killing spree in London during the end of the nineteenth century, he became the first celebrity murderer, the mystery man who eluded police and outwitted his pursuers. To this day there are still conflicting theories about his identity and motives, lending even greater interest to his myth. By the time he had taken his second victim in 1888, the Ripper was already the talk of the country. Crowds of people flocked to the scene of the crime and stood around for hours talking with great excitement about what happened and why. The crimes became a sensation, the news story of the decade, and even over a hundred years later there are still tourists who make a tour of Jack the Ripper crime scenes a priority of their visit to London.

Crowd behavior at scenes of violence has been studied for decades because the collective actions taken (or not taken) seem incomprehensible. It is not unusual with "jumpers," individuals who are contemplating suicide while standing on a high ledge or rooftop, that crowds will gather below along with police and rescue workers. This, in itself, is not surprising given the novelty of the situation; it is understandable that people would be curious about something unusual going on in their neighborhood. But what is absolutely mind-blowing are the incidences when individuals will scream at the top of their lungs for the distressed person to hurry up and jump already. Other members of the crowd will join in the chorus, or even laugh at the situation, and not necessarily a nervous laugh.

Even the police are not immune from such thoughts, all the while they are present in order to save the person's life. One police officer, often called to the scene of suicide jumpers, confessed that sometimes he's just like everyone else. "We're supposed to stop the guy, but that's just for show," he admitted. "Most of us would just as soon see him jump. We don't have to clean up the mess but we do have to go up there and get him down. And who wouldn't like to see someone take a dive?" Apparently this sentiment is shared by various news organizations that repeatedly showed people jumping out of the Twin Towers during the 9/11 attack.

There have been other instances, some studied in great depth, in which bystanders did virtually nothing at all to stop a crime in progress or even call for help. One classic case in New York from the sixties involved a woman, Kitty Genovese, who was coming home late one night when she was attacked and stabbed twice in the back. As she lay wounded, she yelled out, "Oh my God, he stabbed me. Help me!" As she tried to crawl to safety, the attacker resumed his assault on her, stabbing her several more times as she continued to yell for help and tried to defend herself. In all, there were thirty-eight witnesses to her murder, watching through their windows, yet nobody called for help until it was too late. Psychologists concluded that it wasn't so much people's indifference to Kitty's plight but rather that when part of a crowd, individuals behave in ways that are quite different than if they were alone. When interviewed about the incident, the witnesses said they didn't intervene or call for help because they assumed that someone else would do so.

When looking at crowd behavior at the location of crimes that have already been committed, several researchers studied all the homicide scenes that occurred in Richmond, Virginia, during a single year.[32] They found that in 90 percent of the cases, significant crowds materialized, numbering an average of two dozen adults, teenagers, and children. They describe the crowd behavior as generally "carnival-like," with plenty of laughter, socializing, drinking, eating snacks, and raucous behavior, as if they were witnessing an episode of *CSI* on television, only better because there was a real body and blood to view. Also keep in mind that this festive atmosphere occurred even though there were likely bereaved love ones present. Lest you think the presence of food and beverages might be due to mealtimes, the investigators found that it didn't matter if the crime occurred in the morning, afternoon, or late evening—spectators brought their own treats to consume while watching the event unfold. If there was a convenience store nearby, many members of the crowd would send someone to reload their food and alcohol supplies. They also found that once the body was taken away, the crowd immediately dispersed. They were only there to view the dead.

Here's another example of morbid fascination in a group setting. An old man who saw a crowd gathering by a tree in his village in Nigeria wondered what all the commotion was about. He drew closer to the scene to find that a man was attempting to hang himself. Several members of the crowd actually intervened to save the man's life, but this witness to the drama was hardly relieved by the resolution; if anything he was now even more upset: "People were wondering, what kind of thing is this? How can this happen? As for me, I could not believe it, as old as I am, because since I have been moving around, I have never seen somebody trying to take his life in broad daylight. It was amazing."[33]

There is also a depersonalization effect that takes place during such threats of suicide, a phenomenon that is different at every scene depending on the mood and context of the situation.[34] As noted in the case mentioned earlier of the bystander effect, when part of a large group people tend to "disown" their individual conduct and feel less guilty about antisocial behavior as part of a crowd—that's how riots take place and why inhibitions are reduced at crime scenes or threats of suicide. The physical distance between the bystanders and the victim, as well as the cover of darkness, also allow for anonymity and less personal responsibility for behavior.[35]

While mobs and crowds have been known to do some terrible things that individuals within that group would never consider when alone, the vast majority of gatherings at crime scenes, impending suicides, and other disasters are "self-regulating" in that they are usually quite respectful and helpful to the victims, their families, and emergency personnel.[36] Yet with such relatively polite and obedient, even compassionate and altruistic behavior, there is still a natural curiosity that draws people to the scene in the first place: they want to know what happened and make sense of it.

We move next to dealing in death as an occupational pursuit—on both sides of the law. Specifically, in the next chapter we explore more deeply those who kill for a living, their "job" so to speak, as well as those law enforcement personnel who must live inside this dark world to prevent such crimes. I interviewed both professional killers, as well as police officers, who took human lives. In each case, their experiences are revealing in the sense that they are not just interested in observing violence as a spectator but also wish to get much closer to the action.

Chapter 8
Occupations of Violence

"I think the crowds are just curious. It's something new for them, something they just don't see every day."

The speaker is a homicide detective with twenty years' experience. I had asked him to dig deeper, insisting that there must be more at work to explain why murder scenes inspire such passionate interest.

"Yeah," he admitted with a smile. "That's just what we're supposed to tell people who ask." He winked. "They're just like the rookies, you know, they can't wait to see a body. They ask about it all the time when they first start out on the job. You can tell who the new ones are because they're right up front trying to check things out. But I've been doing this for a long time. I've seen way too many bodies. I could care less now."

Whereas this veteran cop has become desensitized to the violence in his profession, a newspaper photographer has a very different reaction. James covers the "breaking news" with his camera. "Breaking news usually involves, literally, something breaking: cars, buildings, people, and the relative calm. I cover the occasional car, train, or plane crash, along with any disaster, drug bust, shooting, stabbing, fire, or accident that might occur in the vicinity."

At every crime scene he visits, there is always a group of curious onlookers standing just beyond the ribbon of yellow police tape, pushing and shoving to get the best view possible. James overhears their conversations, and they run the gamut from "Thank God it wasn't me!" to "The son of a bitch deserved just what he got." He notices that their reactions are often related to class differences between themselves and the victim. There is envy and resentment if it was some rich kid who crashed his father's Ferrari, glee if it was a gang-banger killed in a drive-by shooting, and terrible grief if it was a child in the neighborhood.

"Besides all that," James concluded, "I really do think people just enjoy the mayhem. I've noticed that the more gruesome the scene, the bigger the crowd, and the more papers we sell. Our Web site goes crazy whenever we post photos of blood and gore, even though we try to be tasteful about it. The viewers keep clicking away, hoping for more damage and destruction."

"And what about you, James? How does all this affect you?" I asked him.

"Well, I am a professional lookie-loo. I get paid to be a witness to mayhem for the community. I am extended special privileges as a member of the media to get closer in, to watch first responders work with the wounded. It's a weird path that brought me here, representing that corporate need for a daily dose of mayhem. This isn't what I saw myself doing but something drew me toward the drama of people, the chaos of the world. Perhaps I'm simply repressing my inner caveman, not owning up to my true nature, our nature to love a good fight, to want to vicariously experience giving others pain and suffering. There are many who have trained their minds to reject that 'lust for blood,' but they are the rarity."

As a news photographer, James is a member of several professions that specialize in examining death up close and personal. This is a select group that has either chosen this line of work because of some interest and skills, or because it felt like a calling. In the case of law enforcement personnel and health professionals, they are providing an important service, sacrificing their peace of mind for the benefit of others. Yet some members of these occupations also confess to a very personal interest in their work, one that satisfies a deep craving to get as close as possible to death and its aftermath.

DEATH DEPERSONALIZED—OR UP CLOSE AND PERSONAL

In this chapter we examine more closely some of the "occupations" of death, that is, individuals who work closely in the arena of threatening lives, taking lives, or preventing such occurrences by protecting citizens against greater vulnerability. In all of these cases, whether in the role of killer or law enforcement officer, these professionals are intimately familiar with violence and its effects.

Dr. Jack Kevorkian, aka "Dr. Death," is perhaps best known as a professional death consultant. He specialized in putting people out of their misery. Whether he was driven by altruistic beliefs related to the right of patients to decide their own fate, or a more personal attraction to death, is up for grabs. He brought physician-assisted suicide to the forefront of a national debate on euthanasia and served prison time for his clandestine house calls to patients who asked for his help.

Kevorkian spent much of his early years researching death and execution practices. He volunteered to work nights because more people expired then, providing him with more opportunities to study the death process. He experimented with a number of different euthanasia methods, eventually deciding that carbon monoxide poisoning worked best because "it often produces a rosy color that makes the victim look better as a corpse."[1]

Kevorkian is hardly alone in his fascination for getting as close to death as possible—without going so far that people risk their own safety. "I like to see people cut open," admits Chelsea, a nurse who works in an emergency room. "I think that's why I got into this business in the first place." Apparently she doesn't get enough of that at work because she also watches any television show or movie that features a serial killer. "I'm obsessed with them. I love to learn about them. I think one reason I can watch that stuff is because as a nurse I'm used to thinking about patients as 'objects' rather than people. They are just bodies to be processed, cut, and patched up."

This kind of depersonalization among people who have close encounters with death without undue stress is common among executioners who work on death row. During interviews conducted with the men who perform dozens of lethal injections, it was quite common to hear them speak about the impersonal nature of their jobs merely working switches in a death factory. "Some of the inmates talk about killing people like eating a bag of potato chips," one executioner related, feeling justified that with this kind of attitude by his "clients," they were not really members of the same species.[2]

VIEWS FROM THE OTHER SIDE OF THE LAW

There is a curiosity that most of us feel when we try to make sense of why some people feel no particular compunction about hurting or killing others, often without a moment's doubt or guilt. It is possessing a conscience and feeling concern for others' welfare, even more than consensual law or the Ten Commandments, that lead us to restrain our most aggressive impulses. Yet some people seem to have shed (or been born without) a moral compass, which permits them to do most anything they like with concern only for being caught and punished.

Fred is serving time in prison for multiple burglaries and assaults, as well as sexual offenses against underage girls. He has a lot of time to think in prison and he has been trying to come to terms with his crimes. One thing that disturbs him greatly is recurrent images from violent movies he's seen. "I don't remember having much of a reaction when I watched them at the time but now I can't get them out of my mind. They are feeding my nightmares, especially movies when people are hurting and killing one another. I see my victims over and over again. And then I get worked up. I feel my temper getting out of control and I'm trying to learn to do something about that but it's hard, you know, with all those images and stuff. If we're sitting around in the cell block watching a movie, and a violent scene comes on, I have to get up—right then—or I get tense and feel like I want to do something. I'm afraid it's going to get me in trouble."

Whereas Fred is disturbed by images of violence that might spark his own rage, other "professional criminals" have quite a different take on getting close to death in all its forms. Henry Lee Lucas, who tried to set a world record for serial killing, was put in prison early in his "career," during which time he made it a major priority to learn as much from his and others' mistakes. He became obsessed with learning how people died and how killers got caught.

Lucas was placed on a psychiatric unit initially because he was remorseful after killing his mother and he didn't quite know how to cope

This sweatshirt for sale features the image of Henry Lee Lucas, prolific serial killer, who began his murderous spree to satisfy a compulsive curiosity about death.

with this foreign sensation of guilt. "After I got out of the hospital unit in the prison," Lucas told me, "they put me in the records room. And every record that jumped through there, I would read it, study it, and see who got caught and how that happened. I intended on doing these crimes when I got out. I knew I was planning on killing some more."

Indeed he was. And this education proved invaluable to Lucas as he left scores of bodies in shallow graves across the nation's highways. Just as Lucas studied police procedures in order to protect himself, so, too, do potential victims attempt to deal with their fears by learning about the ways that killers think and operate. This is exactly the motive Jason Moss talked about in *The Last Victim* that led him from such an early age to devote his life to studying serial killers. "People thought I was weird," Moss admitted with resentment. "Friends ridiculed me. Grown-ups thought I was crazy. But I had been so afraid as a kid, so haunted by nightmares of the bogeyman, that I had to do something to protect myself. I decided to become an expert, a world authority, on the behavior of murderers. For me this wasn't just a career choice—it was a way for me to survive."[3]

Except for pathologists and homicide detectives, death is certainly a curious circumstance, literally once in a lifetime. We prepare ourselves for death by trying to appease our fears. There is nothing more mysterious. There is no subject more alluring, especially if we can experience death from afar. And for those who want to know what it's like to be involved in an occupation that flirts so closely with death on a daily basis, we can read about these exploits in the news or entertainment media. It is the next best thing to being there.

TWO SIDES OF THE STORY: PERSPECTIVES OF A KILLER AND A POLICE OFFICER

I had the opportunity to spend considerable time interviewing two very different subjects who spent much of their daily lives embroiled in violence with the prospect of death always present.[4] Matt is a police officer who was involved in a shooting in which an unarmed man was shot several times because he was suspected of reaching for a gun. I spoke with him soon after the shooting took place when he was still trying to come to terms with the consequences of killing an innocent man.

The second case study represents the opposite end of the spectrum. Kyle was a hit man for the Dixie Mafia, a crime organization that runs drugs and prostitution in the South. He was hiding out in the FBI's witness protection program and contacted me to tell his story—which I never completed because he disappeared without warning. To this day I will never know if he was murdered or just got cold feet.

I've chosen both of these individuals to profile different sides of the violence "business." Whereas Matt, and so many other courageous professionals like him, put their lives on the line in order to protect public safety and prevent greater violence, they often pay a high price for this commitment. Matt's story illustrates how easily lives can be destroyed by the fascination that the media and the public have for high-profile news stories in which someone has been killed—through intention, accident, or unfortunate circumstances.

WHEN THE BAD GUYS FALL DOWN

The sound of gunfire stopped as abruptly as it began. There was a lingering smell of firecrackers in the air, strangely out of place on the cold winter night. Everything was cast in muted hues of black and gray.

Gun. Gotta get his gun. First thing, secure the weapon. Just like we're taught. Proceed with caution. Could be faking. Could still be a threat.

Shit, he's still moving. How can he still be moving? All those shots. Can't hear a damn thing. Gun. Get the gun. Just reach down, move it away from his hand. Christ, his fingers are still moving. So many shots. How could he still be moving?

It started in the early morning on a cold winter day. Matt and his partner were patrolling a high crime area that was known for its army of drug dealers who occupied the territory. They had slowly turned onto a street so infested with criminal activity, the police had literally barricaded both ends, going door-to-door like an operation more resembling pest control than law enforcement. Since then the rats had relocated to the doorways and vestibules of the neighborhood, setting up shop as easily as any of the city's street peddlers.

It was quiet in the car. Matt and his partner were concentrating intently, scanning their assigned watch area just like fighter pilots looking for bogies. Matt was riding shotgun in the passenger seat, scanning his side of the road, looking for suspicious activity in the shadows and doorways.

The tour had been quiet so far, except for a 1085—officer needs assistance—a couple of hours earlier. Before they arrived on the scene the disturbance had already been settled. Since then, they had been patrolling the streets, on the lookout for criminals at work. They were particularly on guard for a known rapist in the vicinity who had been terrorizing women with his brutal attacks. Like any of the other bad guys they battled with, he was armed and considered very dangerous.

The day was turning into night.

Can't hear a damn thing. My ears feel like I'm underwater. So many shots. The guy must have had an automatic. Looks like a small one, maybe a .22.

My leg is killing me. Must have been hit. Deal with it later. Just pick up the gun. Just reach down and get it away from his hand.

What the hell? It's soft. Not a gun. A handkerchief! The gun must be tucked inside. These guys are always hiding little guns in their hats, their pockets, their wallets, probably in their underwear too.

No gun. Where's the gun? Where's the damn gun? I saw a gun. Shit, he was firing back. So much noise. My ears are killing me. Can't find the gun. I know I saw one. No doubt about it. Look around the guy.

Matt had seen the suspect hiding in one of the doorways, just the sort of place where a local dealer would be operating, or even the rapist would be lurking. As soon as they had slowed to a stop, the man slipped deeper into the shadows. He had obviously been trying to hide something.

Matt and his partner were weary and cautious as they got out of the car, keeping their eye on the guy in the dark. He seemed to fit the appearance of the rapist they had been searching for, and he certainly acted suspicious.

Oh, shit! How can this be? Where's the gun? There was a gun. He pulled out a gun and started shooting at us, over and over. We couldn't put him down. I could see the return fire. Shit, I caught one in the leg. A round right through my pants.

Oh, my God! It's just a damn bandana. Not a gun. Can't be. I saw the gun firing back at us. I heard the bullets whizzing by us. Shit, I saw the muzzle flashes. It was a firefight.

"Police officers," Matt's partner called out to the man. "Please come out, sir. We just want to talk to you."

Something was wrong. The guy wasn't responding. Instead of coming out, he moved back farther into the recessed area where he couldn't be seen.

Matt and his partner, Eddie, stopped at the bottom of the steps, checking their positions once again. "Sir," Matt tried again, "please come out with your hands visible. We only want to talk to you."

The suspect suddenly turned to face the officers. They could see his outline in the shadows. The single lightbulb was crusted with dirt and grime, so the only illumination just lengthened the shadows. Just as he turned, the man reached into his jacket and started to pull something out.

"Gun!" Matt cried out. "He's gotta gun!"

Can't breathe. Can't catch my breath. I'm gonna have a heart attack. Can't hear a thing. What's wrong? Breathe. Just breathe. Calm down.

Someone called for backup. Can hear the sirens. Take care of the guy. Keep the guy alive. Oh, my God, this poor guy. He looks bad. He looks so bad.

He's gone. The guy is dead. I killed him. I shot him. Shit, why did he reach into his jacket when I told him to come out? I told him to come out and show me his hands. Why didn't he listen? Oh, God, I killed him. I killed a man.

Everything shutting down. Numb. Can't see. Can't feel my fingers. Shit, I'm cryin' like a damn kid. Get it together. Get it together. Stop crying. Don't let them see you crying. Can't stop. Can't move.

A total of two minutes had elapsed since the first shots had been fired. Other cars were arriving on the scene, dozens of them from every end of the precinct. Patrol cars were screeching to a halt, setting up a perimeter for the officers under fire.

A lieutenant walked up to Matt, kneeling over the dead man. He approached cautiously, not because he sensed danger but because he could see that the officer was distraught and sobbing. It looked like he was going into shock.

"Come on, Matt," he said gently, as he tapped him on the shoulder. "Let's go."

Matt remained frozen on his knees, kneeling over the body, holding the man's hand. He was mumbling something to himself, something that sounded vaguely like, "He hadda gun."

"Come on, buddy," the lieutenant tried again, this time helping to lift Matt on wobbly legs. "Let's get you some help."

Everything looked to Matt like he was staring out of a porthole. Ever since the whole thing went down, it felt as if his field of vision had narrowed to the point where he had to turn his head to see anything other than what was directly in front of him. During the gun battle, it seemed to him as if it was just the suspect and him, alone, trying to bring the other one down. The gunshots sounded like cannons booming, nothing at all like the muffled sounds during training when they wore protective earplugs. The muzzle blasts looked like they came from a flamethrower, reflecting off the glossy paint in the vestibule.

The whole incident took just a few seconds, but it was in slow motion just like when you're in a car accident or fall off a bike. You can see it all happening. You know there's nothing you can do to stop it. Just react to protect yourself. And afterward, you think those few seconds seemed to last minutes, or longer. You can recall every single detail, remember every thought that flashed through your brain, as if it might very well be your last moments on Earth.

IT'S WHAT WE'RE TRAINED TO DO

I have been invited to a block party that has some special significance to Matt, his friends, and family. While it was not exactly time to celebrate with the prospect still looming that he would be indicted for the incident, there was still reason to be grateful for the temporary lull in the storm.

The street was blocked off on one end with a volleyball net and wooden horses at the other. There were fifty or so families in attendance, guys standing around drinking Coronas or Miller Lites, the women helping prepare and set out the food, the kids shooting hoops, playing stickball in the street, or clinging to their parents' laps. It was a festive atmosphere, but quiet, controlled, everyone polite, cordial, welcoming.

These were the people Matt grew up with, including his extended family, his neighbors, his partners on the force over the years. There were others around who had something to do with his case, providing support or expertise as it was needed. Sitting at my table was a man who introduced himself with a handshake and the announcement, "I'm the guy who carried the sign."

"The sign?" I repeated, stalling for time, wondering if this was some obscure cop code and it would be immediately found out that I didn't belong here. I knew that almost everyone here was either a cop or a firefighter. By the look of all the blonde and red hair, it was also quite Irish.

"Yeah," they guy said proudly, "you know, I was the guy who carried that eight-foot sign at all the protests and the hearing."

I guessed he was referring to the investigation into the shooting in which a hearing had recently taken place. Matt and his partner, while taking a beating in the media, had been exonerated.

Another guy at the table introduced himself with a bone-crushing handshake. He runs a school for training civilians and police in methods of self-defense. He was wearing a T-shirt that said, "Loyalty above all else." Later, when he walked away, I noticed the inscription on the back: "Except honor." That made perfect sense in light of what he had been explaining earlier in our conversation. "I tell the new cops that every day they go to work they've got to be prepared to turn in their badge and their gun if they're ever asked to do something that they don't feel is right."

Since the police academy provides only the barest basics of what they need to do their jobs, it was this trainer's role to fill in the gaps. Police forces all around the country hire him to come in and teach the things that cops need most to survive and function effectively.

Eventually, the conversation rolled around to Matt's case and its aftermath. In fact, there were debates back and forth at every table I visited. "It was just a mistake," some offered. "No, it was just an unfortunate accident." Others believed that it could have been a lapse in judgment. Still others claimed that the officers did exactly what they were trained to do in such a situation. It was dark. The alleged perpetrator was standing in shadows. The officers had identified themselves repeatedly. The victim had been ordered to keep his hands visible. Instead, he reached inside his jacket and pulled out an object that could very well have been a weapon. If the officers had hesitated, they might have been the ones who were killed. That's why they are told by their supervisors to shoot the bad guy—and keep shooting until he falls down dead.

Another cop approached me. He had heard I was writing about how police officers respond to violence—and recover from it. He told me that they had just run a simulation of the shooting, a reenactment in which two dozen volunteers were told that a man standing in the shadows would reach into his pocket and pull out one of three objects—a handkerchief, a gun, or a handkerchief with a gun tucked inside of it. They would have less than a second to decide what they were facing and then to react. If they made a mistake, either they would die or the suspect would die. "In nine out of ten times, they screwed it up," he said with a laugh, shaking his head. "Don't believe all that crap you see in the movies," the guy told me. "You know, all those practice shooting ranges with pop-up targets. Most departments can't afford that shit."

The sign guy returned to the table and joined us, having overheard the conversation. "I didn't realize people would still be talking about Matt's case," he said with a laugh. "Hey, if I'd known that, I would have brought my sign." He nodded his head regretfully. "Could have set it up right over there," he pointed at a vacant spot on the lawn between the barbeque and the tables that had been set out.

TRIBAL FEUDS AND THE KILLING OF "OTHERS"

They have set up a microphone and speakers so a guy can be the play-by-play announcer of the stickball game. Kids and their parents are spread out all over the street, with a long line of batters patiently waiting their turns. Almost everyone gets a hit, between the little ones trying to field the ball and everyone else running into one another in the crowded street. There are three- and four-year-olds standing dazed on the bases, being cheered on by the others for doing something right, but they have no clue where to run next. Cheers go up from the crowd anytime someone does anything worthy of recognition, whether that was solid contact with the ball or simply good style running the bases.

I am envious of the life they have here in this police enclave. There is a real sense of community that most of us have lost, or never had. All the people Matt grew up with are within easy view. The friends he went to elementary school with are here. The neighbors and all their kids are running around together in a way that it's impossible to tell who belongs to which house, or to which parents. Everyone is taking care of everyone else. They have come together to support Matt. And they see others outside their insulated community as foreign, different—even as enemies who don't understand them and the tough jobs they have, trying to maintain order in a world of chaos.

In the history of the world, it is this suspicion of different "tribes" that has contributed to ongoing violence between people who see others as "not like them." People often respond instinctively with either fight or flight when faced with strangers they perceive as threatening. The metaphors for this are easily identifiable in the horror movies, true-crime books, and video games that are so popular. Serial killers are described as "predators," making it appear as if they are of a different species. The aliens, zombies, vampires, Godzillas, and Freddy Kruegers are viewed as monsters that are expendable, totally justifiable as targets for destruction. That's what makes it so easy for us to enjoy killing them, directly in first-person shooter games, or vicariously as spectators. This belief about "otherness" is also what leads to cultural misunderstandings, and if taken to extremes, even genocide.

Traditionally, there have been some very good reasons for caution in trusting and accepting strangers since there was much greater likelihood that those who came from another tribe (or neighborhood) might very well be approaching as much to hurt or kill you as to trade with you. All of this intertribal conflict between groups of people who see themselves as competitors or enemies is what most contributes to escalating violence. Police officers like Matt are hired to "protect and serve," but as a function of their profession, they sometimes get caught in the cross-fire between the public demand that they put criminals out of business by acting forcefully and the pitfalls of overreacting.

Matt's case was a tragedy on so many levels. First and foremost, an innocent man, someone who was simply entering his apartment, was gunned down because the police were operating on a hair-trigger mentality of shoot first and ask questions later. Yet they were also doing their jobs to the best of their ability. I can't speak for the other officers, but in the short time I knew Matt I found him wounded and guilt-stricken. Even though be believed that he did the best he could in the split second he had to make a decision, he will have to live with the consequences for the rest of his life. This was not a make-believe video game in which he could hit the restart button and initiate a do-over. A man was dead because of his actions, and no justification or excuses he could offer would change that. The experience had killed a part of Matt as well.

WHERE THE BODIES ARE BURIED

Matt's story is tragic on multiple levels, and it is one filled with regret and remorse. The second case I wish to present looks at a very violent occupation that has been so often celebrated in movies and books—the assassin or hit man. The best-seller lists are packed with novels about professional killers—on both sides of the law. Whether about an assassin for the government or one who operates in the shadows of terrorist organizations, these novels are a staple for recreational readers like myself. I devour books with such intrigue and action, although in recent years the plots had become so predictable that it was time to find another genre.

When I was contacted by a real, genuine hit man to tell his story, it was a dream come true. I had already been part of one such project in which I described the tales of a Jewish assassin who operated in Lebanon and Syria during the Israeli War of 1948 and who successfully completed two dozen assignments before he was captured, tortured, and eventually rescued. I found the experience both exhilarating and bewildering because of all the moral issues involved in killing for a cause.[5] But still, there was some justification for such action in a time of war. The experience was made even more complicated by the questions I have to this day about how much of what happened was really true. But that's quite another story.

Now I had been offered another opportunity to explore the dark side of human nature, but this time to interview someone who killed without apparent guilt or moral concerns—for him, it was just a job as ordinary as waste management. There would be no justification of reasons for the killing; it was just a matter of commerce. Yet I heard my heart pounding the first time I spoke with the hit man. This wasn't just something I was reading about but something of which I was now a part. What would you do if you were given the opportunity to interview a professional killer and could ask him any question you always wanted to ask?

DIXIE MAFIA

I learned in the first few minutes of our conversation that Kyle had been offered immunity by the government for agreeing to testify against one of the most notorious families in the Southern Mafia. Kyle knew where all the bodies were buried. Literally. It was his job to dispose of them.

Kyle's father was head of a crime syndicate that operated drug smuggling, extortion, prostitution, gambling, and murder rings in a few Southern states. Kyle was groomed since the day he was born to take over the family business. While he was still in elementary school his father took him to race tracks during the day and they hung out at the family bar at night. By age fourteen, he became his father's driver and confidante. By fifteen, he was expected to "audition" prospective whores, sometimes three or four at a time. At sixteen, his father arranged for him to commit his first murder. Throughout his teenage years, when most kids were in school, Kyle was prepared in every facet of the family business, from negotiating drug deals with Mexican sources and extorting money from local businesses, to the art of hiding dead bodies so they will never be found.

Working under the guise of bounty hunter and bail bondsman, Kyle was the family problem solver and troubleshooter. He was called upon to get someone out of jail, to bribe the police, judges, or politicians, to handle complex negotiations with drug lords, or to assist in mob hits. Kyle had now turned state's evidence and was the star witness in the government's case against his former henchmen. He was a wanted man on the run, hunted by the killers he was threatening to put away.

Picture *The Godfather* meets *The Beverly Hillbillies*. These are people who make tens or hundreds of thousands of dollars on drug or extortion deals. They can't draw attention to themselves or flaunt their profits, so they live in trailers and drive old pick-up trucks. They can't deposit their money in banks or it will alert various law enforcement agencies that are monitoring their activities. So they hide the money in mattresses or holes buried in the woods, not far from where they bury their victims' bodies. The trouble is that they're so high on drugs when they do their deals that they can't remember where they stored their funds.

These are stone-faced killers, direct descendants of the Italian mob, but a distinctly American homegrown product. They may lack the tight organization and hierarchy of the Italian Mob with their far more fluid, decentralized structure, but these Southern killers are no less dangerous. This is the South's very own organized crime syndicate—the Dixie Mafia—with tentacles reaching deep into Arkansas, Louisiana, Alabama, Mississippi, Tennessee, Florida, and Texas. They are now independent from the "official" Mafia. "Daddy didn't need them boys in Chicago anymore," Kyle explained. "He's got his own suppliers, his own distributors, his own protection, and his own hired guns. Now he's as big as those boys in New York. He's at the top of the food chain."

I'VE DONE SOME VERY BAD THINGS

The Swamp Club was a hangout for locals who were tough enough to enter the door. They dealt in everything there with little care for the law, and Kyle saw it all, even when he was just a little boy. They served beer and Jack Daniels, of course, but also any drug you could want or money you wanted to borrow. There was gambling in the back room, and some whores always hanging around like horseflies. By midnight there'd be people passed out all over the place—drunks asleep at the bar, junkies nodding off in the bathroom. Only the whores and hustlers would be up and about, looking for easy marks.

"As far back as I can remember," Kyle continued his story, "I don't ever recall being around anything legal, except maybe my father's lawyer, and he was a drunk to boot, always smelling of bourbon, mouthwash, and aftershave lotion. Among the folks of Pascagoula, he was about the best criminal mind available, a real tricky son of a bitch. He used to wear expensive suits and talk like a Yankee, which sometimes is just what you need to get you out of trouble."

You look at Kyle and see a cross between Sean Penn and Elvis, although it's mostly the long sideburns that might remind you of the latter. Although only thirty years old, his short cropped hair is already peppered with gray. You'd notice his big blue eyes and the last thing you'd imagine is that he is a gangster and killer. If you look even closer, past the perpetual five-o'clock shadow of a face that always needs a shave, you see his mother's heritage of Creek Indian.

It's not easy for Kyle to talk about these things, and not just because he has disappointed his father and betrayed his friends. He doesn't sleep much anymore. When he closes his eyes he sees his father's men holding a gun to his head, making him watch them rape his wife and little girls before they kill them in some horrible way. Then the worst part is that they leave him alive. "I kind of wish they'd go ahead and kill me already," Kyle confesses. "It would be a relief."

The other night Kyle was sleeping on the couch, as he usually does so as not to disturb his wife while thrashing around. Although his wife wonders what is bothering him, so far Kyle has been unwilling to tell her the full story. She knows a lot about what happened, of course. Heck, she was into the sex and drugs and partying as much as he was. Maybe more. But she has no idea about some of the stuff Kyle had to do when he was away.

This particular evening Kyle yells something out loud, piercing enough to startle himself awake. He opens his eyes, disoriented for a moment as to where he is. His heart was thumping so hard, he first wondered if he'd been shot, then suspected he might be having a heart attack.

Kyle lights a cigarette and watches the reflected light from early morning traffic illuminate the smoke trails as they float up to the ceiling. Tears run down his face, although he can't recall what he had been dreaming about. There was just the faintest images of faces looking up at him from their graves.

Suddenly, tiny footsteps shuffle across the floor, and Kyle sees his youngest daughter, Samantha, about to launch herself across the room. Standing there, watching him with concern, the little girl clutches a stuffed animal.

"Daddy," she says, so softly Kyle thinks it might be part of his dream. Samantha takes a tentative step closer.

"Hey, punkin," he answers her, brushing the tears off his face. He stubs out the cigarette and pushes the ashtray under the couch.

The little four-year-old is Kyle's favorite child, although he feels guilty admitting this to himself. She is so adorable with her long blonde hair and huge blue eyes, he aches every time he sees her.

"Why are you crying, Daddy?" Samantha asks as she scampers up to the couch and crawls in her father's lap. She cradles his head in her tiny hands, studying the residual moisture on his cheeks. For some reason, rather than feeling frightened by her father's show of emotion, she feels a special closeness to him. It's as if fluent crying is some special gift they share in common.

"Oh, honey, I just had a bad dream."

Samantha puts her head on her father's chest and squeezes him as hard as she can. Kyle stifles a sob building in his chest, but he knows Samantha can feel it gathering force. She snuggles closer.

Kyle regained control, but just barely.

As he told me what happened, I could hear the catch in his voice, as if that sob was still caught in his chest. This is a man who is barely holding things together. He can't sleep at night, and during the day, he hides inside the house when not at work. Kyle is afraid to go out in public, even to Wal-Mart, for fear the Mississippi boys will shoot him down. He just hopes they do it fast and quiet, some place where his family won't see it happen.

I wonder why, then, that Kyle has agreed to jeopardize the safety of his family and himself. Why is he turning state's evidence against the very people he grew up with? And why is he willing to tell me his story and give such complete access to this world that has forever been hidden from view?

"I ain't no rat," Kyle protests, "but I am a witness to the things I've seen, and also the things I done myself. People ask me why I'm doin' this with you. From the time I can remember that was the one thing you just didn't do. And I still won't tell where all the bodies are buried. There's too many even if I could remember them, which I can't."

"So," I press him, a little more cautious than I would prefer, but I am unwilling to provoke this man who is used to settling disputes with a gun. "If you aren't a rat, then what are you doing this for?"

"Well, I'm doing it for my wife and kids. I'm almost thirty years old. I took a hard look at my life and the stuff I've done. I just remembered a time I was lying in bed with my wife under one arm and Becka, a girl I grew up with, under the other arm. I looked at both of them and thought to myself, it's good to be king. I can sure get used to this. And I did have a string of awful good luck. In any week I slept with more pussy than most men do in a lifetime."

This is how our conversations go. One minute we're talking about his motives for testifying against his family, the next he's telling me about an orgy he participated in with three or four girls at a time or when he and his father beat a man half to death. I wonder how I will know if any of this is really true and how I will confirm it with his case officers, corroborating news stories and witnesses, and the crime scenes. This world is so different from anything I could imagine, a world in which violence is so casually administered it has lost any real entertainment value—except for the news junkies. This is like nothing I had ever heard about the Mafia. This is no Godfather who operates by sanctioned rules agreed upon by the larger international network. This is an independent clan that does what it likes and answers to nobody for its actions.

"Somehow," Kyle continued his explanation, sounding tired and sad, "I had to do a better job of taking care of my family. I don't want my girls to grow up like I did, knowing the things I did. I had to break this family chain, get out from under the weight of it all."

I don't know what to say to him. This is way more than I can handle or make sense of, nothing at all like I expected. I had been so eager to hear what violence was like in real life, especially by an expert who killed people for a living. But I'm just confused by the pity I feel for this man who delivers death without hesitation or compunction.

"I'm not a bad person," Kyle blurted out. "You gotta understand that." It seems like he can almost read my mind even though I'm the psychologist, the one who is used to picking up on the slightest nuances of behavior. He can sense my struggle. I like this man even though he scares the hell out of me. There is a vulnerability about him that invites me to help him find some peace. He is charming and entertaining, not like the sociopath you might immediately suspect, but like a son of the South who, without formal education or book learning, is still smart as hell and wise way beyond his years.

"I've done some very bad things," Kyle admitted with candor. In fact, it amazes me how much he trusts me and how much he is willing to share. "Some of these things I did for honor. And some for money." He hesitated for a moment, then added, "I just wanted to be the man my father was."

I nodded my head not only in understanding but agreement. My guess is that so much of his life revolved around earning the approval of his father. Yet he also seemed to understand that he'd never get what he wanted most.

When Kyle thinks about his father and his family, he doesn't see them as a bunch of killers. They were just ordinary people, trying to scrape by during some hard times.

"My father was a great man among common people. He was an honorable man among thieves. He raised me to be the kind of person who has compassion but no remorse, who has feelings but don't never show them out loud. What kind of chance did I have to be a normal man? That's why I am no more, and no less, a thug."

NOW I'M ONE OF THEM

Kyle was sixteen when he killed a man for the first time. He didn't even know the guy's name. His father just told him they were going on a little trip. On the way to their destination, his father offered Kyle his most important rule: "There are two things you never have to tell a man—when he's lying to you and when he's fucking you. He already knows that!"

It didn't take much to figure out that they were going to kill the man because he was breaking his father's sacred rules. Kyle felt pretty pleased with himself afterward. He made twenty thousand dollars for ten minutes work. None of the money lasted long. There really wasn't much he could do with it anyway. He couldn't be seen tooling around in a new car or wearing fancy clothes. He had all the girls he could dream of, courtesy of his father. About the only thing he could spend money on was his own stash of drugs—pot at first, then cocaine and speed.

Once Kyle became strung out on drugs, he lost all control of his life. With his wife also in trouble—she was in jail—they were in danger of losing their kids. Without telling a soul, his wife approached the United States Customs Service about testifying against the family for an assortment of crimes related to drug smuggling. Kyle was invited to participate as a witness against his former friends or to face prosecution himself.

Kyle and his family literally ran for their lives. Witness protection will not be completely available to them until after grand jury testimony. They left town in a hurry, taking whatever they could fit in their car, leaving their home, their friends, and their family.

"Every friend I had wanted to kill me," Kyle said. "People think drug dealing is easy but it ain't. There's always someone trying to steal from you or cheat you or get you back. And there were a whole lot of them people after me. Still are. Now I don't have no friends at all. I could make new friends but I'd have to lie about my past, so what's the use? If you have to lie to someone then they're not really a friend."

In hiding, Kyle lives in a small town in the South. He works in a factory, lives in a rented house, and drives a ten-year-old car.

"I wake up every day and go to work in the factory, driving with all the others. You work your ass off your whole life and still can't get a house or a new car. I got nothing for my kids. I'm working like a slave for next to nothing."

Kyle doesn't sleep much anymore, although he's been clean and drug free for over a year.

"I guess it must be strange to look at me now. I look in the mirror and see a person plum wore out. My father is now eighty years old, living with a woman forty years younger than he is, a woman who has been his lover for ten years.

"The first time I killed someone I expected some dark angel to swoop down out of the sky and cart me off to hell. But it didn't happen. You get something much worse. You have to live with yourself for the rest of your days."

Kyle's narrative isn't quite the romanticized, exciting version that so often inhabits the books and movies about life as a hit man. He is seriously depressed and feels hopeless, and many would probably believe he got exactly what he deserved after the things he'd done to others, whether he thinks they deserved it or not. As interesting as it might be to catch a glimpse inside the life of a professional killer, it doesn't seem particularly entertaining—just sad and disturbing.

Both of these stories bring to life the realities of jobs that are immersed in violence. In spite of the secret attraction of this type of work, at least as portrayed in movies, books, and video games, both the subjects of my interviews see themselves as victims, whether justified or not. They operate on different sides of the law yet share in common feelings of disillusionment. They feel misunderstood. Of course that's about where the similarities end since Matt's experience with the death of an innocent man was both accidental and devastating to his own life, whereas Kyle never gave much thought to taking a life one way or the other. It was just taking out the trash.

So, what are we to make out of all the different manifestations of violence described thus far in this chapter and the others that preceded it? In Matt's and Kyle's stories we may feel the same kind of morbid curiosity about what it feels like to kill someone as what leads readers and viewers to seek out such vicarious experiences in books, films, television, and video games. As you'll see in the next chapter, this is a very complex set of phenomena that involve scores of different motives, instincts, and interests.

Chapter 9
The Meaning of Mayhem

"Okay, I give up. What *does* all this interest in violence mean?"

I was being challenged by a young woman I'd been interviewing who had a passionate interest in watching violent films, the more graphic the better. She was an avowed feminist who was also a peace activist, opposed to war. She was also a psychotherapist, an intern I was supervising, who worked in a women's shelter to assist survivors of abuse recovering from their trauma. She was the single most unlikely candidate you could ever imagine to be a fan of violent entertainment. I also have to mention that she confided a guilty pleasure in watching cage fighting when she could find it on television when nobody else was around.

This woman, like so many other people I spoke to in all walks of life, casually indulges in spectator violence but without much reflective thought about what that interest means. It is either too disturbing to think about, ruining the pleasure, or it just seems so confusing that there isn't a simple answer present. I would certainly agree with this statement in that the phenomenon *is* complicated and the answers often conflict. In this chapter, I sort out the various theories that help to explain the meaning of mayhem.

COMPLEX QUESTIONS WITH MULTIPLE DIMENSIONS

One of the operating assumptions of hedonistic philosophy through the ages, from Aristotle and Epicurus to Freud, is that human beings are primarily motivated by the pursuit of pleasure and the avoidance of pain. How, then, do we explain the attraction to violence and watching others suffer? One reason may be that almost *any* intense stimulation can be experienced as pleasantly arousing. I'm not referring to masochistic sex but rather to everyday activities that, objectively, are painful—eating spicy foods, grueling exercise, shiatsu massage, and yes, frightful films or literature, and witnessing violence and its effects firsthand. We actually learn to experience painful things as pleasurable or at least only mildly uncomfortable. Or, more likely, it isn't as simple as that: we are capable of experiencing both happiness and sadness, or pain and pleasure, at the same time.[1] And this is just one of many paradoxes related to entertainment violence.

There are also wide variations in responses to the stimulation, just as there is with any other form of human functioning. Some people can't tolerate any form of violence whatsoever and find it difficult to understand why anyone would want to watch others suffer. Others are relatively indifferent: they won't go out of their way to look for violent entertainment but may find it mildly interesting. And a third group finds themselves extremely entertained and aroused by the stimulation. What produces such varied reactions?

Part of what makes this subject so complex and difficult to explain is that there are so many different forces at work, some genetic and evolutionary in origin, and others contextualized by culture, learned behavior, or individual personality and needs. There are, in fact, no less than dozens of different reasons offered for why there seems to be an almost universal attraction to entertainment violence. I've divided the theories according to their roots in biology, culture, or the individual, but it requires combining several of them in order to really get a handle on what might be going on.

BIOLOGICAL INFLUENCES

I have carefully chosen the word *influences* rather than *determinants* or *predictors* or even *factors*, since I believe that our genetic heritage and instincts are only one part of what leads to our feelings, motives, and behavior. We may feel an urge to do something impulsive, to strike out at a perceived adversary or to grab someone in an amorous embrace, but that doesn't mean we usually act on those feelings. Nevertheless, it helps to understand how our attraction to watching violence, and enjoying the experience, is at least partially rooted in the ways we have been programmed by nature in order to survive.

The human brain is designed to focus on violence, programmed to notice its impending signs, and prepared to respond swiftly (fight or flee) to any possible threat. Neurological and hormonal activation that takes place in anticipation of impending violence has a number of noticeable effects that eventually may be seen as pleasurable. These include slowed time and increased sensory acuity, experiences you may recognize when you are in the throes of an exciting film, book, sports event, or video game.

Evolution and the Ancestral Environment

Evolutionary theorists speak of the "ancestral environment" as the original place in which human minds, bodies, and instincts were designed to function. This was a place in which humans were hunter-gatherers, where survival depended on peak physical condition, ruthless stalking and hunting skills, and continual struggles for power and dominance. Whatever this environment was like, whether it resembled the Kalahari Desert or the jungles of New Guinea, it didn't look like where we are now. "We weren't designed to stand on crowded subway platforms," observes one theorist, "or to live in suburbs next door to people we never talk to, or to get hired and fired, or to watch the evening news."[2]

This discrepancy between what we were designed to do and what we do now is one reason why we have deviant and pathological behavior. Whereas it has only been a few thousand years since we relocated from a largely cave-dwelling or hunter-gatherer existence to contemporary urban life, it takes the nervous and endocrine systems, as well as our basic instincts, tens of thousands of years to fully adapt to the demands of the new lifestyle.[3]

Meanwhile, we still crave combat and are prepared for violence even though such instincts are no longer as useful. Moreover, this ancient impulse to fight and hunt and kill is still itching to express itself in a number of ways. Dominance games play out in corporate politics. Competitive sports have become the arena for acting out ritual combat—with tennis rackets, hockey sticks, or golf clubs instead of spears. In even one further degree of evolution from our ancestral environment, we now experience violence vicariously through simulations and spectatorship.

In studying the impact that the endocrine system plays on the evolution of human behavior, sociologist Theodore Kemper discusses the civilizing process that has muted forms of emotional expression over the years, distancing us from our most natural instincts. Most of all, aggression and violence have been controlled as much as possible.[4] Civilization has thus forced people into a more sedentary lifestyle in which we are relatively passive, sheltered, and safe in a protected existence. While providing many benefits, this also leaves us frustrated in failing to express and act out our natural tendencies to solve problems with swift violence. Arousal and excitement, which were once ignited by confronting mortal dangers of battle or the hunt, are now largely left unsatisfied except by professional soldiers and athletes, or through vicarious entertainment.

In his treatise on how various human mental disorders evolved, sociobiologist Brant Wenegrat asks the question why such "a basically peaceful animal stands so ready to adopt murderous ways."[5] He wonders whether this propensity for committing violence was indeed useful sometime in our ancestry or whether, in fact, this behavior developed accidently as a byproduct to other adaptive strategies related to rules of hostility. In almost all cases of within-species fighting, there are certain codes in place to make sure that combatants don't kill each off but rather determine dominance hierarchies. In other words, why was it necessary for only humans to actually kill rivals (and risk greater injury) rather than just driving off competitors to teach them a lesson about who is in charge?

Humans are among the most indiscriminately violent creatures that roam the planet, killing sometimes without apparent motive or purpose. It has only been in the last few hundred years that major attempts have been made to control behavior that is no longer very useful in the present cultural and physical environment. It is actually quite rare to be attacked these days by a horde of ravaging enemies or a pack of animals.

As was shown in the previous chapters, spectator sports from gladiator times onward were designed to provide vicarious outlets for citizens to release pent-up needs for competition and battle that we were bred to perform. With few opportunities in contemporary life to exercise the tools of aggression that were once necessary for survival, the best we are offered are ritualized events in arenas—football or hockey stadiums, boxing or wrestling matches, car or horse races, in which spectators can experience the thrill of combat at a safe distance, without risk of injury. That is, unless you are attending a soccer match between rival towns in Britain or Italy.

There is some evidence charted by researchers that spectators, whose teams or surrogates have earned a victory, also experience a surge in testosterone, the hormone associated with aggressive arousal.[6] If this is the case with sanctioned spectacles like boxing, football, or rugby matches in which combatants attempt to beat one another into submission, then other violent scenes played out would be similarly arousing to spectators, even if such feelings are perceived as shameful or "uncivilized." In fact, these reactions predate civilization as we know it.

Therein lies the attraction of violent spectacles that offend our civilized sensibilities while appealing to the reptilian remains of our brutal heritage. Thus slasher movies, the exploits of serial killers or mass murderers, displays of death and violence in the streets, sports arenas, or films, plug into the visceral thrill of impulses that are both dormant and forbidden. Whereas once upon a time hormones became elevated whenever we faced an encounter that would lead to victory or defeat, nowadays we get comparable kicks by watching others engage in ritualized dominance activities. Quite simply, it is hormonally arousing to observe violence, to experience even painful events whether as a perpetrator, victim, or observer.

Programmed Reenactments

Social commentator and war historian Barbara Ehrenreich acknowledges that while the human instinct toward violence and predation may explain part of the appeal that killing has for our species, it is by no means the only factor. Long before we were masters of the universe, humans were primarily meat for other predators, especially large cats. She claims that the compulsion to reenact the terror of predation—in forms of gladiatorial combat—are not just to identify with the killer but also with the prey. Why else, she wonders, do ancient religious rituals re-create the drama of human sacrifice? "Probably," she answers, for the same reason that "civilized" people today pay to see movies in which their fellow humans are stalked and devoured by flesh-eating ghouls, vampires, and monsters.[7]

So visceral is our reaction to voyeuristic violence that nothing else gets our attention in the same way. We are drawn again and again to revisit the primordial encounter of being stalked and devoured by the beast as a way to celebrate our narrow escape. The "fun" of jacking up our blood pressure is in surviving the death encounter to live another day.

This is most certainly a controversial theory considering how often we hear about our killing instincts, and our propensity toward violence, because of our long-held belief that we are the predators, not the prey. However, it has been only relatively recently that domesticating animals such as horses, inventing weapons, and developing language for cooperative hunting allowed us to change roles and dominate the planet. These skills have allowed us to stand at the top of the food chain.

Homage to Alpha Males

Historically speaking, most societies have been polygamous in which men had multiple mates. It was hardly a democratic affair in which each male was permitted to have access to females for reproductive purposes; on the contrary, a few males controlled access to almost all the females in the tribe. This led to intense competition and a high degree of violence in which only the most vicious and brutal specimens would survive, vanquishing their opponents and enjoying the spoils (the women) as a prize. If this sounds distasteful to you, consider that women conspired in this arrangement as well since they prefer to have mates who are high status and who can help them and their offspring survive in sometimes harsh climates with limited food and resources.

Thankfully, you might think, we are done with this primitive practice. But consider how often you see a relatively unattractive, older man, perhaps fat and bald, driving in an expensive sports car with a much younger, gorgeous woman in the passenger seat. It so happens that whereas men care much more about physical attractiveness in their mates for reproductive purposes, women have been programmed to consider a prospective mate's status, wealth, and resources to take care of offspring.[8]

That helps explain, in part, why serial rapists today are overwhelmingly from the lower socioeconomic class.[9] In the good old days, they would not be permitted to have access to reproduction and, even today, have more limited prospects. They are unconsciously driven to take what they cannot have legitimately. And that also helps explain why rape is considered such a serious crime since not only is the man potentially stealing twenty years of a woman's life (if she should become pregnant and must care for this unsanctioned child), but he is challenging conventional rules that would ordinarily restrict him from procreating at all.

This also leads to the curious question of why some women can't explain their attraction to brutal or violent men, even though their rational minds say there is little constructive virtue that these men can offer. Nevertheless, in our ancient environment, a man with the skills of a boxer, ultimate fighter, or serial killer would definitely have been in control of power and resources. His mates would have the best choice of food, the most comfortable shelter, and his children would have the best chances of survival. In today's world, these genetic celebrities tend to be famous sports figures. Someone like basketball player Wilt Chamberlain, whose main attributes were that he was over seven feet tall and could shoot a ball through a net (once one hundred points in a game!), claimed to have had sex with over twenty thousand women (averaging 1.2 per day since he was fifteen years old).[10] Even if he exaggerated a bit and it's only half that number, that is still strong evidence of the power of celebrity attraction.

Men, as well, can't help themselves for admiring the best physical specimens, the most successful sports figures in violent sports. Current fashion, dress, manner, language, and style are all influenced by the choices of a few individuals in the sports world who are followed by millions of youth, hoping that such imitation will net them a tiny fraction of the mating opportunities afforded their heroes. It may seem sad and even ridiculous, but human beings have been organized around this distribution of resources (and women have been viewed as commodities and still are in many parts of the world) for millennia. At one time, this served a useful purpose in strengthening our gene pool by allowing only the most perfect specimens to reproduce. Now that physical strength and violence are no longer adaptive in terms of success in the material world, there are many other options for developing coveted abilities.

CULTURAL INFLUENCES

Certain biological and evolutionary factors just highlighted have been integrated into our cultural norms, values, and practices. In a sense, violence has been ritualized and institutionalized by cultures as a way to prevent wider bloodshed. We have seen how human sacrifice has been used as a form of sanctioned homicide that has been practiced by religions and cultures all over the world. Whether among the Aztecs or Mayas, the Christians, Hindus, or Jews, the Greeks, Romans, Phoenicians, or Celts, human sacrifices were designed to prevent anarchy and war, as well as win friends and influence among the gods. Since violence can't be denied, its purpose is to be channeled into a form of "cathartic appeasement," to satisfy the bloodlust of the masses without resorting to widespread war.[11]

Cultures thus create their own unique ways of helping their citizens to deal with aggression so that it does not disrupt commerce and productivity. As we have become more civilized, the means by which entertainment violence is supplied has also evolved. We still have our human sacrifices as public spectacles of voyeurism, but they deal primarily with moral floggings of celebrities and elected officials. We still build coliseums, but their modern-day combatants wear pads and play within rules that are designed to prevent serious injuries. We still have ritualized combat and wars, but now they are mostly simulated in gaming environments. Even the "real" wars are often limited in scope and designed to minimize casualties.

That isn't to say that there aren't cults that still practice ritual homicide. Throughout the world, on every continent, there are still groups of people who sacrifice the lives of animals and humans as "food" for their gods. In Haiti the practice of black magic and voodoo often demands blood sacrifices. Throughout Africa there are still tribes that condemn victims to death as an honor to their deities. In parts of Thailand, India, Nepal, and Asia animal sacrifices are included in religious practices. Ditto in Latin America, as remnants of their ancient Inca, Mayan, and Aztec cultures. There have also been dozens of documented cases in the United States of various cults that have launched murder sprees as homage to satanic worship.[12] Serial killer Richard Ramirez was (and is) an avowed instrument of the devil. Likewise, Charles Manson famously recruited his "family" to sacrifice Sharon Tate and others in his mass murder designed to start a race riot.

Cults in the West are only examples of people with shared beliefs that sacrificial rituals are justified in order to satisfy the bloodlust of their perverted religions. Far more likely, these are only excuses by individuals who wish to take others' lives under the guise of some "higher" calling.

Killer as National Icon

Killing is portrayed on television and in movies so frequently that we have developed, in the words of writer Eric Schlosser, a "culture of murder" in which killers have become our national icons, portrayed as heroes in the media for their daring and courage in outwitting the police.[13]

Tired of restraint, rules, boundaries, conventions, we have seen how some people secretly admire those who ignore such limits. When asked why they worship mass murderers and serial killers, fans often say they are attracted to their raw power. These are men who kill indiscriminately, who obey no laws except those they have invented, who hold nothing sacred except their own lust for blood. If that's not enough, they don't even have a guilty conscience.

Doreen Ramirez, wife of the infamous Night Stalker Richard Ramirez who terrorized all of Southern California while on his murderous rampage, is one example of an individual who gravitates toward the dark side of a killer. She is expressing repressed parts of her own psyche. Doreen was a good Catholic girl, a virgin, a sheltered, innocent young woman, who became infatuated with Ramirez during his trial. Although raised with traditional values, Doreen became fascinated with Ramirez's beliefs as an outlaw and Satanist.[14]

John Wayne Gacy,
aka the Clown Killer.

John Wayne Gacy, another serial killer who gained worldwide notoriety, was at one time one of the most famous people in America. "I am the most widely written inmate in the U.S. Prison system," he boasted in a letter written just prior to his execution. "You see, each week I answer about 50 letters, about 15 of them are from people who are writing for the first time. So I'm like Dear Abby to a lot of them and no subject is off limits."[15]

In 1993, when this letter was written, Gacy was the most sought-after interviewee in America, perhaps in the world. Journalists and fans vied for his attention. He had the guards and prison administrator eating out of his hand. He was a celebrity of the highest order. People paid up to ten thousand dollars for one of his primitive paintings. His signature today is still worth hundreds of dollars to collectors. And all of this recognition and attention just because he was such a prolific killer.

Traditionally and historically, being an accomplished predator and killer brought significant rewards. Not only would such successful violence bring trophies and meat, but also a rise in status and power, as well as greater access to resources and potential mates.

As much as we might abhor the violent behavior of killers like Gacy or Ramirez, it is unfortunate but likely true that their brutality and single-minded devotion to murder, without hesitation or regret, would have led others to fear and respect them. Pacifists like myself would have been quickly dispatched with absolutely no opportunity to ever produce offspring.

Gender Socialization

The couple is sitting in the third row, popcorn balanced on their laps and soft drinks nestled safely in their cup holders. It is their second date, and neither of them can remember which one of them suggested they see this particular film. Nevertheless, they are committed to complete the ordeal, however painful it might be. Thus far in the first twenty minutes, the body count has been horrendous. With each progressively more brutal slaying on the screen, the man reacts. He grabs the armrests tightly and holds on for dear life. His face is impassive and he is doing his best to appear bored, although that is hardly what he is feeling inside with his pulse consistently hovering above 120. He can feel his heart pounding as if it is going to explode.

The woman, on the other hand, is squirming and making all kinds of noise—whimpers, gasps, and an occasional scream. It is during the latter that she seems to involuntarily grab her companion's arm and squeeze as tight as she can. She glances over at her date to check his reaction, but he seems unconcerned. Actually, he is quite enjoying that part of the experience when this attractive woman hugs him tighter. A part of him is looking forward to the next victim.

Both men and women learn their prescribed roles from cultural artifacts that are presented as instructional lessons. In the case of horror enter-

In modern times, when observing violence on the screen or on the athletic field, males are supposed to be stoic and unflinching, whereas females hide their faces and scream their heads off, inviting males to reassure them. This induction into traditional gender roles has often been a part of why couples choose violent entertainment for a night's enjoyment, even with the accompanying discomfort. Image © James Blinn, 2009. Used under license of Shutterstock.com.

tainment, men are expected to be stoic, controlled, and withholding of strong emotional reactions, whereas women are expected to scream hysterically and show as much fear as possible. This acts as an invitation for men to provide protection and comfort.

Males learn their appropriate roles in the context of social behavior. Almost all entertainment violence is watched as a group in which boys share experiences. This is true whether watching wrestling or boxing, horror films, or playing interactive video games. Even when games are played alone, the activity itself is a vehicle to talk to others about what happened, the score attained, the nuances of the play, and shared tips to improve performance.[16]

This indoctrination into vicarious enjoyment of violence is one of the developmental tasks for male adolescents. Whereas in olden times young males were expected to master the intricacies of combat, warfare, hunting, and weaponry, urban boys now learn comparable skills for simulated violence. Just as boys play make-believe games of cowboys and Indians or war, they now act out these narratives through video simulations or interactive games online.

Desensitization to Violence

Just as violence has become more invisible in daily life, it has become more pervasive and graphic in entertainment media. The same phenomenon occurred during Roman times when the emperors needed a way to satiate citizen interest once active wars were reduced.

Over time, watching violence has become like an addiction in which it takes more intense stimuli to produce the same levels of arousal. Once you've seen a head explode or skin ripped off a body, it just doesn't produce the same kick to see the same thing again. That is the challenge that Hollywood producers face when they try to meet the public demand for increasingly creative displays of mayhem.

In the arena of video games, once designers realized that their products were starting to appeal to an adult rather than adolescent audience, they had to figure out a way to meet the needs of an increasingly sophisticated set of consumers who demanded greater realism in the virtual reality. "Older guys like me," Trent explained, "we wanted to drive fast cars, shoot things, blow things up, score goals, you know, macho crap. But it has to be real. You have really *feel* it." Trent complains about how it's almost impossible to play the older versions of games because they don't come close to approaching the realism of the newer incarnations, in which the victims of mayhem look like they really are dying. "Anyone who plays first-person shooter games will tell you that you they get lost for hours if it all feels real, but that means that the violence has to be realistic with plenty of blood and guts."

Trent believes that he and his friends have become so desensitized to the violence in the games that it presents a level of reality that is comparable to what he sees on the news every day. "In *Call of Duty*, for example, it could be based on the headlines pulled from newspapers around the world." But it doesn't feel to him like he is only reading about the news, or watching it on television, but he is right *there* in Somalia, Gaza, or Afghanistan. "I just lose interest if a game becomes predictable and familiar," Trent explains. "For instance, if I'm coming over a hill, and there is a guy there waiting for me who always kills me, I know that next time I come over that same hill he'll be in the same place. With online game play, there is no telling where an opponent might be. There's another gamer just like me running around trying to kill everyone else. It's just so satisfying to know there's someone else out there who is pissed off because I keep killing him."

Trent is describing the desensitization he feels as an individual who logs so much experience online that he needs higher doses of graphic reality to feel the kick, but this process of accommodation to the familiar occurs on a cultural level. Just think back to the most disturbing horror movie of the past century, *Psycho*, in which Hitchcock's victim in the shower is never actually shown being stabbed. And then compare that to present incarnations in which you can watch someone being chopped up like a hunk of sushi—then devoured.

Physiological and Emotional Arousal

"I like to watch scary movies because they allow me to see something that is dark and brutal without having to really be there. They make my heart beat faster and my palms sweat. They make me feel utterly hopeless and frightened, but I have to watch. I can't stop watching. It's just such a rush!"

Michelle recalls watching horror films with her sister when they were both young. They would sneak into the spare bedroom and before the movie started, they'd warm each other up by telling scary stories to try to frighten each other. "It used to be so fun, but because my sister was older she liked to take things too far so I'd have nightmares."

Now an adult, Michelle is still chasing that exhilaration that comes from being so terrified that she can't even sleep at night. "I know that a movie is really good when I keep looking over my shoulder on the way home. I'll have nightmares for sure. But these are the best and I keep looking for more."

One of the most basic human drives is the quest for excitement. This goes far beyond the hypervigilance toward novel situations; rather, human beings seem to crave arousal of their neurological and endocrine systems. It is this stimulation that seems to keep our senses running at peak efficiency.[17] When you are watching a predator, monster, or serial killer stalk a victim, especially someone with whom you have strongly identified, you feel all the fear, excitement, and strong emotions without actually putting yourself in danger.[18] Eventually this powerful emotional arousal is experienced (or perceived) as pleasurable enough to the point that you may choose to seek out such violent media in the future. In other words, it is just fun to be scared, which is why people are willing to pay money to go to a horror movie or a haunted house around Halloween.

Horror writer Stephen King claims that fantasy and horror are "salt for the mind."[19] More likely, they are jalapenos. Just like hot peppers, the objective sensation is best described as painful rather than pleasurable when watching or reading some type of violence in action. It hurts—but such sweet pain it is! The brain so craves stimulation, any burst at all, that it actually urges us to keep haunting ourselves through repeated exposures to terror.

King believes that a tale of horror is beyond definition, explanation, or rationalization; it exists purely to arouse people's emotions. Look around you at any monster movie in which aliens drip slime, the living dead decompose, or psychopathic killers chop up victims, and you will see people in the throes of excruciating pain and pleasure. As much as they might be repulsed by sickening and disgusting images on the screen, they are also enjoying the stimulation that is generated. Their hearts are pounding. They peek between split fingers, unable to resist looking when they hear the sounds of screaming.

Arousal for some takes place at a level where violence and sexuality become intermingled. This is not only true for actual serial killers who conduct brutal crimes to stir themselves up, but also for members of the audience who watch the reenactments.

Tanya, a twenty-year-old college student, talks about what happens to her when she watches a violent film: "Any movie where women are being chased or hunted drives me crazy. I could have sex with my boyfriend after any one of them. It takes being a victim one step further . . . it gets me wet. Then when my boyfriend and I are getting it on later I fantasize about the movie."

Esperanza, a mother of two young children, blushes in embarrassment as she reveals similar feelings. "The movie *Se7en* got me sexually aroused. Every time someone was murdered, and they showed what happened to the victims, I would get excited in a . . ." Esperanza blushes and looks away, then continues: ". . . you know, sexual way."

Representative of the male perspective, Nathan talks about the excitement he feels watching gore on the screen. "When I first heard about the Manson murders, all I wanted to do was to see and smell the blood myself. I wouldn't want to kill," Nathan is quick to point out, "but just be in the room to see the death and bodies firsthand. I just want to witness it."

This is, of course, most disturbing to hear someone say out loud, especially if it is indeed representative of how a lot of other people feel. It confirms what some of the killers themselves believe about their own acts, that they are heroes who are envied by the public.

Even if they are right, there is a big difference between having a fantasy to hurt people versus acting on this impulse. Nathan agrees with this point. "I do get aroused by watching violence," he says, "but I would never do that stuff myself."

That might be some small satisfaction but nevertheless shows that as long as the demand for violent enactments remains so high, film producers and publishers will continue to turn out these products that the public obviously finds alluring. Moreover, the arousal that viewers feel isn't just emotional, but sexual as well. Robyn, another college student, admits her secret pleasure that echoes Tanya earlier: "Any movie where women are being chased or hunted drives me crazy. It just takes being a victim one step further. I like what the victim went through and I keep it in my mind when we're having sex."

Vicarious Sensation Seeking

It has only been in relatively recent times that the dangers of the world have been significantly reduced. Sure, you can get hit by a car, struck by lightning, or fall off a ladder, but the odds of getting picked off by a lion or ambushed by a marauding band of enemies is relatively rare. The news media focus on reporting crimes of violence, murders, terrorist attacks, wars, earthquakes, hurricanes, genocide, suicide, physical abuse, outbreaks of killer diseases, but the probability of such events happening to *you* are actually quite remote. During ancient times you would have been lucky to live to your mid-twenties, whereas now you can expect to survive until your eighties or beyond.

Nature afforded us the physical equipment and skills that we needed to survive in such a lethal environment in which we might hunt for food or fend off an attack at any moment. Alas, the only hunting most of us do now is at the grocery store, and the only battles we fight are on the tennis court, at a bridge table, or in office politics.

You may wonder why people choose to deliberately risk their necks by climbing Himalayan peaks, jumping out of airplanes, driving recklessly on the highway, or even picking a fight in which they could get hurt. You might also question why people have a strong interest in pursuing risky, exhilarating activities as simulations or spectators. In the absence of opportunities to exercise our risk-taking "muscles" in which we put our lives in jeopardy on a daily basis, we find alternative means to stimulate ourselves. There is a craving we feel to seek the thrill of suspense, to arouse our heightened sensations that take place during life-or-death struggles. We were bred for this, and our bodies evolved specifically to deal with such situations.

Enter vicarious sensation seeking: the kinds of experiences when we can elevate our arousal levels by pretending that we are in danger. We can do this directly through forms of physical or psychological competition, or indirectly by watching others act as surrogates. Movie producer Clark Peterson believes that the main purpose of horror and violent films is to help people reclaim those feelings of excruciating arousal, but in a way that they remain physically safe at all times. If you consider the phenomenon more closely, it is actually a brilliant solution.

Filmmaker Sam Peckinpah described his method as being all about evoking fear in the audience. "Someone may feel a sick exultation at the violence, but he should then ask himself, what is going on with my heart?"[20] In the film, an easily identifiable character played by Dustin Hoffman is confronted with a moral dilemma. He is a pacifist and intellectual, yet he is driven to revengeful bloodlust during a climax in which he becomes what he most despises. The violence was so bloody and realistic, Peckinpah admitted that even he felt sickened by it. But that was his point—the goal of his work was to elicit such strong emotional responses in the viewer. Ultimately he makes the persuasive case that any of us can be driven to the brink of our animal killer instincts with the right provocation. He had hoped—or at least *said* that was his intention—that he was making a film about the senselessness of violence.

This theme of stimulation featured prominently in the interviews I conducted with viewers. Randy shared that he liked the feeling of being scared. It made him feel more alive. And the more gore there is, the more stimulated he feels. Like Nathan mentioned earlier, Randy distinguished between his strong interest in watching gore from his need to be scared: "I just really need to be stimulated, I guess because my life is so boring. I feel bad about talking about this but I'm relieved to know that I'm not alone, that there are others like me so I feel kind of normal."

Randy also admitted that the whole seduction of the victim by the killer is particularly exciting for him, to the point that he gets an erection and even masturbates thinking about the rape and murder. Does this fantasy activity then stop him from acting on these impulses, or increase the probability that he, or others like him, will do so? The answer is: it depends.

What is it that determines whether watching violence either activates aggressive urges or reduces their intensity? It turns out it is the rare exception in which someone is motivated to act out what is witnessed on the field or on the screen. Most of the time, viewers experience a release of tension and feel reasonably satiated by what they observed, sufficient that there is no particular urge to imitate the pain inflicted on others. In some cases, the viewings can act as a deterrent.

Emotional Catharsis of Aggression

James Patterson, author of numerous novels about serial killers who go to unimaginable extremes to brutalize their victims, supplies one explanation for "the common man's sick fascination" with the spectacle of violent death. In his novel *Cat and Mouse*, a police detective shakes his head as he sees shopkeepers and customers scurry to the scene of a reported murder. "It was the fear of the unknown," Patterson's character observes, "especially the fear of sudden, horrible death, that drew people's interest to the bizarre murders."[21]

Novelists like Patterson or Stephen King have made careers, and fortunes, following the formula of presenting the most graphic horror possible. "Naturally," King explains, "I'll try to terrify you first, and if that doesn't work, I'll try to horrify you, and if I can't make it there, I'll try to gross you out."[22]

Stephen King likens the appeal of horror books and films to the same thrill as slowing down to look at a car accident. Even Henry James and Nathaniel Hawthorne wrote stories that appeal to such voyeuristic violence. "They are still showing us the car accident," King writes, "the bodies have been removed but we can still see the twisted wreckage and observe the blood on the upholstery." Furthermore, he contends, many people feel an undeniable attraction and revulsion toward horrible death: "The two of them mix uneasily, and the by-product seems to be guilt."[23]

It isn't his business, King claims, to tell readers not to feel guilty, nor does he wish to justify his chosen genre. Nevertheless, he does seem defensive and tired of judgments that he must be perverse or damaged because he likes to write about demons, devils, monsters, killers, and death. It is a modest goal King has—merely to entertain, to hold the reader spellbound—and there is no subject more captivating than that of horror. The proof of this is found in the value the public holds for his work: a signed first edition of one of his first works is worth as much as the price of a Hemingway, Steinbeck, Kipling, or Fitzgerald.

It is also King's assertion that the function of horror is not to celebrate death but life. "By showing us the miseries of the damned, they help us to rediscover the smaller (but never pretty) joys of our own lives. They are the barber's leeches of the psyche, drawing not bad blood but anxiety."[24]

When the lights come on or the book is closed, you look around and find no blood-spattered walls or corpses. You are alive, more alive than you've felt in a while. You have been to hell and back. And you have escaped. You have seen death and managed to survive relatively unscathed. And what an alluring rush it is!

Horror provides a vehicle for people to experience their most primitive selves. That is exactly how writers like King are trying to connect with the audience. Spiders, rats, ghosts, monsters in the night—always in the night —and death, especially death, are what crank up the tension, get the juices flowing, and remind you that you are truly alive.

It would appear that we hire people to satisfy the killing urge. We watch reenactments of murder and violence almost every day in movies, television, and books. Yet once we leave behind the violent world we have temporarily inhabited, participating in fantasy blood sport with abandon, we reenter our normal, peaceful lives with a newfound feeling of satisfaction. "It's as if I've gotten out my aggressive urges watching Schwarzenegger or Bruce Willis," one otherwise peaceful man reveals. "I'll go to see anything that has automatic weapons and a high body count. I don't care if there is a plot or not; I just love to see things explode and bodies flying."

This man is puzzled by his own reaction. He is, by nature, an advocate of nonviolence. "I haven't been in a fight since eighth grade," he shrugs. "I don't believe that any of the problems I encounter at work can be solved by hostility and I do my very best to practice civility. But I have to tell you, I just love seeing simulated violence in movies."

The theory that participating in violence as an observer reduces tension, and in turn, provides a cathartic outlet for aggression, is somewhat controversial. Scholars and social scientists have as much evidence to support the opposite hypothesis: that watching people engage in brutal behavior acts as a trigger for others to do the same. This, after all, was the basis for social learning research in which it was observed that children who watched violent shows were more likely to act out their aggressive impulses during unstructured play.[25]

Indeed, one inmate I interviewed, now serving a ten-year term for multiple sexual assaults, is plagued by nightmares that are sparked by things he reads or sees on television. He is awakened by nightmares of violence in which he can't control himself, leaving him in a cold sweat and making it so much more difficult for him to control his aggression in such a violent environment. He is terrified that no matter how hard he tries, the stimulation he sees in the media will trigger another episode of acting out.

It would appear, then, that there is some very complex set of processes and dynamics involved in explaining the fascination with horror and violence. Even the same exact stimulus can provide cathartic release for some people, in which they report feeling a release of tension, while others are

Aggression is not only a natural part of the human condition but was once critical to survival in a very violent physical and social environment. From the earliest age, children negotiate power in their relationships, seeking to establish hierarchies of domination. Bullying, either in the form of physical or psychological abuse, is the remnant of this instinct to attempt control over the others. Since such behavior is no longer (mostly) socially acceptable, people seek outlets for their aggressive urges through vicarious sources such as violent entertainment media. Image © Mandy Godbehear, 2009. Used under license of Shutterstock.com.

stimulated to the point where they feel uncontrollable urges to act out what they've seen or read.

Lost in Fantasy

One of the functions of any kind of entertainment, whether comedy, sports, drama, or horror, is to immerse yourself in the experience. For a few minutes, or hours, you lose track of time—and yourself. You become a character in the narrative, often switching roles as the action changes. One minute you imagine yourself as the one being stalked and victimized, the next you are the one wreaking havoc. Without leaving the comfort of your chair, you can live a hundred different lives. Fantasy states are enhanced when the medium is as realistic and vivid as possible; at times it is even difficult to remember that you aren't in the game.

A thirty-two-year-old professional and father guiltily admitted how much he enjoys losing himself in violent video games. "The first-person games are the coolest. I get to pull the trigger. The first time I saw blood spatter when I killed a guy, it startled me. Almost scared me. For a little while I become this kick-ass kind of guy, which I'm not in real life. But there's something about the realism, the virtual reality, that these games turn me into a real hard-nose for a little while. When I'm by myself, I turn the volume up to drown out everything else and it seems to draw me into the role more intensely."

He feels a real moral dilemma about the pleasure he derives from pretending to kill people in his spare time. "I'm pulling the trigger, blowing people away, getting pumped spilling blood, and I'm thinking, *I like this! It's fun!*" But then he feels torn and remorseful that maybe he shouldn't be doing this. He even questions why he is taking the time to tell me this.

Tina, a woman in her sixties, was so powerfully impacted by seeing Stanley Kubrick's film *A Clockwork Orange* when she was a teenager that she has been haunted by it her whole life. "The film slammed me so hard that, at one point, I ran from the theater and tried to collect myself in the lobby." Tina paused for a moment, taking a breath, still surprised by how deeply she was affected. She is about the most peace-loving, nonviolent person you could ever meet, which is why she is still having such a hard time making sense of her reaction. "You see, there was this strange new sensation, like a magnetic force, which made me want to see *more*. I stood behind the last row of seats, absolutely compelled to watch the rest of the movie. I felt these intense feelings, coupled with an intense physical reaction, that was like a surge equal only to the great sex I would someday experience."

Tina is a psychologist, so I pressed her further to talk about her understanding of his phenomenon. How do you explain your attraction to something that you also find so abhorrent?

Tina nodded, understanding immediately where I was going. She has given this subject a lot of thought and thus formulated a fairly clear answer about the appeal, at least for herself. "These experiences give us the opportunity to project ourselves in the roles of victim and victimizer, dominated and dominator, passive player and aggressor. We don't get this kind of excitement in everyday life. There's also a bonus in that you get a kind of 'high' from the adrenaline rush. Who wouldn't want to have that feeling again and again?"

Tina is describing the kind of identification and empathic transcendence that takes place when you lose yourself in violent entertainment, whether identifying with a sports figure or a character in a film or book. The interesting part, however, is the switch that is made back and forth between imagining yourself as the prey that is being stalked, as well as the killer.

As difficult as it is to admit, it is naughty fun giving in to the "dark side." Entertainment violence is often about transgressing society's most cherished rules. Thou shalt not kill. Thou shalt not engage in violent behavior that is harmful to others (unless part of a sanctioned war). You can be a model citizen, a responsible parent, a community leader, admired for your altruism and selfless giving, and still have a secret fantasy life populated by violent expression.

Managing Apprehension and Fear

There has been another grisly murder in the city. There is a body curled in an unnatural angle lying on the street, partially covered with a blanket. One bare foot can be seen peeking out, its shoe lying a few feet away. A small puddle of blood forms a halo above the corpse's head.

The investigative crime unit on the scene is busy with their work, collecting their evidence and interviewing witnesses. But this is hardly a private affair. In fact, it would appear as if a street performance was under way, a growing audience straining against the yellow tape that marks off the stage. People are talking animatedly, gesturing and pointing toward the crumbled body, occasionally yelling remarks. A few can be seen drinking beer out of paper bags, casually comparing notes about what happened.

The homicide detectives on the scene are always amused by the crowds that are attracted to dead bodies like flies. They recognize that the interest is mostly driven by curiosity but also by fear. I mentioned one detective earlier in this book who no longer feels annoyed by the interest his work attracts because he understands that people attempt to manage their terror by looking at that which unhinges them the most: the reality of death.

A woman in her twenties who works as a customer service representative is drawn to the horror genre because it helps her to work things out related to fears she holds. "You feel all that tension and then, at the end, you let it go. I think it's good to understand what frightens you and to face it rather than ignore it. That takes away the power of the fear."

This theme related to curiosity about death pops up again and again when people talk about their fascination with violence. Cal talked about how he has felt drawn to scenes of violent death since he was a child. "I remember watching the *Faces of Death* movies, which glorified suicides and executions, fatal accidents and physical deformation. It was the taboo nature of it all that first attracted me. I figured if they didn't want me to watch it, it must be really good."

It was curiosity that got Cal hooked on the genre. He wanted to understand this mysterious, terrifying thing that all of us must face at some time in our lives, just before we no longer cease to exist. "My first experience watching these movies was both frightening and exhilarating. The discordant heavy metal music playing along with death and dismemberment made the experience unnerving, yet, for some reason, so satisfying. The pleasure lay in the power that I felt while watching. It wasn't that it made me want to hurt others; in fact, it was quite the opposite. I felt deep sadness for the people who lost their lives and intense guilt for watching the footage. However, in a sense, knowing that I could face death and survive gave me a sense of control over my own mortality."

Yet our fears are actually exaggerated, or at least misplaced. People are terrified of strangers and mistrust those who are different or unknown, yet it is ten times more likely you would be killed by a friend or a relative, not a stranger. The fear of strangers made perfect sense during ancestral times when a visitor represented a significant danger since he might be a scout for another warring tribe. Such individuals who were not recognized were usually just killed on the spot, just to be safe, even though they might very well have had innocent or trading intentions. Nowadays, although people still mistrust and fear "those who are different," 90 percent of whites and African Americans are murdered by a member of their own race.[26]

All the stress and "culture of fear" related to obsessions about race riots, road rage, terrorist attacks, contagious diseases, and violent crime are all based on wildly irrational beliefs and faulty logic. Table 9-1 compares beliefs to reality.

TABLE 9-1: DISTORTED FEARS AND PERCEPTIONS OF DANGER[27]

Fear	Belief	Reality
Breast cancer	Women over 40 believe they have a 1 in 10 chance	Actual odds are 1 in 250
Violent crime	News stories on violent crime have increased 1,000 percent, so crime must be way up	Violent crime is actually down 20 percent from a decade ago
Road rage	Described in media as a "plague" or "epidemic"	Incidence of anger-related accidents less than 1 in 1,000
Plane crash	Fear of flying listed as one of most common disabling phobias	Odds of being killed are less than winning the lottery (1 in 4 million)
Workplace violence	Described in media as a "major threat to safety"	Incidence of people killed at work is 1 in 100,000
School violence	Reported in media as an "epidemic"and increasing at an unprecedented rate	*Any* incident is one too many, but there are no more than a few hundred children seriously injured in any year

The consequence of continual attention to potential dangers is that it creates a state of hyperarousal in which a person is constantly looking over his shoulder or startled at the least provocation. News junkies keep the television on every waking moment, augmented by hourly checks of online sources. "Breaking News!" scrolls across the screen announcing some new disaster, shooting, kidnapping, disappearance, or contagious disease. One could easily get the impression that the world is on the brink of apocalypse or that a band or murderous thugs is waiting to ambush you as soon as you walk out the door.

Managing fears through information and preparation isn't altogether a bad strategy for providing a sense of empowerment. Newly diagnosed cancer patients, for instance, attempt to take charge of their own health and recovery by learning as much about the disease as they can to manage their own treatment. They feel greater control from knowing what they are up against and what options are at their disposal. They are even better prepared to handle a poor prognosis because they have done their homework about what to expect.

On the other hand, curiosity about possible outcomes can easily get out of control. My father is confined to a chair or bed throughout the day, so he spends almost all his time either reading novels about terrorists or homicide or watching the news. There are probably few sources of "information" that are more sensationalized, producing an effect in which he is in a constant panic about the state of the human condition. He has an exaggerated sense that the world is a very dangerous place and he's lucky to be cooped up inside where all the terrorists, murderers, gang members, floods, earthquakes, and bloodthirsty pirates can't get him.

What is ironic is that although many people share the magical belief that somehow their interest in subjects like serial killers will somehow protect them from becoming a victim, what makes these predators so dangerous is that they really don't stand out from the crowd. They don't resemble monsters at all but rather quite ordinary people who hold jobs and carry out everyday lives just like you.

Hunger for Novel Stimulation

Watch a young infant and you will notice how easily her attention is drawn to any sight or sound that is beyond her present experience. A new shape or texture, even a strange voice, immediately commands her complete focus. This built-in proclivity toward novel stimulation is considered one of the more adaptive human defense systems. It is what allows us to anticipate and prepare for danger. This instinct makes us hyperalert to anything detected by our vision, hearing, and other senses that might pose an unforeseen threat. It is also the basis for much of learning when we try to make sense of things beyond our present understanding.

This same propensity toward novel stimulation acts as a powerful motivator to study any occurrence that is considered unusual. If dead bodies, public executions, car crashes, or other acts of violence are not part of your usual routine, then these would be powerfully seductive situations; and frankly, nothing is more alluring than the mystery of death. When you add to this enticement the natural urge that people have to protect themselves against misfortune and danger by studying those circumstances that led to others' demise, then you have an irresistible interest.

If novel stimulation is one potential explanation to account for the human fascination with violence and horror, it hardly supplies a complete and comprehensive answer. If anything, it generates even more questions.

For example, with the amount of murder and mayhem that we are exposed to in the news media, movies, television, and books each year, it's hardly accurate to say that this is novel stimulation; if anything, we've been so accustomed to these events that we are only a little titillated when the action is stoked up another notch.

"I don't really think that people inherently love death and violence," one man explained to me. "I think we are just naturally curious. Whether in real life or the media, we love chasing the unexpected." He further commented that it keeps getting harder and harder to top what has been done before because we've already seen it all. He likens it to a drug addiction: "The first hit is powerful, but after that you need more and more to get the same kick. It is novelty and newness that gets the adrenaline moving."

That's why there are always new editions and revisions of popular video games or remakes of classic horror movies. On the one hand, people like a certain predictability of plot line; on the other, they love surprises within limits. So many of the narratives in media revolve around a theme of restorative justice in which a hapless victim has been wronged and seeks retribution that becomes a kind of justifiable violence to fight back. The formula for most films, books, news stories, and games is ridiculously predictable most of the time, resulting in the feel-good satisfaction that comes from knowing the bad guy got just what he deserved and that good triumphed over evil.

But there is another kind of delight that arises from writers who color outside the lines. In that sense, violence is often used for its shock value, to hit you when and where you least expect it. It has only been in the last few decades that screenwriters, novelists, and newscasters have been "allowed" to play with audience expectations and work around them for the element of surprise. In a sports event, suspense is jacked up to maximum levels: the score is tied, the clock is running out in overtime, and in the last second there is a goal, a basket, or a touchdown to decide the outcome of the game.

Television series end their seasons with cliffhangers that leave the audience wondering for months about what will happen next. Suspenseful books or movies lead you in one direction, knowing you are experienced at figuring out where things are likely to end up; then they play with those expectations until such time that they can fool you by killing off the good guy or letting the bad guy escape. Yet in all their forms, the violence acts as a dramatic device that raises the stakes. And, ultimately, no matter how much carnage you witnessed and how voluminous the body count, you will survive. That exhilaration is a feeling worth returning to again and again.

Multiple Identification: From Prey to Predator

"I like movies with a lot of action," a well-known magician confided in an interview, not at all ashamed of his preferences because he knows he is hardly alone. "I like being able to experience horror at a safe distance. Vampires, for example, are ordinary people in extraordinary circumstances. I can imagine myself as a vampire and I try to empathize with those types of characters."

As mentioned previously, readers identify with multiple characters, not only the victims and the heroes, but also the killers. The same is true with movies or real-life atrocities. It may be shameful and socially unacceptable to admit it, but many people at times imagine what it would be like to take another life, to commit acts of destruction and evil. We may not act on these impulses, but the prospect of doing so is enticing, if disturbing. When

When the movie *Scanners* was first released in 1981 it was considered groundbreaking because of new, more inventive ways of showing heads exploding. It is partially novelty that satisfies audience hunger for new, more explicit forms of violence.

we encounter sociopaths and deviants who do break the accepted rules, we are horrified by their actions and yet fascinated by them.

"When I see a scary movie," one woman explains, "of course I'm pretending I'm the heroine, the one who is struggling for her life against the forces of evil. But sometimes, I catch myself imagining I'm the killer, the one doing the stalking. What makes it so exciting is that I'm rooting for the woman to survive, but also for the killer to get away. Pretty crazy, huh?"

If crazy is defined as deviant from the norm, then this is hardly true for this woman since so many individuals report similar experiences in which they are identifying with both sides of the violent interaction. It is a myth that men are the only fans of violence because of their overheated testosterone, and further, that when they are watching such gruesome stories, they are pretending to be the stalker who is brutalizing the women victims. Certainly this is true for some men, but just as often, others report that although they may repeatedly switch allegiances, often they are imagining themselves to be the prey, regardless of gender.

Likewise, a number of women I interviewed reported that when they watch slasher films, or read true-crime books (and women represent a sizeable proportion of this audience), they are often picturing themselves in the role of the predator as well as the victims.

"It feels good to be scared," a thirty-one-year-old social worker reveals. "It's a rush. You know it's a movie. I like the idea of being chased." Yet she is identifying not only with the victims but also with the killer. "Once he [the killer] is caught, it's not as exciting anymore."

That's one reason why contemporary horror and slasher films don't have neat endings in which the monster is caught. It isn't just the hope of a sequel that drives producers to allow the bad guy to escape, but also because that unfinished business is more evocative and memorable—the killer is still on the loose!

In one study of why women are such avid consumers of horror films, media scholar Isabel Pinedo found that scary novels, television shows, and movies help women to express feelings. "These stories allow us to exercise, rather than exorcise, emotions of tremendous importance that were otherwise denied inappropriate expression."[28] She is speaking specifically about terror and rage, which nice girls aren't allowed to show in public. After all, men are known to be emotionally restrictive, yet there is one emotion they are allowed to show in spades—anger. Women may show sadness, helplessness, disappointment, and all kinds of other feelings through tears, but they are not permitted to express rage or else they will be labeled a "bitch." It is only in the horror films that women get to release their pent-up aggression and initiate some payback.

Multiple Dimensions

After reviewing each of these theories to account for the human curiosity and intense interest in things related to violence, death, and horror, it is clear that we are talking about more than a single phenomenon. In other words, novelty theory may fit for some people in some situations in which they seek sensory stimulation and excitement. For others, in a different arena, they are engaging in vicarious indulgence in the forbidden, whether this involves identifying with the perpetrator or victim of violence. Although each of the subjects appears to be related, and certainly they share some features, we are actually not dealing with a single phenomenon but rather distinctly different processes. I have summarized in table 9-2 each of several common manifestations of vicarious violence, for which a theoretical framework might be most useful in accounting for spectator behavior.

TABLE 9-2: MODELS THAT EXPLAIN ENTERTAINMENT VIOLENCE

Type of Entertainment Violence	Example	Preferred Model
Movies	Horror, stalkers, monsters, war, disaster, murderers	Emotional activation; sensory stimulation; novelty as entertainment; multiple identification
Television	Lurid talk shows; news; reality shows with conflict; cop shows; predator documentaries	Deviant reality as normative through repeated exposure; emotional activation; conditioned responses
Car Crashes	Slowed traffic at accidents; car races	Novelty; curiosity; self-protection; guilt and relief over personal survival
True Crime	Books, articles, and films about true-life crimes	Identification with killer or victims; indulging in forbidden;socially acceptable journey to dark side
Sports	Hockey, rugby, football, wrestling, boxing, mixed martial arts	Catharsis of aggression; identification with players

After reviewing these forms of vicarious violence in which spectators enjoy some satisfaction or entertainment from watching others, several things become increasingly clear:

1. There is an unlimited market for experiences in which spectators can watch people encounter violence or death;
2. Vicarious forms of violence provide many of the same thrills as engaging in the behavior but without the direct threat of harm or reprisal;
3. There are several differences among these various activities that serve unique purposes, whether they are found entertaining or horrifying;
4. Almost all forms of spectator behavior are related to satisfying curiosity, providing a release of tension, stimulating emotional arousal, and allowing for identification with one or more roles;
5. Spectator curiosity toward death and violence seems to be fairly universal, and perhaps culturally useful, but also provokes feelings of guilt and shame.

BECOMING NUMB

So many of the processes just described result from the ways our culture has normalized violence. The attraction to horror and other brutal spectacles is, in part, a learned response to repeated exposures in the media. In the "cultivation theory" of mass media originally proposed by communications theorist George Gerbner, it was hypothesized that repeated exposure to intense stimuli such as violence and murder on television creates over time an alternative reality that is legitimized.[29] If you watch enough, or read enough, about acts of violence and horror, after a while it becomes not only commonplace but normal. The average American twelve-year-old has witnessed thousands of murders, rapes, and savage acts, most of them in the company of his or her parents' benign supervision in front of the television. Over time, we become so accustomed to blood that it no longer seems distasteful. Likewise, the reality of true violence can be experienced as a surrealistic film that doesn't seem to be happening.

Rod Dreher, a film critic who has enjoyed his share of violent movies, was shocked to discover the extent to which he had become numb to the incessant killing he had witnessed on the screen. Books and movies that portray women as victims of degradation, sexual torture, and brutal murder become titillating entertainment for the masses. "This is what happens," Dreher argues, "when one idolizes sensation, when the thrill of being shocked, amused or otherwise stimulated by a film supersedes ethical concern." The lust for blood has reached the point that moral judgment has been suspended. Anything goes for the sake of entertainment. Yet Dreher asks: What is it that we are doing to ourselves when we elevate killers to the role of tragic heroes?[30]

Until there are fundamental changes in the ways our culture glorifies violence, there will continue to be an endless market for stories, true or fictional, that depict acts of death and destruction. As long as children are raised on cartoons and video games that show violent characters, as long as they are exposed to sensationalized deaths in the media, as long as they are raised to idealize aggression, there will continue to be new generations of people eager for bloodshed.

While some would argue that this is a fundamental aspect of human nature, there is little doubt that these tendencies can be modified with restraint and moral responsibility. There is still little consensus, at least among the public, whether this is desirable. Meanwhile, we wait for the next serial killer to make his mark, the next blockbuster slasher movie to break box office records, and the next disaster or act of atrocity to bring out the ghoulish spectators hoping for a glimpse of blood.

Chapter 10

What's Normal and What's Abnormal?

Stacy is soft-spoken and generally fairly quiet unless she has something significant to add to the conversation. A slim, petite woman in her midtwenties, and a newly minted psychotherapist, she is both introspective and trained to examine her innermost reactions to life events. She is liberal in her politics and an avowed feminist. It is, therefore, all the more surprising that she is such an avid fan of violence, a proclivity about which she feels terribly guilty and reluctant to admit. Stacy feels that if her secret got out she would not only be labeled a freak but a fraud because of her strongly espoused ideals for women's empowerment. She is a diagnostician as a function of her profession, so it is difficult for her to avoid labeling herself as somehow abnormal. It was thus quite a surprise for her to learn that her attraction to violence is not only quite common but also quite useful in the grand scheme of things.

"I was drawn to the world of serial killers, and other sadists very early in my childhood," Stacy explained. "My mother had a great interest in crime shows so I often used that time to bond with her. I found that as I grew older I began to watch it on my own and relish the moments when the good guys won and justice prevailed. My fascination is not seeing people destroy the lives of others, but rather what creates a monster."

Stacy is driven by curiosity to understand better what leads some individuals to go so far over the line of civilized behavior. Yet she is also worried about her morbid interest and wonders if there is something wrong with her.

"There are two shows that I think I could watch every day, without ever becoming bored—*Most Evil* and *Deadly Women*. The first one highlights the characteristics that are common to murders and this helps me to understand what might be going on so I don't worry so much. *Deadly Women* is interesting too because it is just so surprising to learn about the ways that women can be so ruthless and sadistic."

Stacy realizes that she is trying to protect herself in some way. She wants to be better informed about potential dangers that could threaten her. She also believes that this preparation will help her to pick a partner who is "safe" and not a potential psychopath. In her work she has seen plenty of women who do end up in very abusive relationships, and it scares her that she could make the same mistake.

"Looking into the lives of these individuals does cause a bit of fear and repulsion, but it also gives me a sense of control. I'm able to say, 'Ah ha, you can't fool me!' I guess in the end I just want to feel safe walking to my car, but some of the things that I watch just fill me with more dread."

Stacy—and many of us—wonder whether the attraction to watching violence is somehow abnormal, or just wrong. Like every other proclivity, human behavior can be plotted along a continuum by which we can make an assessment as to its relative functional versus dysfunctional effects. When an activity enhances the quality of your life, and does so with minimal negative side effects or harm, then there is usually little problem. If, on the other hand, the activity contributes to greater suffering, crosses the line into immoral or illegal behavior, or presents additional difficulties for yourself or others, then it is a different story.

SHAME, GUILT, AND CONFUSION

Sammy is a graduate student who is soft-spoken and shy. He devotes his life to helping others and hopes to develop that passion into a future career. He is slight in appearance and almost deferential in his communication style. You'd barely notice him in a room, but once you get to know him, you'd be struck by his extraordinary sensitivity and caring. Like so many others, he harbors a secret that he has never shared—he absolutely loves watching graphically violent and morbid videos.

"The rush I get from these videos is so fleeting," Sammy confided. "Initially I feel this sense of power and control when I watch them, but then I feel terribly guilty and fearful. Not only do I feel embarrassed about my secret hobby, but I just feel so sad about the ephemeral nature of life.

It gets me thinking about my own mortality and my loved ones. I am left with the feeling that I am not really myself, but a fragile biological system that could potentially cease to function at any moment."

Even with these strong negative feelings, Sammy still feels like the satisfaction he gains is worth the shame and confusion. These feelings of being horrified and shocked by what he sees in gruesome videos gives him a greater sense of control over his life. "Whenever I feel the urge, I can log onto popular Web sites and find clips depicting fatal accidents and animal attacks. I can see images of self-mutilation and terrorist beheadings with the stroke of a few keys. The fact that death is now so accessible almost changes the way I feel about it. Because it is so easy to find, I feel as if my own perception regarding the taboo surrounding death has waned. In other words, the more we speak about death with each other, the more real it becomes, and thus the less frightening it is."

Throughout this book, we have explored how people feel a tremendous amount of confusion about what is considered normal or abnormal regarding their personal attraction to violence. We can easily draw a line at the point where anyone, in *any* circumstance, behaves in a violent manner or attempts to harm anyone else (except for self-protection in a life-threatening situation). It is simply not okay to act on violent impulses to solve problems, express anger, or abuse others. About the only other exception may be during times of war, and even that is highly contentious.

Then there are all sorts of fantasy activities that go on inside people's heads, some of which have a definite violent flavor. It is perfectly normal to have these thoughts—unless they reach the point of becoming obsessive or repetitive. Likewise, frequently ingesting violent movies, shows, books, video games, and so on is not harmful in itself unless there is a potential or actual loss of control.

Many of the people I interviewed admitted to all kinds of things they not only think about, but also act out; yet these are usually in ways that do not put themselves, or others, at risk of being hurt. One example was a car mechanic, Mike, a man in his early twenties, who took a while to feel comfortable enough to confess his secret attraction to blood—quite literally. He described his relationship with his girlfriend, whom he'd been seeing for about a year. They had just begun having sex together.

"She has some kind of medical problem with her vagina or whatever—endometriosis or something like that—which causes her to bleed every time we have sex. It freaked me out at first because when I'd pull out, my penis would be covered with blood."

Over time, Mike got used to the situation. "After a while, it didn't bother me at all." There is a long hesitation at this point while he checks out my reaction. As a psychologist, I'm used to maintaining a pretty good poker face, what we call "hovering attention" combined with patience and empathy. I nodded, encouraging him to continue. "So anyway, I not only began to expect to see the blood after I came, but I kinda got to like it. Know what I mean?"

I nodded, again encouraging him to continue.

"A little while ago, I cheated on my girlfriend, you know, had sex with someone else. And this weird thing happened. I didn't really like it very much because there was no blood. It wasn't nearly as good as with my girl-friend. So really, I can't imagine doing that again with anyone else."

Mike mentioned that his girlfriend never has any pain associated with sex, or complains about anything, even though sometimes the blood gets on the sheets so they have to be careful.

"After sex," Mike continued, this time even more hesitantly, "I like to look at the dried blood on my penis and imagine I've been hurt. I'm all bloody and I like to feel the blood. Hey, do you think there's something wrong with me?"

That's the question we're exploring, isn't it? Is there something wrong or abnormal about Mike because he enjoys sex accompanied by blood? While you give the question some thought, consider that Mike isn't hurting anyone, least of all himself, but he derives pleasure from the sight of blood associated with sex. Interestingly, he doesn't imagine himself in the sadistic role of hurting his girlfriend, or anyone else, but rather he sees himself as the victim.

DEATH PORN

It is one thing to watch acts of violence in fictional re-creations or docu-mentaries, but quite another to seek out such content in real life. During my research I heard about a Web site that featured graphic images and films of torture, beheadings, mutilation, executions, and suicides. Ogrish.com has over two hundred thousand subscribers who are devoted fans of crime scene photographs, decapitations, and the most grisly depic-tions of violence you can imagine. The Web site first became wildly pop-ular after it posted videos of the Daniel Pearl and Nick Berg beheadings in Iraq, each of which received over fifteen million hits. There is a kind of "demonic curiosity" to this morbid interest in watching other people suffer so brutally.[1]

There are blogs and open forums on these Web sites in which people talk about their intense interest in the violence displayed. The question that is asked over and over again is: "Are we sick? Is there something wrong with us because of our fascination with gore?" Media researcher Sue Tait studied some of the responses, a few samples of which are presented below to give you a flavor of what might be going on for some of the viewers.[2]

"Damn, I just clicked on that link, that was the first beheading I saw. It made me quite shocked for like 30 mins, after which I was hunting for more, only watched the Armstrong one too, it's some good shit." It was instant attraction for this individual, who found him or herself hooked after a single "dose" of a graphic execution.

Another viewer describes why he or she keeps going back for more: "After I watch the really brutal videos I get a kind of high that I can't get from anything else . . . the videos get my heart racing and [I'm] breathing all heavy. When I am watching them the rest of the world just fades away for a while and I am totally lost in the moment."

Tait comments that this kind of arousal evokes shock and revulsion, but also intense pleasure. She also notes that people seem to feel better about their own life circumstances when they are reminded about the fragility of life. In a sense, watching death scenes makes people feel more alive, a phenomenon that is often articulated by those who have escaped a close call or returned from a funeral. It has also been famously explored by existential philosophers such as Søren Kierkegaard, Friedrich Nietzsche, Martin Heidegger, Jean-Paul Sartre, and Albert Camus, as well as

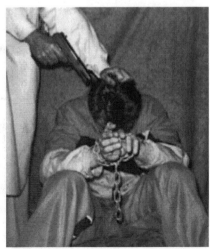

Millions of viewers watched the execution of Daniel Pearl, a journalist who was captured by Pakistani terrorists in 2002 and then beheaded in front of a camera. The video still attracts legions who watch the killing over and over.

the literary giants William Shakespeare, Fyodor Dostoyevsky, and Franz Kafka. Heidegger once observed that it was only by taking death into his life, facing it more directly, acknowledging it, that "I will free myself from the anxiety of death and the pettiness of life—and only then will I be free to become myself."[3]

Contemporary psychotherapists have also been known to employ confrontations with death as a means to help their clients face the emptiness and inertia of their lives. "Despite the staunchest, most venerable defenses," noted psychiatrist Irvin Yalom, "we can never completely subdue death anxiety: it is always there, lurking in some hidden ravine of the mind."[4] Yalom has been known to add dying patients to his therapy groups in order to help other participants consider their own mortality and thus face the time they have left as more precious. "Although the *physicality* of death destroys man," Yalom reminds people, "the *idea* of death saves him."[5] It isn't by denying and ignoring death—but by being more mindful of its presence—that we often feel more motivation to live with greater passion and to appreciate every second as a gift. That is one reason why many people report feeling more alive after encountering death up close and personal. As dramatic and arousing as it is to watch simulations and fictional representations in movies, the effects feel magnified when the mortal outcome is quite real.

One of the first low-budget slasher/gore films, the movie *Snuff* was filmed in South America in the early 1970s. There were rumors for many years that actual people were killed in the making of the film, and there is still some question as to whether *Snuff* and other films like it include real-life murders.

THE INFLUENCES AND EFFECTS OF VIOLENT MEDIA

There has been a half-century of research on the effects of violence in television, movies, and other media with the rather resounding conclusion that it leads to greater aggression, hostility, and antisocial behavior. In fact, violent video games and movies have even been blamed for several school shootings, implying that the young person was activated and stimulated by the fantasy violence enough to get a gun and start shooting classmates to act out the scenarios.

Such simple cause-effects might seem plausible, even logical, but the evidence to support these beliefs is equivocal at best.[6] It turns out that the influence of violence in movies and television may, in some cases, be negligible (but in other cases quite significant). Even more interesting is the theory proposed that the cause-effect relationship is actually backward. In other words, it isn't so much that watching violence encourages people to be more violent themselves, but rather because we have such inborn murderous instincts, we seek out socially sanctioned opportunities to indulge these feelings that are as natural as the urge to mate or socialize with others. To prove this point, David Buss and his colleagues conducted a massive investigation of this hypothesis, including interviews with individuals who were asked to disclose their homicidal fantasies.[7] One twenty-year-old college student admitted that she thought about killing her ex-boyfriend who kept bothering her after they broke up (estimated probability of acting on this plan, according to the subject: 60 percent). A man seriously considered killing his best friend who betrayed him (estimated probability: 80 percent). Another guy who had an altercation with someone on the highway who threatened him (estimated probability of killing him if he hadn't driven away: 90 percent). I must point out that these, and the hundreds of others who Buss interviewed, were normal people like you and me, yet they all had strong impulses to kill someone who threatened, betrayed, or hurt them. Furthermore, when asked what stopped them from acting on their murderous impulses, they most often mentioned that either they didn't have the means available at the time ("If I had a baseball bat with me I would have beaten him to death in a minute") or they were afraid of being caught and punished. "But what if you could have gotten away with it, then what?"

Then there was a long silence.

Evolutionary theory suggests that rather than an aberration, a feeling about which we experience guilt and shame, violence is a significant part of who we are, an adaptive and highly functional instinct that protects us against harm. "Our fascination with blood, our astonishing ability to pick out the angry face in a crowd of hundreds, and our thirst for the details of murders are all features of these defensive armaments."[8] We all have what Buss called a "killing brain," programmed for "homicidal scenario building." Such fantasies, lasting for brief intervals or elaborate scenes, are actually exercises in problem solving: If this person was to become a direct threat to me or my loved ones, what would be the best way to neutralize him?

In fact, such violent fantasies can be quite useful in helping people to work through their aggressive urges without having to act on them. It is the same with enjoying these scenarios vicariously through movies, books, sporting events, and video games.

COPYCAT CRIMES

Stanley Kubrick's masterpiece of violence, *A Clockwork Orange*, spawned several copycat crimes in which youth dressed up like characters from the movie and re-created the gang rape in the film while singing the theme song, "Singing in the Rain." Anthony Burgess, the author of the book, remarked that it was hardly accurate to say the movie caused or promoted the violence but rather introduced a style that was imitated by people who were already prone to aggression and antisocial behavior, and just as likely to act out in some other way. Whether or not that is true, whether other copycat murders and crimes would have been prevented without media violence, is difficult to say.

Martin Scorsese's film *Taxi Driver* shows Robert De Niro's character, Travis Bickle, on a killing rampage, acting out his murderous fantasies, which many would admit have crossed their minds on occasion. John Hinkley Jr. watched the film fifteen times and became obsessed with Jodie Foster in her role as a child prostitute. Like the character in the movie, Hinkley started collecting an armory of weapons, eventually selecting one in order to assassinate Ronald Reagan. After Hinkley's love letters to Jodie Foster went unanswered, he believed this final, desperate act of violence would win her attention and respect. He was right about the first part anyway.

The subtext of this whole episode is actually a familiar theme I have discussed earlier in which a man tries to earn the love of a potential mate by demonstrating his extreme propensity toward violence. However crazy his act, Hinkley was effective in showing a degree of courage and commitment to his cause. Foster may not have been impressed or wooed by this demonstration, but there are other women who would have been. In her study of "prison wives," women who choose to marry murderers or serial killers,

Sheila Isenberg, author of *Women Who Love Men Who Kill,* discusses the way that killers like Ted Bundy, Richard Ramirez, John Wayne Gacy, David Berkowitz, and the Hillside Strangler (actually, Stranglers—two men, Kenneth Bianchi and Angelo Buono, were convicted for the crimes) all had women fall madly in love with them and wish to marry them. Here's one typical letter from a woman suitor, Terry-Sue, sent to Gacy:

> I am a 34 year old black sexy mama. I am looking for a swinging good time whenever you get out. I know you killed them boys but I don't care. . . . P.S.: This is a train letter. Please send it to the rest of your killer friends.

Or another one from Kerri in Milwaukee:

> I've just got over a bad relationship with my x-boyfriend. He was a real bitch—but rather exciting. We would have these wild fights where we would hit each other, scream at the top of our lungs. John, I've got some "great lungs."[9]

Isenberg concluded her interviews with women who fall in love with killers by suggesting that they are drawn to outcasts, especially those who appear "macho" and dominant. What could possibly demonstrate dominance more dramatically than going on a killing spree? There is also an element of tremendous excitement in hanging out with someone who is so prone to potential violence. Yet there is a sense of safety and security in these relationships since the men are locked behind bars.

FUNCTIONS AND MOTIVES

So, what determines whether or not murderous thoughts or attraction to watching violence is "normal"? It isn't *whether* you engage in these activities, but rather *how often* you do so and *how intensely* you participate. There is a qualitative difference between occasionally watching a boxing match or hockey game or playing a shoot-'em-up video game, and immersing yourself in these activities for hours each day. One distinction between a leisure pursuit and a full-fledged behavioral addiction is determined by:

1. How much time you spend engaged in the activity
2. How often you think about the activity even when you aren't involved

3. What impact the participation has on other things you value (e.g., relationships, productivity, self-development)
4. Whether you retain sufficient control to reduce or stop the participation by choice
5. Whether the satisfaction you derive is worth whatever it costs you in terms of time, money, resources, and sacrifices

Motive is definitely part of the picture: What functions does the entertainment violence serve in your life? It is entirely possible that the intense interest in serial killers does not occur because you are perverse or weird, but rather as a defense strategy against a potential danger that is both quite rare and inexplicable. How do you protect yourself against someone who kills without apparent motive? Thus the fascination with serial killers is one way that people attempt to deal with uncertainty and unpredictability.[10] As one example, Mya remarks: "I think that I love a good mystery. This is evident in the types of shows that I watch, the books that I read, and my fascination with the undesirables of society. I like seeing what puzzle pieces, once put together, form someone who can rape, murder, and terrorize others. In the end my interest is connected with how to prevent these actions from occurring."

Considering that one-third of murders in the United States are not solved and remain a mystery,[11] the rate at which serial homicide is solved is even more rare considering that there is no apparent motive, the killer drifts between jurisdictions, and he usually is not known to the victim. This means that it takes considerable investigative skill, resources, and manpower to ever catch such a perpetrator. With the crimes unsolved, and hundreds of serial murderers operating at any one time, it is not unreasonable to devote some time to studying those who have been apprehended in an attempt to decode the pattern.

SECRETS REVEALED

Serial killers who have been somewhat cooperative with law enforcement or writers, or are at least willing to be interviewed, have revealed some of the secrets that guide their behavior—how they choose victims, their modus operandi, and how they dispose of the bodies. I interviewed a contract killer who had this to say:

> The guy started begging us not to kill 'em, crying and all like a child. I just looked at him and was glad it wasn't me sittin' there. The big Mex-

ican walked up behind him and put a pistol up against the back of his head—a little thing—and pulled the trigger. He fell like a brick. The Mexican stooped down and shot him twice more in the head. . . . We loaded the body in the trunk and drove a ways to where Keith had already dug a hole. I told him that it wouldn't fit in there; it was too small. He said watch and learn. We dropped his head in first, then the rest of him. "It only takes a four-foot hole for a six-foot man," Keith told me. Then we shoveled the dirt on top and smoked a joint.

There is something about such descriptions that are involuntarily riveting no matter how horrifying they might seem. When I interviewed Henry Lee Lucas, he admitted that there was really no method to his madness, nor much planning involved. His killings were opportunistic and often impulsive. The most challenging part for him was not the selection of victims, or even the killing itself, but rather what to do with the bodies afterward. Apparently, according to an expert, it isn't easy to dispose of a body. He tried hiding them in the woods, but they were usually found. He tried burning them, but there were always teeth leftover. Finally, he discovered that chopping the body into little pieces and dispersing the parts over a broad area worked best.

As you read this, you have to wonder if this killer could actually be a member of our own species. Can a human being really feel so little about taking a life, and so little remorse afterward? It is indeed a mystery, one that demands attention to figure out. After all, you don't want to be one of the next victims.

Ted Bundy spent considerable time after he was captured talking to authorities about his own preferred style of predation. The fact that he was a law student, an attractive, personable, charming man, that he made himself look harmless and vulnerable by wearing a fake cast on his arm, makes it appear even more hopeless to determine a self-protective pattern. When people are killed at random, for no apparent reason except their availability, what can you do to prevent a similar fate?

Serial killers on television or the movies are portrayed as brilliant schemers, "organized killers," who can outwit and outthink the FBI and police—at least for a period of time. They seem psychologically bent, of course, but also highly intelligent, manipulative, and seductive. Whereas killers like Bundy and Gacy did have reasonable social skills, most serial killers are not particularly bright, nor are they good planners. They manage to elude capture for so long precisely because there is little consistent pattern in their behavior. Sure, they find comfort in their rituals, but more often than not they kill on a whim and don't particularly care who the victim is. That brings little relief to anyone who carefully studies the photographs of the deceased, wondering, "Do I look like that?"

As much comfort as the illusion might bring that you can somehow prepare yourself to recognize a serial killer if you encounter one, they are not visible monsters with telltale signs. "As long as one believes that the evil man wears horns," observed psychologist and philosopher Erich Fromm, "one will not discover an evil man."[12]

A case in point: Gary Ridgway, the Green River Killer—serial murderer extraordinaire—managed to operate for twenty years without being noticed or caught. With forty-eight proven kills to his credit, Ridgway never fit the supposed profile of the disorganized, impulsive, psychopathic killer. He was not a loner or observably deviant or strange. With borderline intelligence measured in the bottom thirtieth percentile of the population, he was also not considered smart enough to be calculating and careful as killers are often portrayed. Yet he still managed to live a completely normal life to all appearances. Even his wife of seventeen years never had a clue. Ditto his family members, who also never suspected a thing. "Ridgway's gift was to bury evil so deeply in the trappings of an ordinary life that it did not exist—except on the nights when he was out polishing his career skills."[13]

Ridgway was disturbingly frank in his eventual confession, sharing the most mundane details of his craft—from how he selected victims to disposing their bodies. Although he preferred to snatch solitary prostitutes because there would be less likelihood of complaints, anyone could become a victim; the only thing that would exempt you as a potential victim was being a direct relative (and that was only because it would raise too much suspicion). Although Ridgway was quite talkative about how he stalked and killed people, as well as how he disposed of their bodies, he was completely at a loss to explain his motive or reasons for murder. All he could do was shrug—he killed because he just felt like it.

So, how do you protect yourself against someone who doesn't fit any known pattern? Ridgway, and others like him, don't necessarily stand out and can even be models of their community (think John Wayne Gacy or Ted Bundy). He didn't keep souvenirs from his victims and told nobody about what he was doing, keeping his leisure pursuits secret for decades. There was virtually no way you could recognize him as a danger—until it was too late—no matter how much you studied the behavior of serial killers.

But here's the good news: considering the population as a whole, the likelihood of you ever coming across such a predator is more remote than being struck by lightning (see table 9-1).

IS WATCHING VIOLENCE REALLY BAD FOR YOU?

In a classic study of how watching violence produces more aggressive behavior in young viewers, psychologist Albert Bandura had children observe others whacking blow-up dolls with bats and then observed their play behavior afterward. Being a good behaviorist, he concluded that aggressive behavior is a socially learned response.[14] This study, and many thereafter, suggested that children (and adults) who watch excessive violence on television or elsewhere are going to be far more likely to grab a bat and start acting out what they saw on the screen. This makes sense in theory, so much so that it has virtually been accepted as truth. Literally hundreds of studies have been conducted to investigate media violence, leading to the "inescapable conclusion that viewing media violence is related to increases in aggressive attitudes, values, and behaviors."[15] In addition, playing violent video games also increases the risk that people will become more aggressive in their behavior. One researcher compares the effects to that of other public health threats like the correlations between smoking and lung cancer or unprotected sex and HIV.[16]

The researchers have identified three main noticeable effects as a result of being a spectator of violence. First, that watching violence on television and other media increases the likelihood that the viewer will resort to aggression when solving problems or resolving conflicts. Second, it generates higher levels of fear in viewers who keep viewing over time; they believe that the world is a far more dangerous and hostile place than those who don't watch violent media. Third, viewers become desensitized and are thus more tolerant of violence when they encounter it in the outside world. These results have led professional organizations like the American Psychological Association to take a strong stand that violence in the media does lead to more aggressive behavior.

How can all this be measured, you might wonder, since the results of self-reports and questionnaires can be skewed and unreliable? People often lie to researchers, as well as underreport shameful or guilt-inducing behavior. To address these problems, Professor John P. Murray and his colleagues used magnetic resonance imaging (MRI) to measure changes in the brain that take place during the viewing of violence.[17] There are all kinds of areas that are lit up like lightbulbs under these conditions, particularly parts of the amygdala and prefrontal cortex. This makes perfect sense that the brain would become activated during exposure to any violent stimuli as a precondition to take evasive action—our minds don't distinguish, at least initially, between real threats and mere simulations.

The average child witnesses more than 100,000 acts of violence in front of the television. Certainly there is a desensitization that occurs, not to mention significantly distorted perceptions of reality. Research has documented that children (and adults) who watch a lot of TV tend to underestimate poverty and overestimate violence in their community. They see the world as a cruel, heartless place in which it's advisable to mistrust strangers, especially those with different skin color. They walk around feeling suspicious, threatened, and paranoid.[18] Image © Ryasick Photography, 2009. Used under license of Shutterstock.com.

A man convicted of assault, now serving time in prison, admitted: "Whenever I see a fight break out in here—and believe me, there's plenty of that going around [laughs]—I just get a rush, man. There's something about seeing a fist slam into the side of somebody's face, crunching a nose or knocking out teeth, that gets my juices flowing. Know what I mean?"

Well, not really. But you get the point.

For some, however, the stimulus of violence on television or in the movies acts as a trigger for their aggression rather than a vehicle for working through their feelings. Walter, in prison for assault and sexual abuse of children, has what he calls "fightmares," in which he wakes up in the middle of the night absolutely terrified, swinging at anything within range. He was sexually abused as a child, as well as subjected to physical abuse, and all of that trauma resurfaces in his dreams or when he watches horror films.

"I just love 'em!" he says. "But I can't afford to watch them. All the psychs like you that I've talked to, they tell me I have piss-poor impulse control. So just watchin' 'em and hearin' certain things gets me all worked up, you know? And believe me, most people don't like it when I get stirred up [laughs]."

CONFLICTING REPORTS

In a compilation of alleged movie-inspired violence from the 1980s, researchers found that it was often difficult to know what was really going on inside viewers' heads when they appeared to act out scenes from movies. Yet one film in which there seemed to be a clear link was the "Russian roulette" scene from *The Deer Hunter*, in which a character held a loaded gun to his head with only one bullet in the chamber. Spectators then bet on whether or not he'd kill himself when he pulled the trigger. There were at least three dozen known cases in which people who'd seen the movie reenacted it themselves for entertainment. They also cited another case from the movie *Born Innocent*, in which three teenage girls attacked and raped another girl with a broom handle. Just a few days after the film aired on television, a group of kids reenacted the same scene using a bottle, with one of them yelling out, "Hey, are you doing it just like they did in the picture?"[19]

In spite of these and other documented cases, it is actually quite difficult to prove a direct link. Defense lawyers have been trying to use movie violence as a way for their clients to plead temporary insanity, that the murders they committed were not really their fault because they were following the scripts of what they watched on the screen. Juries have usually not been persuaded.

The debate over the effects of media violence is both complex and confusing, with fewer definitive answers than you might imagine. It seems obvious that watching violence would make viewers more inclined to act out aggressively; indeed there are many studies that support that apparent cause-effect relationship. Yet there is also research that supports the exact opposite result—that watching violence actually helps viewers *reduce* their potential for acting in similar ways.[20]

There are so many myths, misconceptions, misinterpretations, and misquotations about the data collected that it is hard to sort out what's really happening. In a critical scrutiny of the hundreds of published studies, as well as the commentaries about this research, communication and media scholar David Trend offers several conclusions:

1. Children and adults are enjoying more graphic violence than ever. We are watching more variety, in more different media, for longer periods of time.
2. Crimes of violence are steadily declining each decade. This includes assault, rape, and homicide.
3. In spite of publicized incidents of mass shootings, violence in schools is also going down.
4. The influence of media violence is actually a marginal factor relevant to less than 10 percent of crime.[21]

There are certainly other researchers, critics, and politicians who would strenuously object to these conclusions, citing data and interpretations of their own. But the point is that we really don't know for sure what impact entertainment violence has on viewers.

For some people, in some situations, watching certain media, they feel a marked release of tension and diminished hostility. You can test this yourself by reviewing your own personal reactions to certain violent shows or movies. Sometimes you walk out of a theater wanting to kick something—or someone. Something was triggered in you—anger, frustration, a sense of helplessness or horror, that led you to want to lash out in order to reduce that inner tension. Other times you just feel drained and exhausted, shut down and overwhelmed from what you witnessed. In some cases you might even leave with greater determination and commitment to live a more peaceful life. The particular response is dependent not only on the kind of violence and the way it was presented, but also on the context of what is going on in your life at the time.

I remember one such event as if it were yesterday, even though it occurred forty years ago. It was during the height of the Vietnam War and I was on the verge of being drafted into the army. I didn't particularly object to the idea of going to war. I had watched movies most of my childhood that romanticized fighting and read dozens of books about battles in the Civil War and World War II. It was as if I had been preparing for my own initiation as a warrior. I played army and cowboys and Indians every day after school and on weekends. So the idea of going into battle with a loaded weapon and a license to fight didn't sound too bad.

But here's the really weird part: In spite of what I'd heard and seen about the horrors of Vietnam, I would have gone if only they'd just given me a rifle and let me loose in the jungle. I was terrified of having my head shaved and my fragile identity crushed in boot camp. I believed, like Samson, that if they cut off all my curly locks, I wouldn't recognize myself anymore.

I was still debating what I'd do once I got called to report for induction when I went to see a rather disturbing film. To this day I can still see the theater and the street and remember where I parked my car. I can almost (but not quite) remember what I was wearing. I do remember the friend who accompanied me, and we were both stoked about seeing a cool war movie, one about World War I called *Johnny Got His Gun*.

Well, there was plenty of violence, but it didn't turn out to be much of a "war" movie. In fact, it was the story of a solider who was so catastrophically wounded that there was nothing left of him but a torso and a head that couldn't hear or speak. I have never seen this movie after that first time, but I swear I can still re-create most of the scenes and remember with vivid detail what happened. The wounded soldier, who had no hope, just wanted to die, but the doctors kept him alive as an experiment.

I was so disturbed by this story that I walked out of the theater an absolute wreck. I couldn't talk to my friend about it, but I resolved in that moment, standing outside on a cold winter day in Detroit, that I was done with any fantasies about harming anyone else—with a gun in war or any other situation. I lost my lust for blood as a fantasy at the age of twenty, and it has pretty much remained that way ever since. Not only was I determined not go to war but I also abruptly stopped studying Tae Kwon Do after five years, even though I was about to test for a black belt. As it turned out, I received a deferment from the draft and so I did not have to test my new morality.

In a groundbreaking study on the connection between violent entertainment and subsequent behavior, anthropologist Bruce Knauft investigated a remote New Guinea tribe known for their peacefulness.[22] The highest values among the Gebusi are sharing, cooperation, and mutual compassion. Violent stories and dramas are not permitted as public entertainment, and there is little public tolerance for any conflict or dispute among the tribespeople.

Yet during his lengthy field studies among the Gebusi, Knauft noted a hidden and hushed-up aspect of their culture: they actually have the highest incidence of murder among any known culture—over *forty times* what we are used to, living in the most homicidal country in the industrial world. It is certainly telling that this is also one of the few groups on Earth that does not have alternative outlets for aggression such as violent entertainment. In spite of their goal of eliminating physical aggression within their culture, the behavior has just gone underground.

In her book on violence in the media, philosopher Sissela Bok explains this contradictory phenomenon that disputes consistent claims that watching violent enactments necessarily leads to fewer violent crimes.[23] While there may be some intuitive appeal, as well as modest empirical support to bolster this argument, the picture is a lot more complex. Because the Gelusi go to such extreme lengths to avoid the very mention of violence, even in their entertainment, they remain in denial when people resort to murder. They simply won't speak about it or acknowledge that such crimes exist. No investigations take place. Rarely is anyone found guilty, much less punished for antisocial behavior.

This is not an excuse to justify graphic violence in the media but a reminder that it does serve important purposes as ritualized aggression, catharsis of anger, conflict resolution, and an alternative to actual combat. Among other New Guinea tribes, for example, lethal warfare between warring tribes has been replaced by carefully ritualized enactments in which participants pretend to kill one another, stopping just short of spear penetration. This is not unlike the combat between elk, moose, kob, and other animals that fight over dominance positions but do so without inflicting mortal wounds.

In other critical reviews of the research on how media violence perpetuates criminal behavior, it was actually found that there is little, if any, consistent evidence that the two are definitively linked.[24] I'm not saying there's no connection whatsoever, just that there isn't completely solid research to support the conclusion. Although the research has been presented by experts and media critics as unequivocal, overwhelming, definitive, and consistent, this is not actually the case. A number of methodological problems, overgeneralizations, and exaggerations have led to misconceptions.[25] For example, whereas some studies have found an apparent link between media violence and behavior, the effects varied depending on gender, setting, culture, context, and country. Countries like Japan or Finland have similar, if not higher, consumption rates of entertainment violence than other industrial nations, yet they have very little violent crime.

The reality is far more complex—and interesting. Subsequent studies have confirmed this contagious influence; however, the effects are both small and short-lived.[26] Just as you would expect, people are affected by watching violence, but not nearly as much as you'd think. What we do know, however, is that exposure to violence can produce a condition of hypervigilance in which a person sees potential threats everywhere and attends selectively to incidents and cues that confirm this anxious percep-tion of the world. Strangers are avoided or seen as potential threats.[27] Newspapers and television reports are scanned with an eye toward finding bad news. Physiological triggers, such as release of cortisol (the hormone associated with stress), are easily activated at the slightest provocation, leaving the person eternally wired and jumpy. In extreme cases, people become housebound, collect guns, and watch twenty-four-hour news cov-erage, waiting for the anticipated sign of the apocalypse.

Someone drifts into your lane on the freeway and a siren goes off in your head: "He's trying to kill me!" Any funny look you get is interpreted as a challenge, a cue that predicts impending doom. "He's probably got a weapon and intends to use it on me the first time I let down my guard."

There are all kinds of psychological conditions that can result— generalized anxiety, panic disorder, paranoia, and reactive aggression, which represents exaggerated responses to relatively benign stimuli. Then there are all the other associated physical problems that can result, including ulcers, high blood pressure, tension headaches, stomachaches, and a host of psychosomatic complaints.

Although there are many politicians, religious figures, and moralists who complain that entertainment violence represents the end of civilization as we know it (some made one huge exception for the brutality and graphic tor-ture in *The Passion of the Christ*) responsible for our supposedly out-of-control homicide rate, it is interesting to look at other countries in which violence in the media is ever more prevalent. The Japanese, for instance, go wild over violent movies, yet the number of violent crimes and murders in their country is a tiny fraction when compared to figures in the United States.

In summary, it is difficult to say what is normal and abnormal with respect to entertainment violence, except in terms of whether it is enhancing or detracting to your life. If it leads to greater aggression, hos-tility, and abuse of others, not to mention internal frustration and anger, it is hard to characterize it as harmless. On the other hand, for the vast majority of people who enjoy violent sports, cinema, TV, or books, such a diversion can indeed be both satisfying and relatively harmless.

For a small minority of people, they are indeed activated by watching violence, to the point that they feel seriously disturbed and may act on impulses they can't seem to control. But there is no definitive cause-effect relationship that has been supported by well-designed, replicated research.[28]

Chapter 11
Exploring the Forbidden

A lot of these Christian people, they want to kill too. They're saying to me—I should die—but they want to kill me. They want to kill too. Everyone who writes me—thousands of people only write because they think I killed 500 people. People ask me if they should go out and kill people. I'm not saying that some people don't need to die, but hey, the guards read all my letters.

This was an observation made by convicted serial killer Henry Lee Lucas when I spoke with him in November 1997 at the death row facility in Huntsville, Texas. He was feeling particularly loquacious that day because his lawyer had managed to get some of his alleged murders removed from his case. Apparently when he had been convicted of killing someone in Florida, he had actually been in another state killing someone else. He thought this was hilarious, just another example of the fun he was having leading authorities around in circles.

What could one of the most prolific serial killers in history offer on the subject of entertainment violence, and what was I doing talking to this guy in the first place?

A VISIT TO THE MUSEUM

Residents of the state of Texas would like it to be known that it is not a territory in which to commit a capital crime. Whereas the rest of the country, and most of the Western world, struggles with the morality of killing people as punishment for murder, many Texans have few similar compunctions. Even more to the point, neither do their elected officials, who refuse to stand in the way of what the courts decide.

During the time I visited the Ellis Unit at Huntsville Prison with Jason Moss, my coauthor on *The Last Victim* project, there were not one, but *two* executions scheduled on the same day. There had been thirty-four other inmates whose death sentences had been carried out that year, making this something of a record.[1]

It was either a slow news day or the people of Huntsville take their executions seriously. The headline in the *Huntsville Item*, the local paper, read in large bold type, "Apologizing, Killer Is Put to Death." Even the US standoff with Iraq over its refusal to allow inspectors into their weapons facilities was relatively unimportant compared to the story about the thirty-fifth lethal injection that year. The article reviewed the man's crimes in great detail, how he kidnapped a mother, as well as her eight- and four-teen-year-old daughters, raped them, and would have killed them all, but the little one managed to escape. The article didn't mention, however, that Henry Lee Lucas thought the killer was a standup guy.

It took only thirty-seven minutes for a Texas jury to give him the death penalty, and it took only three minutes for him to die. Dutifully noted in the article were the inmate's last words ("I'm sorry") and descriptions of his last breaths. In another article, there was a story about the little girl who was now in her early twenties. Because she couldn't afford to attend the execution in Huntsville, which was several hundred miles from her home in West Texas, her neighbors took up donations on her behalf so she could travel there to watch him die. This was the entertainment and satis-faction that she had been praying for during these past years of recovery.

Not far from the execution site downtown, Jason and I first decided to check out the local museum that was devoted to their prison, the largest employer in the county. Directly across from the courthouse is the Texas Prison Museum. An older woman sat inside, reading magazines and talking to any visitors who stopped by.

"These people from Germany and other places," she said to us with disgust, "are always arguing with me about killing these murderers."

She was referring to the subject of capital punishment, since this museum holds among its artifacts "Old Sparky," the original electric chair that operated in Huntsville from 1924 until 1964, killing 361 prisoners until it was replaced by lethal injection. The old chair showed little wear and tear for its trouble, all polished wood and ten sets of straps to hold the victim in place.

"What do they think we should do with these people who do those awful things?" the woman asked us. We started to walk toward Old Sparky, to give it a closer look, as the woman kept talking to our backs. "I just wish they'd just keep their damn mouths shut."

We nodded our heads in sympathy and continued to look through the collection on display. On a wall across from the famous electric chair was a framed document titled "Last Meal of #321."

"This is my last meal," wrote J. W. Morrow in careful script, "and damn it, I want it served hot, however many platters and bowls it takes." Listed below was his request for steak, French fries, butter beans, brown grease gravy, biscuits, sliced onion, three large bananas with ice cream, and fluffy coconut pie.

The good people of Huntsville hold a particular fascination with crime and punishment because so much of their lives is dominated by the prison population and the employees who are needed to care for them.

"I was bored and didn't have nothing to do," says Cassie, who serves drinks at the local country club. We had asked her why she decided to take three weeks off to sit and watch every minute of a murder trial in town. "Those babies didn't have a chance," she explained, referring to the children of the mother who now sits on death row, down the street. "I wanted to get up and knock the shit out of her."

"Does that make her a bad person who deserves to die, because she lost it one time?" I ask.

She nodded her head as she continued to wipe the counter that was already sparkling clean. "My sister-in-law was in prison with her, and she said she felt nothing." So it's remorse we like to hear from our convicted felons who are waiting to die.

I asked the waitress what she learned from her experience watching the trial. Then, out of nowhere, she said, "Anybody can kill anyone, anytime."

Before I could ask her what she meant by that, she was called out of hearing range and I never got an explanation. But my guess is that she had given considerable thought to the subject of killing and, as little sympathy as she felt for those who had committed the crimes, she realized that few of us are immune to the possibility of losing control in a fit of rage.

A VISIT TO DEATH ROW

I drove twenty miles outside of town, following directions provided by the prison authorities. In no time we were lost, or at least disoriented by the immense cattle ranches and grazing land that encircles the town. Every time we stopped, we got slightly different instructions about the best way to get to the Ellis Unit, the structure that holds death row. Perhaps the confusion is understandable because there are over a hundred different prison units located around the countryside, each of them with a different name.

The prison information officer looked like a more refined version of the Marlboro Man—without the horse. He was dressed casually in khakis, loafers, and a sport shirt. He smelled like tobacco.

Sam was used to being pestered by the media. An ex-reporter himself, his job was to pacify all interested parties who are doing stories on executions and death row. He is an expert on this subject, having witnessed over 125 executions himself.

To call his office modest would be generous. We were all cramped into a cubicled area, our knees tucked tightly under the chairs. The sounds of the copy machine made talking difficult. Every so often, we heard the beeps of incoming faxes or the phone ringing.

Sam has worked in this job for many years, trying to stay on good terms with everyone—the visiting media, the prison guards, and the inmates, whose cooperation he needs in order to arrange their interviews.

"I wouldn't have thought I could ever talk to these guys," Sam admitted, referring to the killers on death row, "much less be friends with them."

Not liking how that sounded, Sam clarified that he could never be friends with them, but he can see many of them as victims themselves.

"I was talking to this guy," he said further. "Just got his execution date, and we were talking about it. I feel bad for him."

His expression of concern quickly changed to scorn when he thought about most of the killers he has encountered. "The most important thing to remember," he warned "is the word *con* in *convict*. The guy who was executed last night—he was laughing and joking about it. Until the last minute, I don't think he really believed it was going to happen."

Sam looked thoughtful as he played with his mustache. His eyes looked sad. In a sense, his job is to manage these executions in such a way that they provide a satisfying experience for the viewers. There are others who take care of the details of administering death, whereas his role is to provide the public with all the procedural details they hunger for. Sam confided that his biggest problem isn't with the guys locked in prison who mostly behave themselves, but rather with the hordes of other people, mostly women, who admire or worship these inmates.

"They find these guys exciting," Sam said, shaking his head in wonderment. "They're good-looking women too." He made this last comment wistfully.

Sam looked to see if it was safe to continue along these lines and noticed he had a very attentive audience.

"There's just something missing in these women's lives, and, I don't know, they think they can only find it on death row. These women just love the bad boys. I think it's sad."

"What about the celebrity status of the killers?" I asked him. "What are these guys really like?"

"They're just cowards," Sam answered. "What sort of courage does it take to stab a little girl in the back, like that guy last night?"

It frustrates Sam that so many people want to save these guys' lives. He mentioned the story of one European woman who sent a guy on death row twenty thousand dollars for legal fees to get his sentence commuted. Sam just can't believe that people would choose to spend their money that way. "If they want to give away their money," he said, "why not send it to the victims?"

The other thing Sam can't understand is why people are so fascinated by executions in the first place. "There's nothing much to see," he says. "Just two or three small gasps, and that's it. I don't see what the big deal is why so many people care about this stuff." Again, Sam shook his head but admitted that his job depended on this continued obsession with watching prisoners put to death.

"So, then, how has it affected you to watch 125 men die?"

Sam shrugged. "I'll tell you one thing: I haven't lost any sleep over any of them."

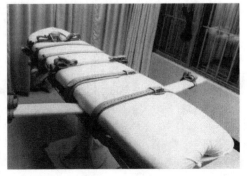

The execution chamber at the facility in Huntsville, Texas, where hundreds of prisoners have been put to death, viewed by family members, relatives of the victims, and reporters who represent the public. While not exactly viewed as a form of "entertainment," it does provide a kind of satisfaction for those who wish to see justice served. Courtesy of the Texas Department of Corrections.

So Sam is the gatekeeper to a world that doesn't interest him. He is amused by all the hoopla that so many people want to gain access to these killers or want to watch them die. He doesn't understand the interest or what people are looking for and, not being the reflective sort, doesn't much care.

PRELUDE TO AN INTERVIEW WITH A KILLER

In the early 1980s the whole country was going "serial killer crazy." During the late 1960s and 1970s, serial murders were headline news: Ted Bundy had been killing in the state of Washington, John Wayne Gacy in Chicago, Charles Manson in Los Angeles, and children were being murdered in Atlanta by Wayne Williams. Even with this backdrop, Henry Lee Lucas stood out as the worst of them all. He was a one-eyed drifter who killed hundreds in unimaginable ways—strangling, beating, shooting, stabbing, raping the victims' dead bodies, and eating their flesh. Furthermore, he played the press and police with the same predator-like skill that he harvested his victims. He thrived on taking polygraphs and loved participating in interrogations, confessing to crimes that he never committed and covering up others. He attempted to destroy the careers of reporters or police who he believed had betrayed him in some way. He changed his stories to suit his moods or the circumstances. He saw himself as the key actor in a drama played out in the media, with millions tuning in for the next installment.

The childhood of Henry Lee Lucas read like a perfect formula for creating a sociopath. His mother was a drunk and a prostitute. She was fond of having sex in front of her young son, sometimes even inviting some of her customers to take her boy as well. One of her most frequent guests initiated young Henry into the joys of torturing and mutilating animals, then having sex with their dead bodies. He was instructed in the intricacies of stalking, capturing, subduing, torturing, and killing things. At age fourteen, Henry branched out and began killing humans; he grabbed a girl his own age in order to have sex for the first time. When she resisted his advances, he strangled her.[2]

Lucas spent the next decade in and out of prison for various burglaries and child molestations he committed, although he later confessed that during this time he was also killing indiscriminately. To this day, nobody really has any idea how many lives he had actually taken; even Lucas couldn't remember and got the details confused.

As much as he enjoyed killing people, most of all Lucas loved the attention from the public. He thrived on the notoriety he received, having lived so obscurely as a drifter throughout most of his life. In fact, he did most everything he could to make himself the most famous man alive—confessing to crimes he didn't commit, leading law enforcement officers on treasure hunts for dead bodies. He represents the classic case of the invisible man dying for attention and willing to do anything to become noticed and admired. Women never noticed him while he was running around loose (except that he seemed creepy), but all that changed once he was captured and credited with setting close to a world record for successive murders. He finally attained the fame he so coveted.

MAN IN THE CAGE

We walked up to the guard tower and were surprised to see female correctional officers in attendance. We yelled up to the top, feeling a bit stupid holding a conversation in this way. The guards directed us to a small shed by the entrance to the Ellis Unit, where an attractive young woman, who looked to be just a few years out of high school, asked for identification. There was a perfunctory search, much less thorough than I imagined, and then we were told to have a seat until we were called.

It was still cold, even just past noon, and the chill cut through my bones, although I may have been shivering with apprehension. I looked enviously at the heater directed toward the young guard's feet. She was ignoring us, talking on the phone to her boyfriend while simultaneously studying the want ads for a pickup truck.

Finally, the public relations guy, Sam, came in to escort us inside. The unit was composed of several dormitory-looking buildings with bars on the windows, surrounded by three perimeters of fence topped with barbed wire. We were led inside, chatting with Sam about the upcoming execution scheduled for that day when, all of a sudden, he said, "There's Lucas waiting for you."

It was a gigantic room containing a long brown counter running down the middle with about fifty chairs in a row. A thick glass and wire-meshed divider separated the room, where the visitors sat on one side, and on the other, the inmates were kept in holding cells until they took their seats at the counter. Below the glass and above the counter was a screen designed to make conversation easier to hear. Since we were the only ones in the room, that would not be a problem.

Sitting in front of us was an old man, a most ordinary man with short gray hair, a short and stocky frame, and ruddy cheeks. His hands were clasped together, hands that had taken the lives of hundreds, and when they moved, I inched back a little from the screen, just on pure instinct.

Lucas was wearing a short-sleeve white shirt, and although it was really cold, he didn't show the slightest discomfort. On the contrary, he looked perfectly composed and relaxed, with a smile on his face. About the only thing that looked sort of weird was his one glass eye, which looked just as dead as the one that was supposedly alive.

It was strange looking at him, not only because I had to concentrate to look only at his right eye, but because his image was obscured by reflections in the glass. The whole time I was speaking to him, it was like I was talking to myself in the mirror. At times, if Lucas would move back or forward, it was like his image became superimposed on my own.

It was completely quiet in the room, except for the sounds of the guards nearby, a woman and two men, chatting with one another. Besides the chill in the air, the only other thing I was aware of was the pounding of my heart.

THE KILLER SPEAKS FOR HIMSELF

The first question I asked was the one that interested me most: "Henry, why do you suppose so many people are interested in you?" I didn't mean to be offensive, but I guessed that he understood that he was not exactly a brilliant intellectual, nor a hunk.

"They're all just living through me," he answered immediately, obviously having given the question a lot of thought. "They don't have the gumption to do what I do."

I assumed by that he was referring to his propensity to kill people.

"They want to be something that they're not," he explained in a bored voice. "They have a fantasy. They want to have the attention I got. They built it up in their minds. They think to themselves, I'd like to do that. They think they'd get away with it." He chuckled as he said that, in a way that was so reminiscent of what the bad guy does in the movies, just before he reaches through the screen and strangles the questioner to death. I inched my chair back a bit more.

"People don't have the courage to do things themselves," he repeated. "It's all their fantasy. It'll just eat you up if you let it."

"What do you mean?"

Lucas talked about the rage he felt when he was younger, how it constantly ate at him until he felt like he'd explode. "I don't know whether to blame my people or not," he said, then coughed into his hand. Again, I moved away from the screen, definitely not wanting to catch a virus from a serial killer. "I killed my mother," he continued matter-of-factly. "But I don't know if it was her fault or not."

He was referring to the sexual, physical, and emotional abuse she inflicted on him throughout his childhood. But since he had just a few months until his scheduled execution date, Lucas was on his best behavior, pretending to show compassion and Christian charity. The veneer didn't last long though, especially when he talked about the so-called civilized people who judged him.

At this point in our conversation Lucas was claiming he hadn't really killed anyone, except his mother, of course, and that was mostly an accident. But he sure had studied the subject of death a lot.

"I've looked at a lot of dead bodies, like, pieces with their heads cut off." As he said this, Lucas made chopping motions with his hands. "Some of them had their bellies open, their guts hanging out, their privates cut off, maggots crawling all over them."

"So," I interrupted him, since he seemed inclined to go on with this for some time, "why do you find this is so interesting?" Jason kicked me under the table since I presume he wanted to hear more graphic details.

"It's an inner feeling you get. It just sparks something in you." As Lucas said this, he looked directly at Jason, seeming to know he'd understand and that I was clueless.

Lucas was talking about the thrill he got, and believed that everyone gets, when looking at a dead body. "It excites you. You try and figure out what happened."

I tried to lead him back on track, asking him about why he was such a celebrity.

"There's so many women out there who want to marry me. But that's only because they want to be with a killer. I have all these women writing me. Even some of the guards. It's a known thing."

"You never had any of this magnetism when you were on the outside," Jason pressed him. I was surprised that Lucas so easily nodded his head in agreement.

"Everyone's capable of killing," he explained. "But not everyone's got the nerve, the push, the rage."

"What do you mean?" Jason asked him to explain further.

"There's two people in everyone—the inside part, which is, like, the conscience, and the outside part. That's the pull. You end up in trouble when you get caught between them." He nodded to himself as if that was a familiar predicament he found himself in.

I could feel tension between Jason and me at this point. I was wanting Lucas to expound on the entertainment violence angle, and Jason wanted to know more about the killing. I could see Lucas watching the two of us, studying us, wondering about our relationship and how he could somehow exploit the situation for his own interest.

After giving Jason a look to back off for a moment, I asked Lucas about his own favorite entertainment, and he shared that he loved watching police stories. "I try to figure out if I would do things that way," he said. "I put myself in the situation. So does everyone."

Yes, Lucas, I wanted to say to him, *but most people identify with the victims or the policemen, not the killers.* But maybe I was wrong.

"People want to be that person," Lucas explained further, "that killer." He paused. "It's not really the person, themself, but the person inside."

Lucas said that everyone needs a release from the tension that builds up inside. "It'll eat at you if you don't find a release. Believe me: I know." There was a definite menacing tone in that warning.

Jason wanted to explore next why a killer gets caught, and Lucas was happy to expound on that subject, one of his favorites. It was interesting how he worded his responses carefully in the second person, as if he were talking about someone else, not himself. It was spooky.

"If you don't leave evidence," he summarized simply, "they can't find you."

"Uh huh," Jason responded neutrally, encouraging him to go on.

"If you don't tell nobody, you won't get caught either." He was referring to his partner during one decade-long killing spree, a guy by the name of Ottis Toole, who had betrayed him. Actually, they blamed each other for various murders, mostly unsure of which ones the other committed. I suppose when you've killed so many people it must be hard to keep them all straight.

"You have to hide the body so it won't be found," Lucas continued the lecture. "It's good to burn a body, but then they still find teeth so you have to hide it real good."

It seemed ironic that he was claiming to be an expert on this topic since he did so little to hide his bodies, just burying them in shallow graves by roadsides.

"Choppin' up a body makes a mess and it leaves evidence. You don't want to have blood."

I could do nothing but nod my head, as if he was passing along a cherished family recipe.

"Everyone urinates. You take the average guy, he messes himself. But a younger girl, they just urinate. The older ones, they do both."

I was too stunned to talk, so Jason casually asked him how a killer finds his victims.

"That's easy. You can find people anywhere—parks, motels, clubs, parking lots, grocery stores. If you like kids, you can go to schools or find them on the streets." He paused for a thoughtful moment, then added, "Of course killing kids ain't right." Then he looked up, as if to say that adults are perfectly fair game.

"You can drive anywhere, see what you want, and just get it. But you gotta have the nerve. If you don't have the nerve, don't bother."

Anything else?

"Yeah, you got to get people away from others 'cause they scream a lot. You make short cuts," he said, showing us in pantomime how to torture a victim with a knife. "You kind of design 'em, is what you call it."

We commented that he sure knew a lot about this stuff, considering he had never killed anyone himself, except his mother, of course.

Lucas smiled.

"Yeah, I'm just good at this stuff. I done solved so many murders, like that little girl in California."

"You mean, Colorado?" He was referring to the case of JonBenét Ramsey.

Lucas nodded his head, proud of his detective work, just like he claimed that all those bodies he showed to the authorities were just his brilliant detective work rather than firsthand knowledge.

For a minute, it felt like we were talking to Hannibal Lecter from *Silence of the Lambs*. Lucas was about to tell us who really killed the Ramsey girl.

"Yup, I know who done it, all right," he said, building up the suspense. "That's an easy one."

"Yeah?" we prodded him further.

"The dad done it. He was just playing with her in the basement and it got out of hand. I seen it on TV and pieced it together."

Lucas was enjoying our conversation earlier about rules for committing perfect murders and he wanted to get back to it.

"Never commit a murder the same way, if you want to get away with it." He seemed to be checking things off in his head. We can't seem to forget that these "rules" follow exactly the ways he committed his own crimes.

"You need to travel a lot, always switch cars, do it different each time, a different way."

Yes, this is *exactly* what he did.

"Do your stuff at night," he said, with that one good eye looking off into the distance as if he was remembering some of his own favorite nights. Then his eye locked back on us, and his usually soft voice became firm: "You gotta pick someone up at night."

He paused for only a moment, then continued his list.

"Find a location for the body away from town. Never leave a body on the side of the road or you'll get caught for sure."

That's exactly what happened with his victim known only as "Orange Socks," since her identity was never learned. Lucas unceremoniously dumped her body right underneath an underpass where it was easily found and connected back to him.

Lucas went on further, checking off another dozen items that any self-respecting serial killer should take into consideration when practicing his craft. Finally, he arrived at the last on his list.

"Most of all," he laughed, then coughed into his hand, "don't confess." Then he started laughing again.

We were writing frantically now, trying to get it all down word for word, because we couldn't believe he was actually saying all this. One of us was writing his words verbatim while the other wrote descriptions of his mannerisms and tone. Since both of us were looking down at our writing pads, he stopped talking. Once eye contact was restored, he was going again.

He repeated what he said earlier, because he considered it so important. "If you tell one person about what you done, it's all over."

Lucas lamented his own impulsive jabbering when he first broke down and confessed to a number of unsolved killings, telling police exactly where to find the bodies, even leading them to the remains himself. In each case, he would talk about how he had killed them and what he did to their bodies afterward.

After spending so many years on death row with nothing but time to think, he had come to regret that his desire for attention was so intense that he broke his number one rule. At the time, though, he was on the verge of a psychotic break, actually feeling remorse for the first time in his life after killing his little girl/wife. Furthermore, he was going through withdrawal after an intense addiction to tobacco and coffee. Only after he broke down were his privileges restored.

Lucas now looked pensive. Time was running out. We had been with him for almost two hours and there was still a lot to cover.

There was an execution scheduled that day and another the next. How do you feel about all that? we asked. Did you know the guy well?

Lucas nodded his head sadly. "He's a pretty good guy. I've known him a long time." Then without skipping a beat, he said, "He killed a woman and her daughter, raped all of 'em too, but he was a good guy."

"They're just killing people here in Texas like crazy," Lucas ranted. "It's gotten worser. It hurts when they take one of 'em away. You know where he's going."

Where they're going to is downtown Huntsville, where the execution chamber is housed. They spend their final week there, without much hope of a postponement at that point, especially since Texas had already executed thirty-five or so that year without a single glitch.

"We'll just end up killin' a bunch of them guards." Lucas looked over his shoulder and nodded in the direction of his overseers. "They take everything from us. They take away our coffee and our privileges and we don't have much hope. Nothing to lose neither."

"Times up! Finish up."

We held our hands up to the glass in a symbol of farewell, just like we've seen them do in the movies. Lucas seemed uncomfortable about any intimacy. He lightly touched the glass and turned away.

ROUND TWO: DEATH ROW AT SAN QUENTIN

"Pliers."

"Huh?" Jason replied, at a loss as to how to respond. Where the hell did *that* come from?

"Pliers are something I think about a lot," Richard Ramirez explained simply.

Jason couldn't believe he was having this conversation. Here he had just recently graduated from college and was taking a break from studying for the LSAT for admission to law school. Now he was sitting within easy reach of the nation's most notorious serial killer, and the guy was telling him about his obsession with pliers.

"Yeah?" Jason prodded him. "Like how?"

"Slowing cracking each knuckle on each finger of a little girl's hand. An Asian girl. The bitch has to be Asian. I love them Asian ones." Ramirez started laughing, providing a particularly gruesome expression when his teeth showed. They were brown, decayed, rotted down to the gums.

Jason had taken careful notes right after their conversations over several days. He had wormed his way into Ramirez's life, earned his confidence, and befriended his wife, who had arranged the meetings at the prison. Jason turned over all his notes so I could write them up and add my own questions and comments. Then I stuck them away in a box for ten years, where they stayed until I opened them this evening. We never got around to doing our follow-up book, and I had forgotten about them.

"You hear me there, boy?" Ramirez said when Jason didn't respond right away.

Jason nodded his head, pretending to listen, but he couldn't stay focused.

"So," Ramirez continued, "I like to use the pliers. *Pop, pop, pop,* that's the sound the knuckles make when you crack 'em. It's cool to watch their eyes when you're doin' it."

Jason was pretending to be one of Ramirez's satanic disciples, the lieutenant in charge of his secret cult, but he had a surprisingly weak stomach. All the while he made appropriate noises and expressions, he distracted himself by thinking about the next question he would ask. He was revolted by what he was hearing but amazed that the killer was talking about these things to him.

". . . and then I stick needles under their fingernails. Hurts like a motherfucker, believe me."

"Uh huh. So tell me, Richard, why do you like Asians so much anyway?"

"They're quiet for one thing," he answered, taking a huge gulp from a bottle of Pepsi that Jason had bought him. It was mesmerizing watching his Adam's apple bounce up and down as he finished the bottle. It was the third one that he finished in the past two hours. It seemed to take frequent bribes from the junk food machines to keep Ramirez talking.

Ramirez paused for a moment to wipe his mouth with the sleeve of his shirt. "They're submissive too," he added. "Sometimes I kinda like that."

Jason nodded again, not sure where to go next. He'd read dozens of volumes on interrogation techniques in preparation for a career someday in law enforcement. He was hoping this experience would bolster his credentials.

"What else?" Jason asked because he couldn't think of what else to say.

"I like to hear 'em scream," Ramirez explained with a casualness that was even more startling than what he was saying. "They are bred to be perfect slaves. Sure, it's hard to understand 'em when they talk, but you can sure understand their screams. Know what I mean?" He actually winked.

"Richard, you think of the best shit," Jason said with a smile. He'd had quite enough of this conversation and, besides, he had run out of quarters to buy more Pepsis. "Wait till I get home and can try some of this shit out myself. Thanks for the advice."

"Hey, man, no problem. You need to find a little girl, one you can hold down by the throat. That's the best way to keep 'em under control while you do what you gotta do."

Jason was staring at Ramirez's hands as he said this. They were huge, twice the size of a normal hand, and they were clenching and unclenching as he spoke, as if they were reliving their favorite fantasies.

"But it's hard to find girls like that, isn't it?" Jason asked. He realized that the killer was testing him, seeing if he'd really follow through, if he'd prove himself. Somehow he had to convince Ramirez that he meant business. "What I mean is that in Vegas we don't have that many girls like that. I go to bus stations mostly to look for runaways. That's where I find my bitches to be future slaves." As he said this he hoped that Ramirez wouldn't recognize that he was borrowing liberally from John Wayne Gacy's methods.

"No shit! The bus station?" Ramirez was impressed, Jason could tell. He had his arms crossed and was staring at the floor, shaking his head. Jason gauged how well his stories were received by the frequency of the head shaking.

"Yeah," Jason answered modestly.

"I never really thought of that." Ramirez reached for the Dr. Pepper that Jason has retrieved for him with the last of his change. He took a long drink.

"They're all over the place," Jason continued in a rush, now excited that he had Ramirez's attention and respect. "All lost and alone. No friends or family. They need someone like me to give them something to live for." Jason remembered this was what Gacy told him was all part of his routine when he picked up boys at the bus stations. "They have no family anymore, so nobody looks for them if they're missing."

Ramirez looked at Jason with a leering smile. "So, do ya fuck 'em?"

"You kiddin'? Sometimes me and the rest of the boys, we take the girl and keep her in a cage that I keep in the closet." At this point Jason pulled out a photo of himself with his college fraternity posing at a party. He told Ramirez that they were all part of his cult that worshipped Ramirez.

"You got any Asian girls?"

The guy was obsessed with that. He wouldn't let up. That made it so much easier to create stories since all he had to do was follow Ramirez's lead and feed him what he wanted to hear.

"Is it like a dog cage that you use?"

"Yeah. They have to curl up like a ball to fit inside."

Ramirez started laughing hysterically. He was making so much noise that he started attracting attention. Jason could see a guard approaching, so they ducked their heads and began to speak in a lower tone. As the time progressed, more and more visitors showed up, cramming into the visiting room. It got to the point they had to yell to hear each other.

"I was never that organized," Ramirez said after a long silence, tapping the Dr. Pepper bottle against the table. He was referring to his mad rampage of randomly picking out houses, breaking in through the windows, and then killing everyone inside after raping the women. He wasn't even particular about what age the victims were—children, teenagers, women in their eighties—it didn't seem to matter to him because he just liked hurting people. "I just would get so excited, I couldn't stop myself. I made a lot of mistakes. I rushed everything. I couldn't help it. Just couldn't stop."

"Yeah," Jason said, trying to think about how to reassure him. Inside he was trying to stop himself from giggling because he was afraid of saying something stupid, like "practice makes perfect."

"Hey," Ramirez added, looking Jason directly in the eyes, "you gotta get some of those girls to write in here, okay?"

"Anything for you, Richard. Anything at all."

I read these words now and picture the young man, just twenty-two, who put himself in these situations because of his insatiable interest in killers and what makes them tick. At the time it seemed like his motive was purely career motivated. After all, Jason was one of the most driven, ambitious people I'd ever met. He'd use anyone to further his goals—including me.

Within ten years Jason would be dead by his own hand, a gunshot to the head. All this stuff had penetrated him, even poisoned him.

VOYEUR OF EVIL

I was looking through some old boxes of research material that I had collected when I was working on the book with Jason and our planned sequel. At some point, before he got caught up in the demands of law school, we had talked about doing this one together.

I don't remember having seen this writing from Jason before, but it's been a long time, over ten years, so perhaps I just forgot about it. All these years since his death I've been trying to unravel what really happened to him, how he fell so far. When I knew Jason, I found him trying at times but essentially a good person. He was responsible and, of course, not altogether trusting of me or anyone else.

He had told me repeatedly he wanted to be an FBI agent, to catch killers and rid the world of the evil that so terrified and fascinated him. But now I wonder. I can see another explanation in his own handwriting that isn't even thinly disguised: "The federal agent has a free hand to get involved in any crime—prostitution, child pornography, serial killing— you name it. I think they enjoy hiding behind their badges so they can get close to the violence, as close as anyone can get."

I realize that Jason is really speaking about his own interests and motives. He makes this clear when he changes pronouns to *we*: "We can go out and make our own cases and find our own trouble. I love this idea. To be able to find a murderer or rapist or bank robber and get to watch him hunt and kill, knowing he's within our sights, that we can take him down."

Jason admitted that he might just be rationalizing and justifying his own "voyeuristic thrill." Finally, he confessed to this in the last-surviving communication from him:

> I am a voyeur of evil, darkness. I am drawn to what others fear. I get a sensational adrenaline rush from the excitement of hanging out with these killers. It's like looking at a real-life monster. I feel so aroused. I feel my heart pounding and my hands shaking. I'm actually sitting next to someone who killed again and again. It's addicting. And I enjoy the struggle of trying to deal with these feelings.

Ultimately, Jason lost that struggle.

Chapter 12
What the Future Holds

In many ways this task of trying to answer the question of why people are so drawn to violence as entertainment is beyond any simple explanation. There are just too many reasons to account for the interest, depending on the individual and the context. There is also little consistency in the studies investigating the phenomenon, which makes definitive conclusions quite challenging.[1]

Even when you ask people why they do the things they do, most of the time they don't know. They just make something up. Or they tell themselves something that bears little resemblance to what might really be going on. People lie all the time, every hour of the day, to themselves, to others, and to researchers trying to figure out the motives that underlie human behavior.[2] People even lie to their therapists and doctors when they are paying them specifically for help.[3] They exaggerate or minimize their symptoms. They provide a very selective history. And especially, they disguise or hide things about themselves that are shameful. Furthermore, even professional interrogators, law enforcement personnel, Secret Service agents, and psychotherapists are not particularly good at recognizing truth from lies, even with all their training.[4]

Apart from the challenges of uncovering true and honest motives for behavior that often elicits a certain amount of guilt and shame, there is also another complexity to this subject that defies easy answers. Yet there is a semblance of truth in what we've learned. Rather than trying to interpret or create meaning from the "data" and stories presented in this book, much less from your own memories, it might be far more reasonable to describe the phenomena as a series of "lived experiences." Psychologists, communication and media scholars, social critics, and scientists have been wrestling with the meaning of entertainment violence for centuries. There have been theories offered that the interest is really about repressed sexuality, existential terror, social anxiety, cultural conditioning, gender role identification, instinctual aggression, fear of murderous impulses, and all the others mentioned earlier. But the simplest explanation is the one that is most often ignored—that people derive pleasure from feeling more alive when they encounter death in some sanitized or artificial form that keeps them out of direct danger.

LIKE SALT ON FOOD

There is little doubt that the desire—perhaps the *need*—to explore terror, violence, and death—has been around as long as human beings have inhabited this world. It appears to be an eternal human urge. We can deny, moderate, and attempt to control the interest in violence all we want, but there are both instinctual and cultural forces at work that have shaped this

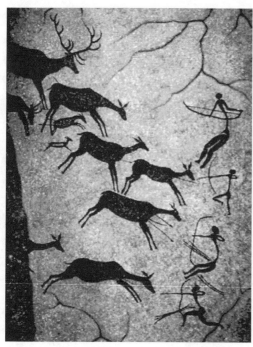

The earliest-known cave paintings from over 20,000 years ago in Lascaux, France, depict violence in the form of animals being slaughtered or tribal members being killed. Such murals were not only a form of entertainment for the cave dwellers, but also were believed to hold supernatural properties.[5]

attraction over millennia. It is not something that is done *to us* out of corporate greed or evil forces but rather because people want it, hunger for it, and need it for the functions it serves. "Whether one blames supply or demand," observes communications researcher David Trend, "the market for media violence remains intact, vibrant, and growing."6

People are willing to pay for violent entertainment, and this has created a burgeoning market in movies, television shows, news broadcasts, true crime and fiction, Internet sites, video games, and sports events. The latest incarnation recognized by movie theater managers is that on slow midweek nights, they can pack the seats at premium prices with mixed martial arts fights broadcasts. "Movies will always be our bread and butter," commented one theater executive, "but this brings in a different clientele and broadens the base of the people we can bring into our theater."7 Bring in a different clientele, indeed, since they can charge triple the price of a movie for audiences to watch a fight.

Second, people take great pleasure in most violent media forms precisely because they are staged and not real. Yet there is often a kind of aesthetic beauty to the narratives, photography, and special effects that make the images appear *as if* they are real. Slow motion, stop action, quick-paced montage, simultaneous camera shots from multiple angles, editing, soundtrack music, special effects—these all heighten the illusion and magnify the authenticity of the scenes. In one sense the violence has been transformed into mere abstractions and sensory stimulation—sound, lights, explosions, movement, action, excitement.

Trend likens the phenomenon to the way that everyone enjoys the taste of salt for the way it spices food and brings out flavors, even though we know it isn't good for us. Similarly, the appetite for entertainment violence is fed by the media, not just created by it. The achievements of contemporary filmmakers are that they are now able to create scenes that are virtually indistinguishable from what could be real. In addition, they are able to construct narratives that elicit strong emotional reactions in the audience for the film's characters—sympathy, pity, anger, hate, and vicarious pain. Whether in news media or fictional representations, it is the emotionalism of victims that attracts the most interest. This is the salt on the food that may, in fact, not be that bad for us after all. In many ways it is the empathic connection to others' suffering that fuels the kind of moral indignation leading to action achieving greater social justice.

Because violence is so provocative and disturbing, it acts as a memory anchor, something that remains indelibly etched into the brain's neurons. Most people who were alive during moments of national trauma—John F.

There are particular visual images that, once seen, can never be forgotten. What makes them so memorable is often their horrifying representations that seem beyond anything that could ever be imagined. This haunting photograph of the Buchenwald concentration camp in Germany shows victims on the verge of starvation. It became one of the seminal memories of the Nazi atrocities and brought world attention to a level of systematic violence never seen before. Courtesy of the US National Archives and Records Administration, College Park.

Kennedy slumping in the back of the limousine, Lee Harvey Oswald grabbing his stomach, the *Challenger* spacecraft exploding, or bodies falling (or jumping) from the World Trade Center Towers—will never forget these accompanying images. It is the same with images from films or books. If you've ever seen *Pulp Fiction*, *The Wild Bunch*, *Halloween*, *Schindler's List*, or *The Exorcist*, it is likely that certain scenes and visuals have stayed with you. There's a reason for this: the human memory is selective in what it prioritizes for long-term storage. Debt is one example: people tend to have an unusual capacity for remembering who owes them money, whose turn it is to buy lunch, who owes them favors, and similar exchanges that help them keep score. Likewise, recalling violent acts—real or simulated—memorializes the plight of those who have suffered. Remembering crimes or acts of injustice, especially those that involve murder or genocide, is crucial in order to help prevent them from happening in the future.

NEVER AGAIN

Whether in fairy tales, fables, mythology, historical cases, or fictional narratives, violence often presents moral lessons. "Little Red Riding Hood" is about mistrusting strangers, who might rape, kill, and eat you. Classic children's movies like *Sleeping Beauty* or *The Wizard of Oz* are terrifying with their wicked witches who threaten to torture and kill people unless they manage to find the resourcefulness and courage to defeat evil. The torture of Jesus Christ teaches compassion and personal sacrifice for the greater good. "Jack and the Beanstalk" is the story of a boy committing trespassing, burglary, and murder, but it offers a lesson on the dangers of curiosity. They are dramatic and provocative stories that are designed to be remembered; as such, violence not only drives the plot but is central to the themes explored.

Human history is scattered with extraordinary acts of brutal violence in which hundreds, thousands, even millions of people have been slaughtered in the name of some misguided political or religious agenda. Massacres, genocide, terrorism, and wars have been launched every decade since the beginning of recorded history, each one directed by those in power to oppress, marginalize, or destroy others who have been labeled as "outsiders." Whether during the Crusades, the Holocaust, Cambodian killing fields, My Lai, or the Rape of Nanking, "intergroup savagery" has not been the exception but the rule. Genocide and mass murder result from cultural norms that make extreme violence not only tolerated but also encouraged by members of the society.[8] Once an out-group is identified by

In this illustration, Little Red Riding Hood is looking innocently at the wolf that is rubbing up against her in a seductive manner. Many of the most classic children's tales and fables have strong violent themes that are intended to cement important moral lessons. "Cinderella" and "Snow White" are stories about child abuse. "Rapunzel" is about a girl who commits theft and is punished through torture and imprisonment. "Little Red Riding Hood" has been interpreted as a story of rape in which the girl invites the assault through her own negligence.[9]

those in power, whether Nazis, Khmer Rouge, Crusaders, Stalinists, or Ku Klux Klan, fear is instilled in the masses. They are warned that unless they act quickly and decisively to exterminate the vermin, they will spread like the plague.

Genocide can only take place when passive spectators remain entertained by the mass killing, or at least indifferent to the victims' fate. Acts of mass murder can only take place when bystanders collude with the perpetrators, believing that it is in their own best economic interests to destroy those labeled inferior or a threat. In one of his many books about genocide, Daniel Goldhagen mentions dozens of cases among Poles, Turks, Germans, Serbs, Hutus, Soviets, and Pakistanis who supported violence in their countries. Yet when spectators did become directly involved in opposing the injustice, such as that which occurred in Denmark during World War II, they were able to stop the bloodshed and prevent harm to their Jewish population.[10]

Whether among the Nazis, Khmer Rouge, or other perpetrators of genocide, there develops a group support system in which murder itself becomes a form of entertainment. During the German occupation of South West Africa (now known as Namibia) in the early 1900s, the governor of the colony ordered that all members of the Herero tribe be killed on sight. There is one case described in which German soldiers came upon a nine-month-old baby crying on the ground. They formed a circle around the infant and began tossing him around like a ball, laughing uproariously at his increasing terror. When one solider fixed the bayonet on his rifle and speared the baby through the body, the soldiers thought this was the funniest thing they'd ever seen. Goldhagen cites dozens of similar accounts in Indonesia, Bangladesh, Burundi, Kenya, Cambodia, Turkey, Germany,

This image of Austrian Nazis and local residents shows their delight in watching the humiliation and degradation of Jews who were forced to scrub the pavement on their hands and knees. Taken in March 1938, the violence would soon escalate to the point that mobs began beating and killing the "outsiders" for entertainment and to enforce new laws that led to mass exterminations. Courtesy of the US National Archives and Record Administration, College Park.

Bosnia, Guatemala, Rwanda, and Darfur, in which perpetrators laughed, joked, and found great amusement in the violent death of their victims.[11]

JEKYLL AND HYDE

This investigation into entertainment violence is ending much differently than I had imagined. Originally I had assumed that the attraction to brutality in one form or another was evidence of the perversity and evil in our world. When there is so much to celebrate that is beautiful and peaceful in the world, why would anyone choose to watch the most disgusting, degrading, and brutal inhumanity? I was fully prepared to accept the countless reports and research that supposedly demonstrated unequivocally a link between enjoying violence as a spectacle, whether at the scene of a crime or in true-crime books, and subsequent increased aggression. I believed that there was nothing more revolting and inappropriate than adolescents spending their free hours in simulated kill games in which they pretend to blow things up and indiscriminately kill as many people as possible. I also believed that this is what leads to increased violence, school shootings, bullying, and all that is wrong with the next generation. Likewise, the proclivity of people to become riveted by brutal sports or ultraviolent films seemed to be further proof that our world is sinking into the sewer. The news continuously reports stories of atrocities, genocide, war, terrorism, and murder, as if we are on the verge of chaos and wanton self-destruction.

The lessons I learned from this study, based on a review of the research and interviews with so many different people, is that the phenomenon is a lot more complex than I thought. It turns out that it is entirely possible that violence-as-entertainment might actually be *preventing* physical violence in some cases. Watching fights, reading about crime, studying murder, viewing films and playing violent video games—these may very well be serving an important function to help us deal with our aggressive impulses.

There is no denying that we are among the most successful killers that have ever inhabited the planet. Through the invention of tools like clubs, bows and arrows, and, later, automatic weapons, land mines, flamethrowers, nuclear bombs, and remote-controlled drones, we have become the most effective killers in history. We are able to target particular individuals via satellite from thousands of miles away. We can wipe out whole villages, or even cities, with a single destructive act. In addition, we are all the descendants of the most violent ancestors who managed to survive and defeat anyone else who was more peacefully inclined. Through thousands of generations, our gene pool has honed our instincts to respond swiftly and decisively to any perceived or imagined threat. We are the perfect products of evolutionary engineering that designed us to become the perfect specimen of killing machines. Yet these abilities and skills are no longer needed in our present world at least most of the time. We may retain the impulse to respond violently to any problem requiring a solution—eliminate a rival, obtain a desired resource, or neutralize a threat—but the cost of such actions is quite risky, not only for our own health in risking injury or death, but to the stability of our community.

We are able to restrain our impulses to hurt others, or enjoy others' pain, only if and when we understand what is going on behind the scenes and within our genetic programming. Just because we have instincts to kill doesn't mean we must act on them, nor should we excuse such actions in others, except in the most extreme circumstances such as war or self-defense. That is why for the first time in human history, we routinely imprison or execute killers, rather than allow them to rise to positions of ultimate power. But then again, perhaps not much has changed in that regard when we consider particular political and military figures who have killed with impunity and still enjoy privileged positions. And popular politicians are sometimes selected because they were war heroes (Presidents Washington, Grant, Eisenhower, and Kennedy, for example).

Oliver Stone, who has made extremely violent films like *Platoon* and *Natural Born Killers*, believes that the appeal of violent entertainment is that it plays into our most natural instincts. "This is what we are; we're animals, we were animals, this is our Darwinian chain; we have aggression in us. This is part of our nature."[12] Nevertheless, Stone remains optimistic, even hopeful, that even with our "natural born killer" instincts, we have the capacity—if we have the will—to practice caring, compassion, and respect for others. He believes it is greater consciousness that will ultimately lead us to a more peaceful and nonviolent world. This same thought is echoed by another film director, John Carpenter: "Horror," he observed, "is the universal language." And horror films have a job to do—"to prevent violence by offering an entertaining vision of it."[13]

This explanation may not be as self-serving as you might imagine. Psychiatrist Robert Simon likens the Jekyll and Hyde metaphor to the reality that each of us has within us the *potential* for violence.[14] He also suggests that there isn't nearly as much difference as we might think between ourselves and those who cross the line into evil. He cites dozens of cases in which otherwise normal-appearing individuals who led remarkably ordinary lives, even model citizens, turned out to be serial rapists, murderers, spies, and con artists. Henry Hubbard was a thirty-year-old veteran of the police force who was secretly raping women in his spare time. Killer John Wayne Gacy won awards for his civic contributions and work with injured children. Ted Bundy was the kind of nice young man—ambitious, handsome, and educated—whom many women would have been delighted to bring home. Spies Robert Hanssen, John Walker, and Aldrich Ames were successful in their treacherous efforts precisely because they fit in so well within the CIA establishment. They seemed just like anyone else because they were!

We may claim the behavior of Hitler, Stalin, Pol Pot, or any of the killers mentioned earlier is thoroughly incomprehensible, but it is even more disturbing to realize how much they were *almost* just like you and me. The "Mr. Hyde" who crossed the line from fantasy into action is the main distinguishing feature, whether the results of poor impulse control, a florid sociopathic personality disorder, or some mental illness. Yet almost everyone *thinks* about hurting others, seeking revenge, even destroying living beings out of curiosity or because it might seem amusing. It is our compassion, empathy, and moral responsibility that prevent us from doing any crazy thing that pops into our heads—but the urges are still there nevertheless. At times they might seem disturbing and frightening, other times dormant and benign. But the fact that we have within us powerful aggressive and violent instincts is what makes watching violence as a form of entertainment so compelling.

Echoing this idea, one man I interviewed used identical language to describe his own experience, a theme I heard again and again. "There is a Jekyll and Hyde in all of us," he said. "Viewing violence touches something in people, the emotional, raw part, almost like a drug." In a summary of his theory on the origins of evil, Robert Simon concludes that "bad men and women do what good men and women only dream about doing."[15]

There are some who can only shake their heads at ideas such as this. Even though the majority of people do enjoy—or at least are curious about—one form of entertainment violence or another, whether that involves drama, sports, reality television, true crime, suspense fiction, or rubbernecking at a crime scene or car accident, there are also those who display quite different responses. One person I interviewed, a political scientist who studies conflict, admitted that he can't tolerate watching any form of violence or abuse whatsoever. He avoids any movie or television show that might contain such content and finds it difficult to understand why anyone would actually enjoy such carnage. "It just makes me sick, literally," he said, shaking his head. "I feel nauseous and just have to look away."

It is interesting why some people have an aversion to watching violence while others find it so alluring. In some ways, it is like anything else in which there is a broad range of reactions to what people like in their food, leisure, work, or entertainment preferences. Our individual physiological systems are all wired a bit differently—and react to stimulation in different ways. In part, the diverse responses are related to culture and how we were brought up within our families. It isn't much of a stretch to assume that someone who was spanked or bullied a lot as a child, or who suffered child abuse, might have different reactions to watching violence than someone never exposed to that suffering. A war veteran might have different responses than someone who grew up in a family of peace protesters. There are thus those among us who feel an irresistible compulsion to seek out as much violent entertainment as they can find, while others invest considerable effort in avoiding any form of human conflict whatsoever. Regardless of such preferences, there has always been tremendous diversity in what people enjoy for fun, which is why we have hundreds of cable channels, thousands of new movies released, dozens of popular sports, and an endless variety of entertainment options.

DECLINE IN VIOLENCE

We have seen how homicide and extreme acts of violence have featured prominently in human history, whether mass murder, atrocities of war, or individual murder. One of the oldest complete specimens of ancient humans, the Iceman, discovered in the Austrian Alps frozen in a glacier, was shot with an arrow and likely bled to death from the murderous attack. What is really interesting, however, when looking at rates of murder throughout the human life span and across cultures, is that societies that don't have violent television, movies, and video games, or handguns and automatic weapons, have much higher rates of killing among their citizens.[16]

You would have to agree that compared to our ancestors who routinely sacrificed people, sentenced them to torture, murdered with impunity, collected slaves, raped unattached women, practiced systematic genocide, launched pogroms to wipe out minorities, enjoyed gladiatorial mayhem, witch burning, or crucifixions, we are a relatively peaceful species. A lot of the religious moral codes, documented in the Bible and the

Koran, advocated death by stoning for merely talking back to your parents, being gay, having an affair, or worshipping an alternative deity. Certainly some of these violent activities are still going on in parts of the world but at least not so commonly in developed countries. Murder rates have fallen dramatically in recent decades, all the while entertainment violence has proliferated. "Far from causing us to become more violent," observes psychologist Steven Pinker, "something in modernity and its cultural institutions has made us nobler."[17]

Homicide rates have indeed been steadily declining in recent years, roughly half of what they were thirty years ago. The number of mass killings has been reduced by 90 percent, murders virtually eliminated altogether when compared to 24 per 100,000 to less than 1 per 100,000 today, and tribal wars are a tiny fraction of what they once were during medieval times.[18] And this is with all the new technological innovations in the various ways that entertainment violence is presented in the media. Granted, we have the occasional mass murder or suicide bombing that claims dozens of lives in a single act of madness, but basically we are far more protected from violence than ever before in human history.

The most gruesome depictions of brutality on film still can't come close to the real-life violence that was once put on display at the Coliseum or local public gallows. I say this fully recognizing that some filmmakers are trying to push way beyond the limits of tastelessness. The Japanese filmmaker who premiered *Ichi the Killer* at the Toronto Film Festival supplied vomit bags to the audience because the film was deemed so disgustingly violent. While called a gimmick, nevertheless, at least one member of the audience did puke during the movie—and another one fainted.[19]

After building a persuasive case and a new theory to account for why humans are so attracted to violence and so prone to curiosity and interest in murder, evolutionary theorist David Buss concludes on the upbeat note that just because we have certain instincts and impulses and proclivities doesn't mean we have to act on them, or even allow them to compromise efforts to promote greater peace and cooperation and compassion toward others.[20] "Murder is one strategy on a menu of solutions to a predictable set of adaptive problems that were frequent in the lives of our ancestors."[21] We no longer live in such environments, nor are violent actions adaptive the way they once were. There are consequences for anyone who surrenders to instinctual aggressive drives. Sometimes they are channeled into forms of verbal abuse, deceit, manipulation, and social aggression, which assist ambitious people who want to work their way up the food chain but are not allowed any longer to actually kill others who stand in their way.

The whole purpose of the horror is to horrify—not just the audience but the status quo. Each successive generation, from the most crude "creature features" of the early years to the ultra-realistic splatter films of today, is designed to break the bonds of acceptable norms. These films are all about generating controversy and pushing the limits, not just to boost ticket sales but, in many cases, as subversive artistic expression. Many critics would now agree that some of the creative and subversive films of our generation would be classified within the horror genre, such as Alfred Hitchcock's *Psycho*. The film's brutal murder in the shower is considered one of the most famous scenes in cinema history.[22]

MORAL CHOICES OVER INSTINCTS

I was moderator for a panel at a conference that included Albert Bandura, the father of social learning theory and perhaps the single most prominent researcher in the area of media violence and its effects.[23] He has long been a proponent of reducing aggressive behavior in children and adults by restricting their exposure to the modeling effects that take place on television and in behavior they observe in others. In his later years he has been interested in applying these concepts to reducing violence by confronting what he calls "moral disengagement."[24]

Given some of the recent research that puts into doubt definitive, absolutist statements about the effects of observational aggression, I asked Bandura how he accounted for the ongoing and increased attraction to entertainment violence even though the amount of hostility, war, and murder was being reduced each decade. Bandura strenuously disagreed with any implication that we are ruled by instincts rather than moral choices we make. He acknowledged that people have the capacity to be ruthless and savagely cruel, but also they can moderate and eliminate this behavior. He cited numerous examples including the practices of the Amish or the Quakers, who abhor violence and will not participate in war because of their religious beliefs. He also mentioned the Swiss and the Swedes as examples of fairly radical evolution. The Swiss were once known as the most fearsome mercenaries in the Vatican forces, until they adopted a position of strict neutrality and nonparticipation in war. Likewise, the Vikings, ancestors of the Swedes, used to be serial rapists, plunderers, and murderers until they reinvented themselves.

It is moral standards that dictate behavior. Aggression and violence have more to do with ideology than biology, Bandura argued. Violence can be justified in all kinds of different ways by bending a flexible moral code to suit one's personal needs and agenda—and perpetuate its continuance (see table 12-1).

TABLE 12-1:
MORAL JUSTIFICATIONS FOR VIOLENT BEHAVIOR

- "I was just following orders." This is the old displacement of responsibility excuse.
- "I was just doing my job." Similar to the previous rationalization, this one defends violence as sanctioned by the organization or society.
- "Others were doing it." Safety in numbers. This is also easily refuted by what your mother told you growing up: "If your friends were going to jump off the Empire State Building, would you follow?"
- "It will save other lives." This is the reason given for starting most wars.
- "God told me to do it." This is the credo of most terrorists to avoid personal responsibility. They feel personally exonerated because some external force was driving the behavior.
- "I don't remember doing it." This is a common excuse heard on the witness stand, rehearsed by legal counsel.
- "I didn't mean to do it." At least this acknowledges minimal responsibility even if it is deftly deflected, as if it doesn't count if it wasn't intentional.
- "He/they deserved it." Behavior is justified by some kind of payback or revenge.
- "They brought it on themselves." Blaming the victims is often used as a justification for genocide.
- "They weren't people, just blips on my screen." In this modern age of warfare with drones controlled from a computer screen, it is easy to pretend that killing is just a video game.
- "I didn't see it, so maybe it didn't happen." Denial is a wonderful thing.
- "They're not quite human." This excuse works well for abusing or torturing animals, but also any group of people who are perceived to be "nonhuman." In the case of the Nazis, this included Jews, gypsies, the disabled, and gays.

A team of researchers was interested in the ways that players of ultraviolent video games justify their enjoyment of vicarious murder and mayhem.[25] They discovered excuses similar to what is summarized in table 12-1. The participants in the study were asked about their thoughts and feelings during the violent play (e.g., "What's it like to kill someone like that?"), as well as how they explain their strong attraction to the activity, often for many hours each day. The explanations offered are quite interesting:

- "It's not real." Some said that the whole question didn't make sense because it was "only" a game and so they thus didn't feel any concerns or moral dilemmas.
- "I want to win." You have to do what you have to do in order to win the game. It doesn't really have anything to do with killing but rather with competition.
- "It's self-defense." Kill or be killed. They believe they are forced to commit violent acts or else they will become victims themselves.
- "They're just creatures in a game." They aren't killing people but rather characters that have been created.

While it is certainly true that there are those among us who can be cruel and violent, whether in real life or simulations, there are many more individuals who consistently demonstrate compassion, kindness, and altruism in their everyday behavior.

VIOLENCE UP CLOSE AND PERSONAL

As in any of the violent entertainment media described in this book, from television, movies, music, or true-crime books to video games, enjoyment can only take place when moral issues like those just mentioned are resolved. This sort of cognitive processing is what makes all the difference in explaining why most people do not become aggressively aroused and potentially violent after playing video games or watching murderous films, while a small minority do feel a loss of control. More specifically, there are certain thought patterns that are associated with acting out in violent or hateful ways:

1. *Egocentricity.* People who overpersonalize the behavior of others, who constantly conclude, "This is about me," are far more likely to become angry and violent. If someone cuts them off on the

highway, it feels like a personal affront. If someone accidently says or does something, there is an exaggerated focus on the impact on oneself.

2. *Perceived offense.* The same individuals who are most likely to inflate their own self-importance are also inclined to overreact to imagined slights. There is a hair trigger that is provoked by the belief that some injustice or disrespect has taken place.

3. *Self-protection.* The best defense against a perceived threat or transgression is to go on the attack, especially if one adopts a hostile frame of reference in which mistrust toward others is the dominant attitude: "People are always trying to take advantage of you," "You have to stand up for yourself and show people you won't take their crap," "If you give people the chance, they will inevitably try to screw you."

4. *Externalization.* When things go wrong, or don't work out as expected, there is a tendency to blame others or outside forces: "It's not my fault," "I can't help it," "He made me do it," "She provoked me," "He should have known better," "It was just bad luck." In each case, there is a diffusion of personal responsibility for one's behavior.[26]

Among those who think in these characteristic ways, exposure to violent stimuli can definitely trigger aggressive action, especially if they have spent considerable time immersed in a fantasy world where brutality and conflict are pervasive. The various internalized beliefs just described lead some individuals to react in ways that are quite different from the way most of us act.

Many of these justifications for committing violence against others can only occur when individuals find or create ways to live with themselves in such a way that they feel like their behavior was justified in some way. When researchers Albert Bandura and Philip Zimbardo interviewed executioners who work on death row, one overarching theme was related to the diffusion of responsibility and abdication of control over the situation.[27] "I had a job to do," one veteran executioner explained, "that's what we did. Our job was to execute the man and we were going to do it in a professional manner." Also note the use of the plural *we*, which makes it sound like he was part of a larger process in which he was just a small cog in the wheel. If anything, executioners see themselves as law-abiding citizens who provide an important service. "The act may seem barbaric," another executioner said, "but it isn't carried out by barbaric people. We try to carry out the act with as much dignity and respect for all people involved." There is pride in their work and a feeling that they are only working on behalf of the majority will, which is actually quite true.

Another common coping mechanism, often used in an attempt to live with the consequences of killing others in war, is the use of euphemistic language that sanitizes acts of violence. Common expressions include *surgical strike*, referring to a bombing that is relatively focused on killing people in a particular area; or *collateral damage*, which refers to the killing of innocent civilians; or *friendly fire*, which means to kill one's own team members.[28] It is the same process when US senator Orin Hatch proclaims, "Capital punishment is our society's recognition of the sanctity of human life."

Yet when people are forced to encounter—up close and personal—the effects and consequences of violence, they're more likely to accept responsibility for their behavior. That's why photos of atrocities like the My Lai Massacre or the abuse of prisoners at Abu Ghraib erode public support and commitment to war, and why officials are weary of allowing photographers on the scene.

It is through personalizing and humanizing violence that it can be reduced, if not eliminated. Bandura cites the case of the moral courage shown by one helicopter pilot at the scene of My Lai in which over five hundred old men, women, and children were murdered in cold blood, mowed down by soldiers with bloodlust coursing through their veins.[29] Captain Hugh Thompson tried to stop the carnage and murder of innocent civilians. After his attempt to radio the commanding officer failed to stop the killing, he lowered his helicopter to block the advance on one hut where he saw a mother huddling with her infant child. He ordered his gunner to shoot any of their own soldiers who tried to hurt the family and then he helped to evacuate the survivors. When asked why he did this, he responded: "I couldn't have done otherwise. I have a two-year-old at home."

It is thus common humanity that links us and protects us from trying to hurt others who are perceived as different. Genocide and extreme acts of violence are not just initiated by tyrants and dictators but because such behavior is tolerated by the larger social system. Bandura believes it is possible to reduce, if not eliminate, most violence even with the enticement of violent entertainment so pervasive in the media. If it is moral disengagement that permits acts of violence, degradation, and oppression of our fellow human beings, then it is more proactive moral initiative that encourages us to take a stand against any such behavior.

RECOVERY FROM ATTRACTION TO VIOLENCE

Enjoying violence and horror during simulations may very well help us to deal with aggressive urges that have been part of our genetic heritage. But that doesn't mean such instincts must control us. There is considerable evidence to show that self-control is not only possible but actually what defines us as human beings. Robert Wright, in fact, makes the case that it is the moral choices we make that help us to moderate our baser instincts and live in closer harmony with not only those among our "tribe" but all members of our global community.[30]

There is reason for optimism about the future of our species, even with threats of global warming, continued wars and genocide, oppression of marginalized people, discrimination against minority groups, and crimes of violence. There is even the possibility that violence in the media can act as a deterrent rather than stimulus for further aggression. One prison inmate and violent offender mentioned previously, Thomas, admitted that he used to watch horror films all the time. "I never really thought about it much, but I used to get a lot of stimulation from them and was a regular viewer of the latest horror films."

Thomas paused for a moment, giving serious consideration to the question about how he is affected now. He was a successful businessman in the outside world, prior to his conviction. He is bright and articulate and apparently filled with remorse for his behavior abusing children. Recently he had been in treatment with a therapist for nightmares and traumatic stress because he was reliving persistent violent events. "I'm aware that my reactions to violence have changed a lot," he finally said. "I don't know . . . maybe my own involvement . . . my own direct experiences with violent acts . . . I guess something just died within me."

Again Thomas hesitated, struggling to make sense of what he was feeling. "I think what I'm saying is that I just have this strong negative reaction to violence now, whether here [in prison] or on the tube. I don't know if it's me who is changed, or if maybe it's just that I'm more afraid of it and my own potential to hurt people."

If he can be believed—and he does seem sincere—Thomas is one example of how human beings do have the capacity to moderate their aggressive urges and attraction to violence. Of course, he's in prison, and the recidivism rate of violent offenders is quite high in terms of the probability that they will commit heinous acts once released. Nevertheless, ultimately higher-level morality is about personal choices that are made within a context of changing social values.

For Thomas, it took one particular event that got his attention in a way that nothing had before. I'll let him finish the story in his own words:

> When I saw that Hawaiian, the one that they jumped in the yard, they had smashed his head in with a dumb bell. He just dropped like a rock, his head cracked open. It swelled up like an elephant, brains and shit everywhere. He was just lying there dying in his own shit. Something just happened to me when I saw that. I was just filled with complete disgust and rage. They never should have let him out there alone in the first place. It was like an execution sentence. He just died right in front of me and I'm a mess. I want to lash out at the prison but I'm afraid of my own potential violence. It scares the shit out of me. I don't know. Maybe they'll come after me next because they can see I'm different now.

In the culture of prisons, where violence reigns supreme, it is virtually impossible to create an atmosphere that would reward Thomas for his attempted changes and support them over the long run. I have since lost touch with him, but I wouldn't be surprised if he was picked off as the next victim.

Still another example is Greg, who is serving time for bombing a federal installation. "I like to see things explode," he explains with a shrug. He used to get really stirred up by violent movies and television, but he can't stand to watch them anymore. "They do something to me. There's something inside me that gets wound up tight and it feels like it needs a place to blow when I see that stuff. I just get so angry that I have to do something."

Greg is an example of someone who *is* activated by watching violence—and he knows it. Such self-awareness is what allows him to exert self-control so that he has weaned himself from violent stimuli; this includes not only the tendency to act on his impulses but even any continuing interest he has in watching it. Similar to Thomas, the impetus for his change occurred as a result of being a witness to a murder, up close and very personal—so close he was actually splattered with blood and bone fragments. Violence for him suddenly became very real and it sickened him.

Greg's recovery from violence took place by confronting another one of his worst fears: math. He had always been a lousy student in school, but numbers and arithmetic terrified him the most. In order to survive in prison and rechannel his aggression, he found an old math book that someone had thrown away. He began studying it, surprised that with sufficient concentration and focus, he could actually make sense of the logic. He felt that numbers helped him maintain control. They were orderly and predictable and clean. He worked his way through algebra, then geometry, and finally multivariate analysis. And this was a man who had never finished high school!

"When I get out of here in a few years," Greg says, "I really don't want to screw up. I'm scared of what I could do so I got to stay away from stuff that's a trigger for me."

It is clear from these examples that violent media is definitely not "entertainment" for some people. In spite of recent evidence that it can be relatively harmless for most of us, there are those among us who are triggered by brutal displays. The question is whether such individuals can exhibit sufficient control to avoid the stimuli that they find most disturbing.

PROJECTIONS INTO THE FUTURE

Certainly violent media will remain with us, just as it has since the earliest cave paintings depicting hunts and battles. Even if it were legislated into extinction or forbidden by judges or censors, people would go "underground" on the Internet or elsewhere, the same way that cockfights are held at secret locations. With mobile devices becoming smaller and more readily available, it has become easier for people to indulge in their favorite forms of entertainment with relative privacy.

For everyone like Thomas or Greg who has been activated by violence on the screen, there are ten or a hundred times as many people who need the outlet to help them reduce their aggression and potential to be hurtful to others. Better that they do so via fantasy outlets and through behavior that is sublimated into other forms of aggression considered more socially acceptable.

At the very least we have to admit that violent entertainment has been part of almost every culture and community throughout recorded history. The one thing that has changed most is that rather than drawing violent scenes on cave walls, it is now possible to view such carnage on mobile phones, the Internet, televisions, computers, movie screens, and streaming video or images transported electronically to any device imaginable. Now that video-recording devices are so easily affordable, almost anyone can record scenes of violence with a mini-camera or even with a camera phone. Check out YouTube and you will find an endless variety of violent entertainment options—close to a hundred thousand videos available on the subject. Search for "extreme violence" on the Internet and in less than a minute you can watch executions, suicides, gang fights, shootings, rapes, terror attacks, a bullfighter being gored to death, and even a peewee hockey game that turned into a brawl with parents cheering on their kids. Select a relatively benign subject to review, perhaps a safari experience in Africa, and the most popular offering (sixty million views!), "Battle at Kruger," shows a ferocious war between a pride of lions, crocodile, and herd of buffalo, all fighting over a captured prey.[31] With such a staggering variety of options, accessible anywhere at anytime, such forms of entertainment are not going away soon.

If you consider the ways other media have evolved in the last few decades, it isn't much of a stretch to predict that vehicles of entertainment will also become utterly transformed. Who would have predicted a generation ago that vinyl records would be replaced by eight-track tapes, then cassettes, CDs, and now electronic downloads? Who would have anticipated that printed newspapers and magazines would be on the verge of extinction, that film would be replaced by digital images, or that computers could be compressed from the size of a small building to a mobile phone?

Satellite radio provides greater variety of programming than conventional broadcasting—and without the restrictions that apply to them. Likewise, cable and premium television stations can show violence (as well as sex and profanity) with a degree of freedom that traditional stations can't imagine, much less ever get past the censors. TiVo and digital-recording devices make it possible for viewers to replay exactly what they want, when they want, and without any interruptions, feeding a "cultural attention deficit disorder" that results from being bombarded with too many choices.[32] Technological innovations like high definition, 3D, computer-generated images, and incredible special effects now make it difficult to tell what is simulated and what is real. The increasing popularity of reality television shows represents another kind of violence in which viewers are titillated by others' conflict, humiliation, and verbal sparring. All of these developments, and so many more on the horizon, will make it increasingly easier for people to sit in the privacy of their homes (or anywhere else) and immerse themselves in the fantasy or realities of violence.

It is easy to talk about the effects and consequences of increased media entertainment, whether steeped in sex, violence, or drama. There are increased physical problems that result from people getting less exercise and active engagement with nature. Carpal tunnel syndrome, repetitive stress disorders, lower back pain, eyestrain, and headaches are becoming increasingly common for those who spend hours each day in front of screens, whether for work or pleasure. Then there is the psychological desensitization or arousal that can occur when someone spends hours each day immersed in a fantasy violent universe.

According to media researcher Laura Triplett, this desensitization to pervasive violence eventually legitimizes and normalizes it to the point where people don't even blink anymore when they encounter extreme examples of it in daily life.[33] In one dramatic case, a homeless man who had been stabbed lay bleeding to death on the sidewalk in New York while hundreds of people walked by, a few even stopping to take photos and video (uploaded on YouTube of course). One passerby even stopped to lift the guy up and look under his body, then unceremoniously dropped him back on the ground as he continued on his way.[34] Although several experts offered familiar explanations of the "bystander effect," in which people assume others will intervene, or that people just didn't want to get involved, Triplett sees this as a clear example of how we have become so saturated with violence that even a dying body doesn't elicit much reaction.

If those are the potential problems, what is the solution? With all the accessibility and variety of vicarious entertainment, it is going to become increasingly more challenging in the future to remain active, to get out of the chair and into the outside world. It is so much easier to watch others having adventures than create one for yourself. Whether feeling bored, anxious, lonely, or distracted, with the touch of a button or keystroke you can enter an alternative world filled with stimulation—sex, violence, beauty, drama, conflict—and never get your hands dirty. It is going to take concerted effort for almost anyone to disengage from these passive forms of entertainment, especially those that aim for the kind of maximum stimulation that is possible with extreme violence. Just as online porn has now become one of the biggest addiction problems in modern life, watching violence can also become chronic and habitual.[35]

Triplett sees the saturation of extreme violence in the media as actually a hopeful sign for the future. "I think we've reached a plateau," she commented, "a kind of boomerang effect."[36] Just as the gladiatorial games eventually died out because the spectators became bored with the status quo and required progressively more novel and interesting enactments of violence, so, too, are contemporary audiences losing interest in some forms of entertainment. She cites the reality show *Fear Factor* as an example in which the producers had to keep upping the ante of horror and outrageous stunts in order to maintain dwindling viewership. When it wasn't enough to have the show's contestants bob for rats in a vat, eat live spiders, consume raw bull's testicles, or zip themselves inside a body bag with hundreds of giant, hissing cockroaches and flesh-eating worms, the show was cancelled. "I think the same thing will happen with watching all violence in the media," Triplett observed, perhaps a little too optimistically.

It is true that throughout history there have been recurrent cycles in which entertainment violence in sports, drama, and literature has waxed and waned. It is also the case that there are increasing social consequences for indulging in violent entertainment—at least in some sectors. The movements of social justice, feminism, political correctness, religious conservatism, social civility, public altruism, and anti-war have all helped to create a backlash of sorts.

Yet if we are truly entering a new era of increased social consciousness and anti-violence rhetoric, advances in technology make accessibility to

This frozen moment in time captures the instant in which these three young women were being offered an opportunity to watch a video of a goat sacrifice on a young man's phone. The young man believed this extraordinarily bloody footage would impress the girls and perhaps earn him a date. Even more remarkable is that this was taking place in Nepal, where mobile devices were just beginning to become widely available. Now it is possible for almost anyone to capture a fight, execution, or any violent episode, watch it at one's leisure, and then share it with the world.

media far easier and more private. "Mobile phones and devices are now the lifeline to the universe," commented communications scholar Andi Stein.[37] "Technology is evolving so quickly it is almost impossible to predict what will happen next. Everything is now about individual access to personal devices, all with complete privacy. There are new devices along the horizon that are not yet conceived, much less invented, that will make it possible for people to have unprecedented access and variety to anything they want to consume for entertainment."

Just think: once upon a time there were three big inventions that ruled entertainment: radio, film, and television. That's it! Now every few years brings a new development—personal computers, MySpace, BlackBerries, YouTube, TiVo, iPods, iPhones, Netflix, Facebook, iPads, virtual reality, and whatever is next on the horizon. Stein predicts that there will be less reason for people to ever leave the comfort of their homes in order to enjoy their favorite entertainment. Why spend a hundred bucks to go see a live sporting event at your local stadium, with all the hassles of crowds, traffic, parking, and lousy seats, when you can watch it in 3D on your screen at home, complete with interactive options that allow you to vote on what the coach should call for the next play?

TRENDS FOR THE FUTURE

Ultimately, our subject of violence as entertainment is intimately connected to two main ideas. The first is that human beings enjoy suspense and seek arousal of sensations in a variety of forms, even if they might be disturbing or terrifying.[38] There are all kinds of ways that individuals seek adventure, exploration, or excitement that include significant dimensions of suffering along the way; even pain is sometimes experienced as pleasurable. This is especially the case with those who have a high need for excitement in that they have learned to interpret fear in positive ways.[39]

Second, the subject of death is compelling with all its mystery, permanence, and corresponding uncertainty. However much the reality of death is denied, disguised, hidden, and avoided, there is an irresistible urge to peel back the curtain and peek into the beyond. In both sanitized and sensationalized forms, news and entertainment media feed this fascination. Discussing this phenomenon, one writer observed that essentially we "create celebrities so we can watch them die. We prefer to watch them die young and beautiful and perfect for paintings, video games, action figures. . . . We don't just grieve for celebrities anymore; we indulge in orgies that turn the dead into the people we need them to be so we can assuage our anxieties about death."[40]

When all is said and done, I feel optimistic and encouraged about the future related to our subject. Most communities and cultures are becoming significantly less tolerant of violence on their streets and in their own homes. Domestic violence is receiving increased attention—and interventions to reduce the physical and psychological mistreatment. Child abuse, spouse abuse, elder abuse, and bullying in schools are being examined on a scale that has never been seen before. Just as violence has been glamorized and promoted in our culture, it can also be discouraged more aggressively.[41] There have been recent court cases in many states challenging so-called free speech in which violent video games and other media are prohibited from being sold to minors.

There have even been incidents in which publicized displays of extreme violence have led to a backlash against further brutality. When the public

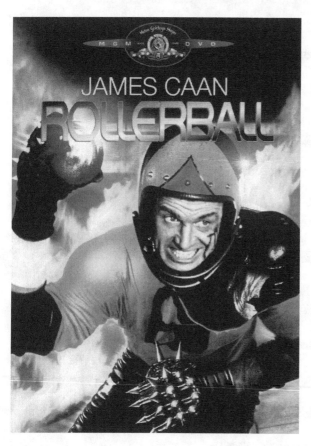

The futuristic vision of spectator sports in the twenty-first century was portrayed in the film *Rollerball* (1975), in which the roller derby match evolved into a brutal fight-to-the-death. Combatants on motorcycles and wielding weapons would attempt to score on the opposing team while causing the most mayhem possible. This was conceived as a way to pacify the masses during a time when crime and war was all but eliminated.

flogging of a girl by the Taliban was posted on YouTube, there were numerous protests in the streets condemning such brutality, literally "transforming Pakistan's collective mind-set at a crucial time."[42] The girl, who allegedly violated some sexual indiscretion, was forcibly held down while she was whipped over thirty times, screaming, "They are killing me! They are killing me!" Also of interest is that not only did this video spur social action to reduce further violence and abuse, but YouTube stepped in to restrict viewers under the age of eighteen from watching the film, presenting a warning that the content may be "inappropriate for some users."[43] A cynic might say that this only increased interest in watching the forbidden film.

The Centers for Disease Control, National Institute of Mental Health, the Office of the US Surgeon General, the World Health Organization, as well as many other organizations, have taken on youth violence as a major priority. Violence in the workplace, incivility at universities, and cyberbullying on the Internet are also being addressed aggressively with new programs. Gang membership and violence are actually going down in many of the nation's largest cities. In Los Angeles, for example, a city with a reputation as a haven for the Bloods, Crips, Surenos, and other violent groups that emigrated from Asia, Latin America, and elsewhere, police are seeing a reduction in membership and acts of violence. In 2005, an article in *Time* magazine reported: "Los Angeles is in terrible shape—again. The city's street gangs, which had been relatively quiet . . . are back with a vengeance."[44] The article reported a 143 percent increase in gang membership, a 23 percent increase in murders, and "more violence for the sake of violence" than had been seen before. These and other stories give the impression that LA is on the verge of anarchy, in danger of complete annihilation from earthquakes and armies of hoodlums.

Yet new trends paint a quite different story in which homicides and gang membership have been cut in half in the last few years, a pattern that is unfolding nationwide.[45] Violent crime is down almost everywhere, with homicides in major cities cut 50 to 75 percent, juvenile crime down by two-thirds, and domestic violence cut by 20 percent.[46] Even with spikes in violent crime for any brief period, in any particular region, the trend is heading progressively downward. This is all the more remarkable as lethal weapons (handguns versus spears) have become more readily available. It is also all the more interesting considering that the general *perception* is that crime rates and homicides are spiraling out of control, all because of the pervasive saturation of violence in the media.

Around the world, genocide and sex trafficking are receiving increased attention. As a global community, themes of social justice and human rights are coming more into the forefront. Violence in the media may be proliferating, but this is clearly not the case in the world at large. It is our conscience, our morality, our sense of right and wrong, and our consensual laws that allow us to compartmentalize instinctual aggressive urges and channel them into outlets that avoid harming others. Even if there is some debate, and perhaps evidence, that violent media may result in a degree of self-harm, that is not so different than other guilty pleasures. Yet we have seen how enjoying violence as entertainment serves some critical functions—to the individual and society at large.

It is indeed the fear of death, the need for stimulation, and instinctual aggression that are at the core of our fascination with violence. There may come a day when human beings no longer require such stimulation to excise our demons and purge ourselves of hostility. In the meantime, we live in the prisons of our own making, defined by our personal codes of honor and morality, as well as the choices we make for how we entertain ourselves.

Notes

PREFACE

1. Robert Graysmith, *The Girl in Alfred Hitchcock's Shower* (New York: Berkley, 2010).

2. Kaiser Family Foundation, "Study of Media and Health: Television/Video," January 2010, http://www.kff.org/entmedia/mh012010pkg.cfm (accessed April 10, 2010).

3. To mention a few of these organizations that have released statements objecting to violence in the media and the toxic effects: American Academy of Pediatrics, American Medical Association, American Psychological Association, American Psychiatric Association, National Academy of Sciences, National Center for Disease Control, Federal Trade Commission, US Surgeon General.

4. Jeffrey Kottler, *Private Moments, Secret Selves: Enriching Our Time Alone* (New York: Ballantine, 1990).

5. Jeffrey Kottler, *The Assassin and the Therapist: An Exploration of Truth in Psychotherapy and in Life* (New York: Routledge, 2010); Jeffrey Kottler and Diane Blau, *The Imperfect Therapist: Learning from Failure in Therapeutic Practice* (San Francisco: Jossey-Bass, 1989); Jeffrey Kottler and Jon Carlson, *Bad Therapy: Master Therapists Share Their Worst Failures* (New York: Routledge, 2002); Jeffrey Kottler and Jon Carlson, *Duped: Lies and Deception in Psychotherapy* (New York: Routledge, 2011); Jeffrey Kottler and Jon Carlson, *The Client Who Changed Me: Stories of Therapist Personal Transformation* (New York: Routledge, 2006).

6. Jeffrey Kottler, *Divine Madness: Ten Stories of Creative Struggle* (San Francisco: Jossey-Bass, 2006).

7. Jeffrey Kottler, *Travel That Can Change Your Life* (San Francisco: Jossey-Bass, 1997); Jeffrey Kottler, *Making Changes Last* (New York: Routledge, 2001).

CHAPTER 1

1. Hans Kruuk, *The Spotted Hyena: A Study of Predation and Social Behavior* (Chicago: University of Chicago Press, 1972).

2. Isabel Pinedo, *Recreational Terror: Women and the Pleasures of Horror Film Viewing* (Albany: SUNY Press, 1997), p. 3.

3. Patricia Lawrence and Philip Palmgreen, "Uses and Gratifications Analysis of Horror," in *Horror Films: Current Research on Audience Preferences and Reactions,* ed. James Weaver and Ron Tamborini (Mahwah, NJ: Lawrence Erlbaum, 1996), pp. 161–78.

4. Sigmund Freud, "The Economic Problem of Masochism" in *On Metapsychology,* ed. Angela Richards (1924; New York: Penguin, 1985), pp. 409–26.

5. Victor Nell, "Cruelty's Rewards: The Gratifications of Perpetrators and Spectators," *Behavioral and Brain Sciences* 29, no. 3 (2006): 211–57.

6. Jody Keisner, "Do You Want to Watch? A Study of the Visual Rhetoric of the Postmodern Horror Film," *Women's Studies* 37 (2008): 411.

7. "Bazooka Joe," http://www.youtube.com/watch?v=Jfiewrx3s4Y (accessed April 20, 2010).

8. Tony Thompson, "Crush Videos Plumb Depths of Perversion: Torturing Small Creatures to Death on Screen Is the New Porn," *Observer*, May 19, 2002, http://www.guardian.co.uk/uk/2002/may/19/ukcrime.tonythompson (accessed April 25, 2010).

9. Melvin Lerner, *The Belief in a Just World: A Fundamental Delusion* (New York: Springer, 1980).

10. David Buss, *The Murderer Next Door: Why the Mind Is Designed to Kill* (New York: Penguin, 2005), p. 24.

11. Mark Pizzato, *Theatres of Human Sacrifice: From Ancient Ritual to Screen Violence* (Albany: SUNY Press, 2005).

12. Irvin Yalom, *Staring at the Sun: Overcoming the Terror of Death* (San Francisco: Jossey-Bass, 2008), p. 5.

13. Ibid.

14. Rachel Shaw, "Making Sense of Violence: A Study of Narrative Meaning," *Qualitative Research in Psychology* 1 (2004): 131–51.

15. Stephen King, *Danse Macabre* (New York: Berkley, 1981), p. 68.

16. W. James Potter, *The 11 Myths of Media Violence* (Thousand Oaks, CA: Sage, 2003).

17. Stacy Smith and Barbara Wilson, "Children's Comprehension of and Fear Reactions to Television News," *Media Psychology* 4 (2002): 1–26.

18. "Crime Statistics," Center for Victims of Violence and Crime, 2005, http://www.cvvc.org/ViolenceImpacts/CrimeStats.php (accessed April 12, 2010).

19. King, *Danse Macabre,* p. 21.

20. Ron Tamborini and James Weaver, "Frightening Entertainment: An Historical Perspective of Fictional Horror," in *Horror Films: Current Research on Audience Preferences and Reactions,* ed. James Weaver and Ron Tamborini (Mahwah, NJ: Lawrence Erlbaum, 1996), p. 12.

21. Virginia Woolf, *The Essays of Virginia Woolf* (New York: Harcourt Brace, 1987), p. 217.

22. Laurent Bouzereau, *Ultraviolent Movies: From Sam Peckinpah to Quentin Tarantino* (Secaucus, NY: Citadel Press, 1996), p. 11.

23. Robert Simon, *Bad Men Do What Good Men Dream: A Forensic Psychiatrist Illuminates the Darker Side of Human Behavior* (Arlington, VA: American Psychiatric Press, 2008).

CHAPTER 2

1. Much of the gladiator material in this chapter is based on the research in two excellent books: Fik Meijer, *The Gladiators: History's Most Deadly Sport* (New York: Thomas Dunne Books, 2003); Rupert Matthews, *The Age of Gladiators: Savagery and Spectacle in Ancient Rome* (Edison, NJ: Chartwell, 2003).

2. Ibid.

3. Ibid., p. 235.

4. Dolf Zillman and Rhonda Gibson, "Evolution of the Horror Genre," in *Horror Films: Current Research on Audience Preferences and Reactions,* ed. James B. Weaver III and Ron Tamborini (Mahwah, NJ: Lawrence Erlbaum, 1996), pp. 15–32.

5. Victor Nell, "Cruelty's Rewards: The Gratifications of Perpetrators and Spectators," *Behavioral and Brain Sciences* 29 (2006): 211–57.

6. Meijer, *The Gladiators.*

7. Ibid., p. 155.

8. Ibid., p. 163.

9. Kathleen Coleman, *Contagion of the Throng: Absorbing Violence in the Roman World* (Dublin: Dublin University Press, 1996).

10. Oscar Brockett, *History of the Theatre* (Boston: Allyn and Bacon, 1995).

11. Denise Martin and Joe Flint, "Spicy 'Spartacus' Slays 'Em for Starz," *Los Angeles Times,* March 23, 2010, p. B1.

12. Michael Newton, "Written in Blood: A History of Human Sacrifice," *Journal of Psychohistory* 24, no. 2 (1996): 104.

13. The same day I wrote this paragraph there was a news story of an eight-year-old girl in Uganda whose body was discovered partially dismembered as part of a ritual sacrifice to bring wealth and health to the killers. She was the thirtieth victim during the year. Jason Straziuso, "Ritual Sacrifice of Children on the Rise in Uganda," *Huffington Post,* April 10, 2010, http://www.huffingtonpost.com/2010/04/05/ritual-sacrifice-of-child_n_525207.html (accessed April 13, 2010).

14. Barbara Ehrenreich, *Blood Rites: Origins and History of the Passions of War* (New York: Metropolitan, 1997).

15. Patrick Tierny, *The Highest Alter: Unveiling the Mystery of Human Sacrifice* (New York: Penguin, 1989).

16. Michael Harner, "The Enigma of Aztec Sacrifice," *Natural History* 46 (1977): 46–51.

17. Newton, "Written in Blood," pp. 104–31.

18. Ross Hassig, *Aztec Warfare: Imperial Expansion and Political Control* (Norman: University of Oklahoma Press, 1995).

19. Jimmy L. Shreeve, *Human Sacrifice: A Shocking Expose of Ritual Killings Worldwide* (Fort Lee, NJ: Barricade, 2008).

20. Straziuso, "Ritual Sacrifice of Children on the Rise in Uganda."

21. Allison Hope Weiner, "Facing the Music: The Metalheads Catch Heat When Three Boys Kill a 15 Year Old Girl," *Entertainment Weekly*, August 23, 2001, http://www.ew.com/ew/article/0,,171585,00.html (accessed April 18, 2010).

22. Bill Mears, "High Court Debates Dog Fighting Videos," cnn.com, October 6, 2009, http://www.cnn.com/2009/CRIME/10/06/scotus.dogfighting/index.html (accessed April 25, 2010).

23. Martin S. Bergmann, *In the Shadow of Moloch: The Sacrifice of Children and Its Impact on Western Religions* (New York: Columbia University Press, 1992).

24. Shreeve, *Human Sacrifice*, p. 24.

25. Tierney, *The Highest Alter: The Story of Human Sacrifice.*

26. Augustine, *Confessions* (New York: Penguin, 1961), pp. 122–23.

27. Matthews, *The Age of Gladiators.*

CHAPTER 3

1. Kathi Diamant, *Kafka's Last Love: The Mystery of Dora Diamant* (New York: Basic Books, 2003), p. 69.

2. Harold Schechter, *Savage Pastimes: A Cultural History of Violent Entertainment* (New York: St. Martin's Press, 2005), p. 59.

3. Jamie Russell, *Book of the Dead: The Complete History of Zombie Cinema* (Surrey, UK: FAB Press, 2005); J. Hoberman and Jonathan Rosenbaum, *Midnight Movies* (New York: Da Capo Press, 1991), p. 125; Tim Cavanaugh, "We the Living Dead: The Convoluted Politics of Zombie Cinema," February 2007, http://reason.com/archives/2007/01/25/we-the-living-dead (accessed April 15, 2010); Annalee Newitz, *Pretend We're Dead: Capitalist Monsters in American Pop Culture* (Durham, NC: Duke University Press, 2006).

4. Cavanaugh, "We the Living Dead."

5. Jane Austen and Seth Grahame-Smith, *Pride and Prejudice and Zombies* (San Francisco: Chronicle Books, 2009).

6. Seth Grahame-Smith, *Abraham Lincoln: Vampire Hunter* (New York: Grand Central, 2010).

7. Frank Spiering, *Lizzie* (New York: Random House, 1984), p. 41.

8. Beth Potier, "Once Upon a Time . . ." *Harvard Gazette*, April 10, 2003.

9. Maria Tatar, *Annotated Classic Fairy Tales* (New York: Norton, 2002).

10. Schechter, *Savage Pastimes*, p. 4.

11. Hervey Allen, *Israfel: The Life and Times of Edgar Allan Poe* (New York: Farrar and Rinehart, 1934), p. 408.

12. Mel Gordon, *The Grand Guignol: Theatre of Fear and Terror* (New York: Amok Press, 1988), p. 18.

13. Walter M. Kendrick, *The Thrill of Fear: 250 Years of Scary Entertainment* (New York: Grove, 1991), p. 206.

14. Howard Chua-Eoan, "Too Many Eyes in the Sky?" *Time*, May 11, 1998, p. 30.

15. Christian Davenport and Allan C. Stam, "What Really Happened in Rwanda?" *Miller-McCune*, December 2009, pp. 61–64.

16. Erica Scharrer, "Media Exposure and Sensitivity to Violence in News Reports: Evidence of Desensitization," *Journal of Media Communication Quarterly* 85, no. 2 (2008): 291–310.

17. Tom Weyr, "Marketing America's Psychos," *Publishers Weekly*, April 1993, p. 38.

18. Jason Moss and Jeffrey Kottler, *The Last Victim: A True Life Journey into the Minds of Serial Killers* (New York: Warner, 1999).

19. Laurent Marechaux, *Outlaws: Adventures of Pirates, Scoundrels, and Other Rebels* (Paris: Flammarion, 2009).

20. These events were described to me in an interview with Jason's wife during a series of interviews in my home in 2008 and in a meeting with the film executives who produced the movie version of the book, *Dear Mr. Gacy*.

21. Bruce Bawer, "Capote's Children," *New Criterion* 3 (1985): 9–43.

22. David Schmid, *Natural Born Celebrities: Serial Killers in American Culture* (Chicago: University of Chicago Press, 2005), p. 279.

23. Ruth Pat-Horenczyk and Danny Brom, "The Multiple Faces of Post-Traumatic Growth," *Applied Psychology: An International Review* 56 (July 2007): 379–85.

24. Jeffrey Kottler, *Divinie Madness: Ten Stories of Creative Struggle* (San Francisco: Jossey-Bass, 2006).

25. Kate Hefferon, Madeleine Grealy, and Nanette Mutrie, "Post-Traumatic Growth and Life Threatening Physical Illness: A Systematic Review of the Qualitative Literature," *British Journal of Health Psychology* 14 (May 2009): 343–78; Nick Gerrish, Murray Dyck, and Ali Marsh, "Post-Traumatic Growth and Bereavement," *Mortality* 14 (August 2009): 226–44; Christopher Peterson, Nansook Park, Nnamdi Pole, Wendy D'Andrea, and Martin Seligman, "Strengths of Character and Post-Traumatic Growth," *Journal of Traumatic Stress* 21 (April 2008): 214–17.

26. Nancy Karanci and Ceren Acarturk, "Post-Traumatic Growth among Marmara Earthquake Survivors Involved in Disaster Preparedness as Volunteers," *Traumatology* 11 (December 2005): 307–23; Anat Ben-Porat and Haya Itzhaky, "Implications of Treating Family Violence for the Therapist: Secondary Traumatization, Vicarious Traumatization, and Growth," *Journal of Family Violence* 24 (October 2009): 507–15.

27. Horenczyk and Brom, "The Multiple Faces of Post-Traumatic Growth."

CHAPTER 4

1. Adam Tschorn, "Outside the Cage," *Los Angeles Times*, September 10, 2008, http://articles.latimes.com/2008/sep/07/image/ig-mma7 (accessed April 25, 2010).

2. Mark Pizzato, *Theatres of Human Sacrifice: From Ancient Ritual to Screen Violence* (Albany: State University of New York Press, 2005), p. 51.

3. Ibid.

4. Norbert Elias, *Quest for Excitement: Sport and Leisure in the Civilizing Process* (Dublin: University College, 2009).

5. Matt Taibbi, "Why Sports Are for Losers," *Men's Journal*, December 2010, p. 78.

6. Mark Rountree, "Violence Helps Sell Extreme Fighting," *Mixed Martial Arts Weekly*, September 30, 2005.

7. Arthur Raney and William Kinnally, "Examining Perceived Violence in and Enjoyment of Televised Rivalry Sports Contests," *Mass Communication and Society* 12 (July 2009): 311–31.

8. Ibid.

9. Dolf Zillman and Rhonda Gibson, "Evolution of the Horror Genre," in *Horror Films: Current Research on Audience Preferences and Reactions*, ed. James B. Weaver III and Ron Tamborini (Mahwah, NJ: Lawrence Erlbaum, 1996), pp. 15–32.

10. J. Farber, "Blood, Sweat, and Fears: Why Are Horror Movies Such a Slashing Success?" *Seventeen*, July 1987, pp. 108–109.

11. Dolf Zillman and James B. Weaver, "Gender-Socialization Theory and Reactions to Horror," in *Horror Films: Current Research on Audience Preferences and Reactions*, p. 85.

12. "Dogfighting a Booming Business, Experts Say," July 19, 2007, http://www.cnn.com/2007/US/07/18/dog.fighting/ (accessed April 9, 2010).

13. David Von Drehle, "Can Attack Dogs Be Rehabilitated?"*Time*, December 7, 2009, pp. 45–48.

14. Winston Ross, "Cracking Down on Cockfighting: Why the Bloodsport Remains a Thriving Industry," *Newsweek*, March, 24, 2008.

15. Ernest Hemingway, *Death in the Afternoon* (1939; New York: Simon & Schuster, 1994), p. 21.

16. Ivan Maisel, A. Kim, and K. Kennedy, "Sport? Not a Sport? This Week: Bullfighting," *Sports Illustrated* 96, no. 20, p. 20.

17. Brett Drake and Shanta Pandey, "Do Child Abuse Rates Increase on Those Days on Which Professional Sporting Events Are Held?" *Journal of Family Violence* 11, no. 3 (September 1996): 205–18.

18. Kevin Young, "Sport and Violence," in *Handbook of Sports Studies*, ed. Jay Coakley and Eric Dunning (Thousand Oaks, CA: Sage, 2000), pp. 382–406.

19. For an extensive list of fan violence, see Wikipedia, "List of Violent Spectator Incidents in Sports," http://en.wikipedia.org/wiki/List_of_violent_spectator_incidents_in_sports (accessed April 12, 2010).

20. Torben Grodal, "Video Games and the Pleasures of Control," in *Media Entertainment: The Psychology of Its Appeal*, ed. Dolf Zillman and Peter Vorderer (Mahwah, NJ: Lawrence Erlbaum, 2000), pp. 197–213.

21. M. Cabral, J. Jensen, A. Vary, and J. Young, "Spring's Hottest Games," *Entertainment Weekly*, February 5, 2010, p. 45.

22. Jereon Jansz, "The Emotional Appeal of Violent Video Games for Adolescent Males," *Communication Theory* 15, no. 3 (2005): 219–41.

23. Kristin Fitzmorris, "Violent Video Games: Insights into Why and How Players Use Them," masters thesis, September 2009, Johns Hopkins University.

24. Chris Baker, "It's Not Just about Killing Hookers Anymore," *Slate*, April 29, 2008, http://www.slate.com/id/2190207/ (accessed April 21, 2010).

25. J. Jensen, "Games," *Entertainment Weekly*, November 27, 2009, pp. 76–77.

26. William Abner, "An Almanac of Pimps, Orcs, and Lightsabers for March," *InformIT*, March 3, 2006.

27. Jonathan Samuels, "Thousands Download Illegal Ultra-violent Game," *Sky News*, February 27, 2008.

28. John L. Sherry, "Violent Video Games and Aggression: Why Can't We Find Effects?" in *Mass Media Effects Research: Advances Through Meta-analysis*, ed. Raymond Preiss et al. (Mahwah, NJ: Lawrence Erlbaum, 2007), pp. 245–79.

CHAPTER 5

1. David Edelstein, "Now Playing at Your Local Multiplex: Torture Porn," *New York Magazine*, January 28, 2006.

2. Michael A. Arnzen, "Who's Laughing Now? The Postmodern Splatter Film," *Journal of Popular Film and Television* 21, no. 4 (1994): 176–86.

3. P. Rainer, "First Blood: It's Rocky versus the World," *Los Angeles Herald Examiner*, October 22, 1982.

4. Clark Peterson was interviewed at his home in December 2009.

5. Erica Scharrer, "Media Exposure and Sensitivity to Violence in News Reports: Evidence of Desensitization," *Journal of Media Communication Quarterly* 85, no. 2 (2008): 291–310.

6. Lev Grossman, "Zombies Are the New Vampires," *Time*, April 20, 2009, p. 61.

7. Walter M. Kendrick, *The Thrill of Fear: 250 Years of Scary Entertainment* (New York: Grove, 1991).

8. Radu Florescu and Raymond McNally, *Dracula, Prince of Many Faces: His Life and His Times* (New York: Back Bay, 1989).

9. Mike Benton, *The Comic Book in America* (Dallas: Taylor Publishing, 1989).

10. Fredric Wertham, *Seduction of the Innocent* (New York: Rinehart, 1954).

11. Isabel C. Pinedo, *Recreational Terror: Women and the Pleasures of Horror Film Viewing* (Albany: SUNY Press, 1997).

12. Ibid., p. 39.

13. David Schmid, *Natural Born Celebrities: Serial Killers in American Culture* (Chicago: University of Chicago Press, 2005), p. 17.

14. Mihaly Csikszentmihalyi, *Beyond Boredom and Anxiety* (San Francisco: Jossey-Bass, 2000).

15. H. Selby, "Why Watching Scary Movies Can Be So Much Fun," *Las Vegas Review Journal* (August 26, 2000): 15B.

16. David M. Buss, *The Murderer Next Door: Why the Mind Is Designed to Kill* (New York: Penguin, 2005).

17. Harold Schechter, *Depraved: The Definitive True Story of H. H. Holmes, Whose Grotesque Crimes Shattered Turn-of-the-Century Chicago* (New York: Pocket Star Books, 2008).

18. Lest this spark your imagination enough that you might want to visit this site out of curiosity, I must warn you that I was punished for my snooping. As soon as I clicked on a blog to read the comments posted by fans about the reasons for their fascination, my computer was invaded by a virus that virtually killed it beyond redemption.

19. Barry S. Sapolsky and Fred Molitor, "Content Trends in Contemporary Horror Films," in *Horror Films: Current Research on Audience Preferences and Reactions*, ed. James B. Weaver and Ron Tamborini (Mahwah, NJ: Lawrence Erlbaum, 1996) pp. 33–48.

20. Christine Spines, "Horror Films and the Women Who Love Them," *Entertainment Weekly*, July 31, 2009, p. 31.

21. Ibid., p. 32.

22. Ibid., p. 33.

23. Peter Brunette, "Interview with Quentin Tarantino," in *Quentin Tarantino Interviews*, ed. Gerard Peary (Jackson: University Press of Mississippi, 1998), p. 33.

24. Graham Fuller, "Answers First, Questions Later," in *Quentin Tarantino Interviews*, ed. Gerard Peary (Jackson: University Press of Mississippi, 1998), p. 60.

25. Stephen Farber, "Peckinpah's Return," in *Sam Peckinpah Interviews*, ed. Kevin. J. Hayes (Jackson: University Press of Mississippi, 2008), p. 39.

26. Steve Biodrowski, "Wes Craven: Alive and Shocking!" *Cinefantastique*, November 1, 1991, p. 11.

27. Walter Kendrick, *The Thrill of Fear*, p. xix.

28. Ibid.

CHAPTER 6

1. Personal correspondence with Jason Moss, 1994.

2. David Schmid, *Natural Born Celebrities: Serial Killers in American Culture* (Chicago: University of Chicago Press, 2005).

3. Deborah Cameron and Elizabeth Frazer, *The Lust to Kill* (London: Polity Press, 1987).

4. Laurent Marechaux, *Outlaws: Adventures of Pirates, Scoundrels, and Other Rebels* (Paris: Flammarion, 2009).

5. Robert I. Simon, *Bad Men Do What Good Men Dream: A Forensic Psychiatrist Illuminates the Darker Side of Human Behavior* (Arlington, VA: American Psychiatric Press, 2008).

6. J. M. Tyree, "Splatter Pattern," *Film Quarterly* (Fall 2008): 82–85.

7. Jasmin Teuteberg, "America's Favorite Serial Killer: The Creation of Sympathy in the Perception of Criminals in Television Crime Narratives Exemplified by the Series *Dexter*," Stockholm University masters thesis, 2009.

8. Laurent Bouzereau, *Ultraviolent Movies: From Sam Peckinpah to Quentin Tarantino* (Secaucus, NJ: Citadel Press, 1996).

9. Tim Adams, "The Stephen King Interview, Uncut and Unpublished," *Guardian*, September 14, 2000.

10. Julie Weist, "Serial Killers as Heroes in the Media's Storybook of Murder," masters thesis, University of Georgia, 2003.

11. Ibid.

12. David Kauzlarich, *Introduction to Criminology*, 9th ed. (New York: Roman & Littlefield, 2010).

13. Weist, "Serial Killers," p. 56.

14. Joel Norris, *Henry Lee Lucas: The Shocking True Story of America's Most Notorious Serial Killer* (Zebra, 1991).

15. Barrie Gunter, "Media Violence: Is There a Case for Causality?" *American Behavioral Scientist* 51, no. 8 (2008): 1061–1122.

16. "The Night Stalker's Wife," CNN, July 28, 1997, http://www.cnn.com/US/9707/28/nightstalker.wife (accessed April 10, 2010).

17. Ibid.; Katherine Ramsland, "Serial Killer Groupies," TruTV, http://www.trutv.com/library/crime/criminal_mind/psychology/s_k_groupies/6.html (accessed April 11, 2010).

18. Sheila Isenberg, *Women Who Love Men Who Kill* (New York: Simon & Schuster, 1991).

19. Peter Fimrite and Michael Taylor, "No Shortage of Women Who Dream of Snaring a Husband on Death Row," *San Francisco Chronicle*, March, 27, 2005.

20. James A. Fox and Jack Levin, *Extreme Killing: Understanding Serial and Mass Murder* (Thousand Oaks, CA: Sage, 2005).

21. Jason Moss and Jeffrey Kottler, *The Last Victim: Inside the Minds of Serial Killers* (New York: Warner, 1999).

22. Ramsland, "Serial Killer Groupies."

23. Richard Wrangham and Dale Peterson, *Demonic Males: Apes and the Origins of Human Violence* (Boston: Houghton Mifflin, 1996).

24. Marecheux, *Outlaws*, p. 10

CHAPTER 7

1. Empower Nepali Girls, "About the Foundation," http://www.empower nepaligirls.org (accessed April 10, 2010).

2. A. J. McKnight and B. Adams, *Driver Education Task Analysis*, vol. 1 (Washington, DC: National Highway Traffic Safety Administration, 1970).

3. Ronald Bailey, "Don't Be Terrorized," http://reason.com/archives/2006/08/ 11/dont-be-terrorized (accessed April 10, 2010).

4. Justin Vallejo and Lauren Williams, "Family of Neil Gledhill Shocked at Callous Rubberneckers," *Daily Telegraph*, April 2, 2009.

5. D. Harwell, "Hooked on Tragedy," *St. Petersburg Times*, July 31, 2009, http://pqasb.pqarchiver.com/sptimes/access/1816434131.html?FMT=ABS&FMTS =ABS:FT&date=Aug+2%2C+2009&author=DREW+HARWELL&pub=St.+Peter sburg+Times&edition=&startpage=E.1&desc=HOOKED+ON+TRAGEDY (accessed April 15, 2010).

6. Jennifer Stoudt, "A Nation of Gawkers," *Albright Reporter*, Spring 2009, http://www.albright.edu/reporter/spring2009/gawkers.html (accessed April 15, 2010).

7. Rupert Matthews, *The Age of Gladiators: Savagery and Spectacle in Ancient Rome* (Edison, NJ: Chartwell, 2003).

8. Entering "car crashes" into a YouTube search nets 14,700 choices. "Police chases" nets 3,200 options. http://www.youtube.com/results?search_query=car +crashes&aq=f (accessed April 11, 2010).

9. Harry Teng and Jonathan P. Musinick, *An Analysis on the Impact of Rubbernecking on Urban Freeway Traffic* (Charlottesville, VA: Center for Transportation Studies, 2004).

10. Tom Vanderbilt, *Why We Drive the Way We Do (and What It Says about Us)* (New York: Knopf, 2008).

11. Ibid.

12. Mary Roach, "Slow-Moving Vehicle," *New York Times*, August 10, 2008.

13. Andrea Glaze and James Ellis, "Pilot Study of Distracted Drivers," Center for Public Policy, Virginia Commonwealth University, January 2003.

14. Jamie Doward and Chris Slater, "Giant Screens at Crash Sites to End 'Rubbernecking' Danger," *Guardian*, August 2, 2009, http://www.guardian.co .uk/uk/2009/aug/02/car-accidents-prevention (accessed April 12, 2010).

15. Kathleen McGowan, "Seven Deadly Sentiments," *Psychology Today*, Jan-

uary/February 2004; Lionel Tiger, "Torturers, Horror Films, and the Aesthetic Legacy of Predation," *Behavioral and Brain Sciences* 29, no. 3 (2006): 244–45.

16. Pieter Spierenburg, *Spectacle of Suffering* (Cambridge: Cambridge University Press, 1984).

17. Harold Schechter, *Savage Pastimes* (New York: St. Martin's Press, 2005), p. 99.

18. Matthews, *The Age of Gladiators*.

19. "The Death Penalty in 2009," Amnesty International, http://www.amnesty.org/en/death-penalty/death-sentences-and-executions-in-2009 (accessed April 17, 2010).

20. A much more detailed and lengthy description can be found at executedtoday.com, the Web site that specializes in describing executions. "1757: Robert-Francois Damiens, Disciplined and Punished," http://www.executedtoday.com/2008/03/28/1757-robert-francois-damiens-discipline-and-punish (accessed October 14, 2010).

21. Henry Edgeworth, "The Execution of Louis XVI, 1793," http://www.eyewitnesstohistory.com/louis.htm (accessed April 15, 2010).

22. Kevin Fagen, "A Witness's Account of Beardslee's Execution," *San Francisco Chronicle*, January 19, 2005, p. D1.

23. "Bids to Witness Execution," *New York Times*, March 2, 1986, http://www.nytimes.com/1986/03/02/us/bids-to-witness-execution.html (accessed April 11, 2010).

24. A. Freinkel, C. Koopman, and D. Spiegel, "Dissociative Symptoms in Media Eyewitnesses of an Execution," *American Journal of Psychiatry* 151 (1994): 1335–39.

25. Bjorn Carey, "Beheadings Are Out, but Watching Executions Is in Vogue," *Live Science*, August 2005, http://www.livescience.com/history/050815_execution_evolution.html (accessed April 18, 2010).

26. Annulla Linders, "The Execution Spectacle and State Legitimacy: The Changing Nature of American Execution Audience, 1833–1937," *Law and Society Review* 36 (2002): 607.

27. Larry K. Brown, *You Are Respectfully Invited to Attend My Execution* (Glendo, WY: High Plains Press, 1997).

28. Kirk W. Fuoss, "Lynching Performances, Theatres of Violence," *Text and Performance Quarterly* 19, no. 1 (1991): 1–37.

29. James W. Clarke, "Without Fear or Shame: Lynching, Capital Punishment, and the Subculture of Violence in the American South," *British Journal of Political Science* 28 (1998): 269–89.

30. W. Fitzhugh Brundage, *Under Sentence of Death: Lynching in the South* (Chapel Hill: University of North Carolina Press, 1997).

31. Ida B. Wells-Barnett, *On Lynchings* (New York: Humanity Books, 2002).

32. Robin. D. Lacks, Jill A. Gordo, and Colleen M. McCue, "Who, What, and When: A Descriptive Examination of Crowd Formation, Crowd Participation, and Participation with Law Enforcement at Homicide Scenes in One City," *American Journal of Criminal Justice* 30, no. 1 (2005): 1–20.

33. "Man Furious with Bystanders Who Aborted His Suicide Bid," *Daily Sun*, November 25, 2006, http://theclick.us/2006/11/man-furious-with-bystanders-who-aborted-his-suicide-bid/ (accessed April 13, 2010).

34. Tom Postmes and Russell Spears, "Deindividuation and Antinormative Behavior: A Meta-analysis," *Psychological Bulletin* 123 (May 1998): 238–59.

35. Leon Mann, "The Baiting Crowd in Episodes of Threatened Suicide," *Journal of Personality and Social Psychology* 14 (October 1981): 703–709.

36. Mark Levine, "The Kindness of Crowds," *Economist* 390, February 28, 2009, pp. 83–84.

CHAPTER 8

1. Jack Kervorkian, "A Brief History of Experimentation on Condemned and Executed Humans," *Journal of National Medical Association* 77, no. 3 (1985): 215–26.

2. Michael J. Osofsky, Albert Bandura, and Philip G. Zimbardo, "The Role of Moral Disengagement in the Execution Process," *Law and Human Behavior* 29, no. 4 (2005): 389.

3. Jason Moss and Jeffrey A. Kottler, *The Last Victim: A True Life Journey into the Minds of Serial Killers* (New York: Warner, 1999).

4. As mentioned in the preface, all names, details, and identifying information have been changed to protect the anonymity of the individuals I interviewed.

5. Jeffrey A. Kottler, *The Assassin and the Therapist: An Exploration of Truth in Psychotherapy and in Life* (New York: Routledge, 2010).

CHAPTER 9

1. Eduardo B. Andrade and Joel B. Cohen, "On the Consumption of Negative Feelings," *Journal of Consumer Research* 34 (2007): 283–99.

2. Robin Wright, *The Moral Animal* (New York: Pantheon, 1994).

3. Ibid.

4. Theodore D. Kemper, *Social Structure and Testosterone* (New Brunswick, NJ: Rutgers University Press, 1990).

5. Brant Wenegrat, *Sociobiology and Mental Disorders* (Menlo Park, CA: Addison-Wesley, 1984).

6. P. C. Bernhardt et al., "Testosterone Changes during Vicarious Experiences of Winning and Losing among Fans at Sporting Events," *Physiological Behavior* 65 (1998): 56–62.

7. Barbara Ehrenreich, *Blood Rites: Origins and History of the Passions of War* (New York: Metropolitan, 1997).

8. Alan S. Miller and Satoshi Kanazawa, *Why Beautiful People Have More Daughters* (New York: Perigee, 2007).

9. Randy Thornhill and Craig T. Palmer, *A Natural History of Rape: Biological Basis of Sexual Coercion* (Cambridge, MA: MIT Press, 2000).

10. Wilt Chamberlain, *A View from Above* (New York: Random House, 1994).

11. Rene Girard, *Violence and the Sacred* (Baltimore: Johns Hopkins University Press, 1972).

12. Michael Newton, "Written in Blood: A History of Human Sacrifice," *Journal of Psychohistory* 24, no. 2 (1996): 104–31.

13. Eric Schlosser, "A Grief Like No Other," *Atlantic Monthly*, September 1997, pp. 37–76.

14. "The Night Stalker's Wife," CNN, July 28, 1997, http://www.cnn.com/US/9707/28/nightstalker.wife (accessed April 10, 2010).

15. Jason Moss and Jeffrey Kottler, *The Last Victim: Inside the Minds of Serial Killers* (New York: Warner, 1999).

16. Jeffrey H. Goldstein, ed., *Why We Watch: The Attractions of Violent Entertainment* (New York: Oxford University Press, 1988).

17. Norbert Elias and Eric Dunning, *Quest for Excitement: Sport and Leisure in the Civilizing Process* (Oxford: Blackwell, 1986).

18. W. James Potter, *The 11 Myths of Media Violence* (Thousand Oaks, CA: Sage, 2003).

19. Stephen King, *Danse Macabre* (New York: Berkley, 1981), p. 121.

20. Laurent Bouzereau, *Ultraviolent Movies: From Sam Peckinpah to Quentin Tarantino* (Secaucus, NJ: Citadel Press, 1996), p. 127.

21. James Patterson, *Cat and Mouse* (New York: Grand Central, 1998), p. 251.

22. Stephen King, *Bare Bones: Conversations on Terror with Stephen King* (New York: McGraw Hill, 1988), p. 50.

23. Stephen King, *Night Shift* (New York: Doubleday, 1978), p. xv.

24. King, *Danse Macabre*, p. 198.

25. Albert Bandura, *Aggression: A Social Learning Analysis* (Englewood Cliffs, NJ: Prentice-Hall, 1973).

26. US Department of Justice, "Homicide Trends in the U.S.," 2007 http://www.ojp.usdoj.gov/bjs/homicide/race.htm.

27. Barry Glassner, *The Culture of Fear: Why Americans Are Afraid of the Wrong Things* (New York: Basic Books, 1999).

28. Isabel C. Pinedo, *Recreational Terror: Women and the Pleasures of Horror Film Viewing* (Albany: SUNY Press, 1997).

29. George Gerbner et al., "Living with Television: The Dynamics of the Cultivation Process," in *Perspectives on Media Effects*, ed. Jennings Bryant and Dolf Zillman (Hilldale, NJ: Lawrence Erlbaum Associates, 1986), pp. 17–40.

30. Rod Dreher, "Movie Violence: When Is Enough, Enough?" *South Florida Sun-Sentinel*, October 12, 1997.

CHAPTER 10

1. Jonathan Friday, "Demonic Curiosity and the Aesthetics of Documentary Photography," *British Journal of Aesthetics* 40 (2000): 356–75.

2. Sue Tait, "Pornographies of Violence? Internet Spectatorship on Body Horror," *Critical Studies in Media Communication* 25, no. 1 (2008): 91–111.

3. Martin Heidegger, quoted in T. Z. Levine, *From Socrates to Sartre: The Philosophic Quest* (New York: Bantam, 1984), p. 332.

4. Irvin Yalom, *Staring at the Sun: Overcoming the Terror of Death* (San Francisco: Jossey-Bass, 2008), pp. 5–6.

5. Irvin Yalom, *Existential Psychotherapy* (New York: Basic Books, 1980), p. 30.

6. Barrie Gunter, "Media Violence: Is There a Case for Causality?" *American Behavioral Scientist* 51, no. 8 (2008): 1061–1122.

7. David Buss, *The Murderer Next Door: Why the Mind Is Designed to Kill* (New York: Penguin, 2005).

8. Ibid., p. 13.

9. Sheila Isenberg, *Women Who Love Men Who Kill* (New York: Simon & Schuster, 1991), p. 213.

10. Buss, *The Murderer Next Door*.

11. Thomas Hargrove, "Unsolved Homicide Analysis: A Look at What Kinds of Murders Get Solved," Scripps Howard News Service, May 23, 2010.

12. Erich Fromm, *The Anatomy of Human Destructiveness* (New York: Holt, Rinehart, and Winston, 1973), p. 574.

13. Blaine Harden, "The Banality of Gary: A Green River Chiller," *Washington Post*, November 16, 2003, p. D01.

14. Albert Bandura, *Aggression: A Social Learning Analysis* (Englewood Cliffs, NJ: Prentice-Hall, 1973).

15. John P. Murray, "Media Violence: The Effects Are Both Real and Strong," *American Behavioral Scientist* 51, no. 8 (2008): 1212.

16. L. Rowell Huesmann, "The Impact of Electronic Media Violence: Scientific Theory and Research," *Journal of Adolescent Health* 41 (2007): S6–S13.

17. Murray, "Media Violence."

18. James A. Fox and Jack Levin, *The Will to Kill: Making Sense of Senseless Murder* (Boston: Allyn and Bacon, 2001).

19. Wayne Wilson and Randy Hunter, "Movie-Inspired Violence," *Psychological Reports* 53 (1983): 435–41.

20. David Trend, *The Myth of Media Violence: A Critical Introduction* (Malden, MA: Blackwell, 2007).

21. Ibid.

22. Bruce M. Knauft, "Reconsidering Violence in Simple Human Societies," *Current Anthropology* 28, no. 4 (1987): 457–82.

23. Sissela Bok, *Mayhem: Violence as Public Entertainment* (Reading, MA: Addison-Wesley, 1988).

24. See Christopher J. Ferguson, "Media Violence Effects: Confirmed Truth or Just Another X-file?" *Journal of Forensic Psychology Practice* 9 (2009): 103–26; Joanne Savage, "The Role of Exposure to Media Violence in the Etiology of Violent Behavior: A Criminologist Weighs In," *American Behavioral Scientist* 51 (2008): 1123–36.

25. Jerald J. Block and Bradford R. Crain, "Omissions and Errors in 'Media Violence and the American Public,' *American Psychologist* 62 (2007): 252–53.

26. P. Niels Christensen and Wendy Wood, "Effects of Media Violence on Viewers' Aggression in Unconstrained Social Interaction," in *Mass Media Effects Research: Advances Through Meta-analysis*, ed. Raymond W. Preiss et al. (Mahwah, NJ: Lawrence Erlbaum, 2007) pp. 145–68.

27. Jeffrey A. Kottler and David Chen, *Stress Management and Prevention: Applications to Daily Life* (Belmont, CA: Wadsworth, 2007).

28. Gunter, "Media Violence," pp. 1061–1122.

CHAPTER 11

1. The number of executions since 1997 has steadily declined as more prisoners are sentenced to life in prison without parole. Nevertheless, there has been an average of twenty-five inmates executed each year since then. Texas Execution Information Center, http://www.txexecutions.org/stats.asp (accessed April 17, 2010).

2. Joel Norris, *Henry Lee Lucas: The Shocking True Story of America's Most Notorious Serial Killer* (New York: Zebra Books, 1991).

CHAPTER 12

1. Cynthia Hoffner and Kenneth Levine, "Enjoyment of Mediated Fright and Violence: A Meta-Analysis," *Media Psychology* 7, no. 2 (2005): 207–37.

2. Salman Akhtar and Henri Parens, eds., *Lying, Cheating, and Carrying On* (New York: Jason Aronson, 2009).

3. Jeffrey Kottler, *The Assassin and the Therapist: An Exploration of Truth in Psychotherapy and in Life* (New York: Routledge, 2010); Jeffrey Kottler and Jon Carlson, *Duped: Lies and Deception in Psychotherapy* (New York: Routledge, 2011).

4. Paul Ekman, Maureen O'Sullivan, and Mark Frank, "A Few Can Catch a Liar," *Psychological Science* 10 (1999): 263–66.

5. Gregory Curtis, *The Cave Painters: Probing the Mysteries of the World's First Artists* (New York: Anchor, 2007).

6. David Trend, *The Myth of Media Violence: A Critical Introduction* (Malden, MA: Blackwell, 2007), p. 118.

7. Richard Verrier, "I Went to the Movies and a Fight Broke Out," *Los Angeles Times*, April 20, 2010, p. B1.

8. Joanna Weiss, "Fear of Fairy Tales," *Boston Globe*, September 21, 2007.

9. Donald G. Dutton, *The Psychology of Genocide, Massacres, and Extreme Violence* (Westport, CT: Praeger, 2007).

10. Daniel J. Goldhagen, *Worse than War: Genocide, Eliminationism, and the Ongoing Assault on Humanity* (New York: Public Affairs, 2009).

11. Ibid.

12. Laurent Bouzereau, *Ultraviolent Movies: From Sam Peckinpah to Quentin Tarantino* (Secaucus, NJ: Citadel Press, 1996), p. 69.

13. Ibid., p. 189.

14. Robert I. Simon, *Bad Men Do What Good Men Dream: A Forensic Psychiatrist Illuminates the Darker Side of Human Behavior* (Arlington, VA: American Psychiatric Press, 2008).

15. Ibid., p. 3.

16. David M. Buss, *Evolutionary Psychology: The New Science of Mind* (Boston: Allyn and Bacon, 2008).

17. Steven Pinker, "A History of Violence," *New Republic*, March, 19, 2007.

18. Manuel Eisner, "Modernity Strikes Back? A Historical Perspective on the Latest Increase in Interpersonal Violence (1960–1990)," *International Journal of Conflict and Violence 2*, no. 2 (2008): 288–316.

19. Tom Mes, *Agitator: The Cinema of Takashi Miike* (Surrey: FAB Press, 2004).

20. Buss, *Evolutionary Psychology*.

21. David M. Buss, *The Murderer Next Door: Why the Mind Is Designed to Kill* (New York: Penguin, 2005), p. 34.

22. Susan Kandel, review of *The Girl in Alfred Hitchcock's Shower* by Robert Graysmith, *Los Angeles Times*, March 23, 2010, p. D9.

23. Albert Bandura, Cloe Madanes, and Jeffrey A. Kottler, "Moral Disengagement," Evolution of Psychotherapy Conference, Anaheim, CA, 2009.

24. Albert Bandura et al., "Mechanisms of Moral Disengagement in the Exercise of Moral Agency," *Journal of Personality and Social Psychology 71*, no. 2 (1996): 364–74.

25. Christoph Klimmt et al., "How Players Manage Moral Concerns to Make Video Game Violence Enjoyable," *Communications 3* (2006): 309–28.

26. Aaron T. Beck, *Prisoners of Hate: The Cognitive Basis of Anger, Hostility, and Violence* (New York: HarperCollins, 1999).

27. Michael J. Osofsky, Albert Bandura, and Philip G. Zimbardo, "The Role of Moral Disengagement in the Execution Process," *Law and Human Behavior 29*, no. 4 (2005): 386.

28. Albert Bandura, "Moral Disengagement in the Perpetration of Inhumanities," *Personality and Social Psychology Review 3* (1999): 193–209.

29. Bandura et al., "Mechanisms of Moral Disengagement in the Exercise of Moral Agency."

30. Robert Wright, *The Moral Animal: Why We Are the Way We Are* (New York: Pantheon, 1994).

31. "Battle at Kruger," YouTube, http://www.youtube.com/watch?v=LU8DD Yz68kM (accessed May 3, 2010).

32. Michael Hirschorn, "The Future Is Cheese," *Atlantic Monthly*, March 2009, pp. 39–41.

33. Laura Triplett, interview conducted April 26, 2010.

34. Associated Press, "Man Bleeds to Death as People Walk Past," *Los Angeles Times*, April 27, 2010, http://www.latimes.com/news/nationworld/ nation/la-na-ny-left-to-die-20100427,0,4202400.story (accessed May 1, 2010).

35. Wendy Maltz, "Out of the Shadow: What's the Prevalence of Porn Doing to Our Psyches?" *Psychotherapy Networker* (December 2009).

36. Laura Triplett interview.

37. Andi Stein, interview conducted April 27, 2010.

38. D. Zillmann, J. Weaver, N. Mundorf, and C. Aust, "Effects of Opposite-Gender Companion's Affect to Horror on Distress, Delight, and Attraction," *Journal of Personality and Social Psychology* 51 (1986): 586–94; Hoffner and Levine, "Enjoyment of Mediated Fright and Violence: A Meta-Analysis."

39. M. Zuckerman, "Sensation Seeking and the Taste for Vicarious Horror," in *Horror Films: Current Research on Audience Preferences and Reactions,* ed. James B. Weaver and Ron Tamborini (Mahwah, NJ: Lawrence Erlbaum, 1996), pp. 147–60.

40. Stephen Marche, "Aren't We Enjoying All This Celebrity Death a Little Too Much?" *Esquire*, December 2009, p. 98.

41. Sissela Bok, *Mayhem: Violence as Public Entertainment* (Reading, MA: Basic Books, 1998).

42. Alex Rodriquez, "ID of Girl in Taliban Flogging Video in Question," *Los Angeles Times*, April 29, 2010, p. A3.

43. "Woman Publicly Flogged in Pakistan," YouTube, http://www.youtube .com/verify_age?next_url=/watch%3Fv%3DUbrkTeVJlnQ (accessed May 2, 2010).

44. Terry McCarthy, "LA Gangs Are Back," *Time*, June 13, 2005, http://www .time.com/time/magazine/article/0,9171,1000677,00.html (accessed April 18, 2010).

45. Timothy Hagen, "LA Consequential," *New York Times*, March 2, 2010, http://opinionator.blogs.nytimes.com/2010/03/03/l-a-consequential/ (accessed April 18, 2010).

46. Gregg Esterbrook, *The Progress of Paradox: How Life Gets Better While People Feel Worse* (New York: Random House, 2004); Michael Shermer, "As Good as It Gets," *Los Angeles Times*, April 30, 2010, p. A19.

References

Abner, William. "An Almanac of Pimps, Orcs, and Lightsabers for March." *InformIT*, March 3, 2006.

Adams, Tim. "The Stephen King Interview, Uncut and Unpublished." *Guardian*, September 14, 2000. http://www.guardian.co.uk/books/2000/sep/14/stephen king.fiction (accessed April 21, 2010).

Allen, Hervey. *Israfel: The Life and Times of Edgar Allan Poe.* New York: Farrar & Rinehart, 1934.

Anderson, C. A., N. L. Carnagey, and J. Eubanks. "Exposure to Violent Media: The Effects of Songs with Violent Lyrics on Aggressive Thoughts and Feelings." *Journal of Personality and Social Psychology* 84 (2003): 960–71.

Andrade, Eduardo B., and Joel B. Cohen. "On the Consumption of Negative Feelings." *Journal of Consumer Research* 34 (2007): 283–99.

Ansen, D. "Shock and Yawn." *Newsweek*, October 26, 2009, pp. 48–50.

Arnzen, Michael A. "Who's Laughing Now? The Postmodern Splatter Film." *Journal of Popular Film and Television* 21, no. 4 (1994): 176–86.

Augustine. *Confessions.* New York: Penguin, 1961.

Austen, Jane, and Seth Grahame-Smith. *Pride and Prejudice and Zombies.* San Francisco: Chronicle Books, 2009.

Bailey, R. H. *Violence and Aggression.* New York: Time-Life, 1976.

Baker, Chris. "It's Not Just about Killing Hookers Anymore." *Slate*, April 29, 2008. http://www.slate.com/id/2190207/ (accessed April 21, 2010).

Bandura, Albert. *Aggression: A Social Learning Analysis.* Englewood Cliffs, NJ: Prentice-Hall, 1973.

———. "Moral Disengagement in the Perpetration of Inhumanities." *Personality and Social Psychology Review* 3 (1999): 193–209.

————. "A Murky Portrait of Human Cruelty." *Behavioral and Brain Sciences* 29 (2006): 225–26.

Bandura, Albert, Cloe Madanes, and Jeffrey A. Kottler. "Moral Disengagement." Evolution of Psychotherapy Conference, Anaheim, CA, 2009.

Bandura, Albert, et al. "Mechanisms of Moral Disengagement in the Exercise of Moral Agency." *Journal of Personality and Social Psychology* 71, no. 2 (1996): 364–74.

Barbanel, J. "Nassau County Limits Sale of Crime Trading Cards." *New York Times*, June 16, 1992, p. B5.

Bawer, Bruce. "Capote's Children." *New Criterion* 3 (1985): 39–43.

Beck, Aaron T. *Prisoners of Hate: The Cognitive Basis of Anger, Hostility, and Violence*. New York: HarperCollins, 1999.

Behrendt, Ralf-Peter. "Cruelty as a By-product of Ritualization of Intraspecific Aggression in Cultural Evolution."*Behavioral and Brain Sciences* 29, no. 3 (2006): 226–27.

Benton, Mike. *The Comic Book in America*. Dallas: Taylor, 1989.

Bergmann, Martin S. *In the Shadow of Moloch: The Sacrifice of Children and Its Impact on Western Religions*. New York: Columbia University Press, 1992.

Biodrowski, Steve. "Wes Craven: Alive and Shocking!" *Cinefantastique*, November 1, 1991, p. 11.

Block, Jerald J., and Bradford R. Crain. "Omissions and Errors in 'Media Violence and the American Public.'" *American Psychologist* 62 (2007): 252–53.

Bok, Sissela. *Mayhem: Violence as Public Entertainment*. Reading, MA: Addison-Wesley, 1988.

Bouzereau, Laurent. *Ultraviolent Movies: From Sam Peckinpah to Quentin Tarantino*. Secaucus, NJ: Citadel Press, 1996.

Brockett, Oscar. *History of the Theatre*. Boston: Allyn and Bacon, 1995.

Brown, Larry K. *You Are Respectfully Invited to Attend My Execution*. Glendo, WY: High Plains Press, 1997.

Brundage, W. Fitzhugh. *Under Sentence of Death: Lynching in the South*. Chapel Hill: University of North Carolina Press, 1997.

Brunette, Peter. "Interview with Quentin Tarantino." In *Quentin Tarantino Interviews*, edited by Gerard Peary. Jackson: University Press of Mississippi, 1998, pp. 30–34.

Buss, David M. *Evolutionary Psychology: The New Science of Mind*. Boston: Allyn and Bacon, 2008.

————. *The Murderer Next Door: Why the Mind Is Designed to Kill*. New York: Penguin, 2005.

Cameron, Deborah, and Elizabeth Frazer. *The Lust to Kill*. London: Polity Press, 1987.

Center for Victims of Violence and Crime. http://www.cvvc.org/.

Chamberlain, Wilt. *A View from Above*. New York: Random House, 1994.

Christensen, P. N., and W. Wood. "Effects of Media Violence on Viewers' Aggression in Unconstrained Social Interaction." In *Mass Media Effects Research:*

Advances through Meta-Analysis, edited by R. W. Preiss et al. Mahwah, NJ: Lawrence Erlbaum, 2006, pp. 145–68.

Chua-Eoan, Howard. "Too Many Eyes in the Sky?" *Time,* May 11, 1998, p. 30.

Cialdini, R. B., et al. "Basking in Reflected Glory: Three (Football) Field Studies." *Journal of Personality and Social Psychology* 34 (1976): 366–75.

Clarke, Clark W. "Without Fear or Shame: Lynching, Capital Punishment, and the Subculture of Violence in the American South." *British Journal of Political Science* 28 (1998): 269–89.

Coleman, K. M. *Contagion of the Throng: Absorbing Violence in the Roman World.* Dublin: Dublin University Press, 1996.

———. "Fatal Charades: Roman Executions Staged as Mythological Enactments." *Journal of Roman Studies* 80 (1990): 44–73.

———. "They, Too, Enjoyed Watching Violence and Death." *New York Times,* July 7, 2001, p. 9.

Csikszentmihalyi, Mihaly. *Beyond Boredom and Anxiety.* San Francisco: Jossey-Bass, 2000.

De Becker, G. *The Gift of Fear* New York: Dell, 1997.

Diamant, Kathi. *Kafka's Last Love: The Mystery of Dora Diamant.* New York: Basic Books, 2003.

Doward, J., and C. Slater. "Giant Screens at Crash Sites to End Rubbernecking Danger." *Guardian,* August 2, 2009. http://www.guardian.co.uk/uk/2009/aug/02/car-accidents-prevention (accessed April 21, 2010).

Drake, Brett, and Shanta Pandey. "Do Child Abuse Rates Increase on Those Days on Which Professional Sporting Events Are Held?" *Journal of Family Violence* 11, no. 3 (September 1996): 205–18.

Dreher, Rod. "Movie Violence: When Is Enough, Enough?" *Sun-Sentinel,* October 12, 1997.

Dutton, Donald G. *The Psychology of Genocide, Massacres, and Extreme Violence.* Westport, CT: Praeger, 2007.

Edelstein, D. "Now Playing at Your Local Multiplex: Torture Porn." *New York Magazine,* January 28, 2006. http://nymag.com/movies/features/15622/ (accessed April 22, 2010).

Ehrenreich, Barbara. *Blood Rites: Origins and History of the Passions of War.* New York: Metropolitan, 1997.

Elias, Norbert. *Quest for Excitement: Sport and Leisure in the Civilizing Process.* Rev. ed. Dublin: University College, 2009.

Elias, Norbert, and Eric Dunning. *Quest for Excitement: Sport and Leisure in the Civilizing Process.* Oxford: Blackwell, 1986. Empower Nepali Girls. "About the Foundation." http://www.EmpowerNepaliGirls.org (accessed April 10, 2010).

Evans, R. "Justice Seen, Justice Done? Abolishing Public Executions in 19th Century Germany." *History Today* 46 (April 1996): 20–25.

Farber, J. "Blood, Sweat, and Fears: Why Are Horror Movies Such a Slashing Success?" *Seventeen,* July 1987, pp. 108–109.

Farber, Stephen. "Peckinpah's Return." In *Sam Peckinpah Interviews*, edited by Kevin J. Hayes. Jackson: University Press of Mississippi, 1969, pp. 29–45.

Ferguson, Christopher J. "Media Violence Effects: Confirmed Truth or Just Another X-file?" *Journal of Forensic Psychology Practice* 9 (2009): 103–26.

Fimrite, Peter, and Michael Taylor. "No Shortage of Women Who Dream of Snaring a Husband on Death Row." *San Francisco Chronicle*, March, 27, 2005.

Fitzmorris, Kristin. "Violent Video Games: Insights into Why and How Players Use Them." Masters thesis, Johns Hopkins University, Baltimore, MD, September 2009.

Fox, James A., and Jack Levin. *Extreme Killing: Understanding Serial and Mass Murder*. Thousand Oaks, CA: Sage, 2005.

———. *The Will to Kill: Making Sense of Senseless Murder*. Boston: Allyn and Bacon, 2001.

Friday, Jonathan. "Demonic Curiosity and the Aesthetics of Documentary Photography." *British Journal of Aesthetics* 40 (2000): 356–75.

Fritz, B. "Video Game Borrows Page from Hollywood Playbook." *Los Angeles Times*, November 18, 2009, p. B1.

Fromm, Erich. *The Anatomy of Human Destructiveness*. New York: Holt, Rinehart, and Winston, 1973.

Fuller, Gerard. "Answers First, Questions Later." In *Quentin Tarantino interviews*, edited by Gerard Peary. Jackson: University Press of Mississippi, 1998, pp. 49–65.

Fuoss, Kirk W. "Lynching Performances, Theatres of Violence." *Text and Performance Quarterly* 19, no. 1 (1999): 1–37.

Geier, T. "R-Rated Bugs Your Kid Will Beg to See." *U.S. News & World Report*, November 10, 1997, p. 74.

Gerbner, George, et al. "Living with Television: The Dynamics of the Cultivation Process." In *Perspectives on Media Effects*, edited by Jennings Bryant and Dolf Zillman. Hilldale, NJ: Lawrence Erlbaum Associates, 1986, pp. 17–40.

Girard, Rene. *Violence and the Sacred*. Baltimore: Johns Hopkins University Press, 1972.

Glassner, Barry. *The Culture of Fear: Why Americans Are Afraid of the Wrong Things*. New York: Basic Books, 1999.

Goldberg, V. "Death Takes a Holiday, Sort Of." In *Why We Watch: The Attractions of Violent Entertainment*, edited by J. H. Goldstein. New York: Oxford University Press, 1998, pp. 27–52.

Goldhagen, Daniel J. *Worse Than War: Genocide, Eliminationism, and the Ongoing Assault on Humanity*. New York: Public Affairs, 2009.

Goldstein, Jeffrey H. "Immortal Kombat: War Toys and Violent Video Games." In *Why We Watch: The Attractions of Violent Entertainment*, edited by J. H. Goldstein. New York: Oxford University Press, 1998, pp. 53–68.

Gordon, D. "Horror Show." *Newsweek*, April 3, 2006, pp. 60–62.

Gordon, Mel. *The Grand Guignol: Theatre of Fear and Terror*. New York: Amok Press, 1988.

Grant, A. "King of Horror." *Scholastic Scope* 44 (1995): 13–14.

Grodal, Torben. "Video Games and the Pleasures of Control." *Media Entertainment: The Psychology of Its Appeal*, edited by Dolf Zillman and Peter Vorderer. Mahwah, NJ: Lawrence Erlbaum Associates, 2000, pp. 197–213.

Grossman, Lev. "Zombies Are the New Vampires." *Time*, April 20, 2009, p. 61.

Gunter, Barrie. "Media Violence: Is There a Case for Causality?" *American Behavioral Scientist* 51, no. 8 (2008): 1061–1122.

Guttmann, A. "The Appeal of Violent Sports." In *Why We Watch: The Attractions of Violent Entertainment*, edited by J. H. Goldstein. New York: Oxford University Press, 1998, pp. 7–26.

Harden, Blaine. "The Banality of Gary: A Green River Chiller." *Washington Post*, November 16, 2003, p. D01.

Harwell, Drew. "Hooked on Tragedy." *St. Petersburg Times*, August 2, 2009, p. E1.

Hassig, Ross. *Aztec Warfare: Imperial Expansion and Political Control*. Norman: University of Oklahoma Press, 1995.

Hoffner, C. A., and K. J. Levine. "Enjoyment of Mediated Fright and Violence: A Meta-analysis." In *Mass Media Effects Research: Advances Through Meta-analysis*, edited by R. W. Preiss et al. Mahwah, NJ: Lawrence Erlbaum, 2007, pp. 215–44.

Huesmann, L. Rowell. "The Impact of Electronic Media Violence: Scientific Theory and Research." *Journal of Adolescent Health* 41 (2007): S6–S13.

Isenberg, Sheila. *Women Who Love Men Who Kill*. New York: Simon & Schuster, 1991.

Jansz, Jereon. "The Emotional Appeal of Violent Video Games for Adolescent Males." *Communication Theory* 15, no. 3 (2005): 219–41.

Jensen, J. "Games." *Entertainment Weekly*, November 27, 2009, pp. 76–77.

Kauzlarich, David. *Introduction to Criminology*. 9th ed. New York: Rowman & Littlefield, 2010.

Keegan, R. W. "The Splat Pack." *Time*, November 30, 2006, pp. 66–70.

Keisner, Jody. "Do You Want to Watch? A Study of the Visual Rhetoric of the Postmodern Horror Film." *Women's Studies* 37 (2008): 411–27.

Kemper, Theodore D. *Social Structure and Testosterone*. New Brunswick, NJ: Rutgers University Press, 1990.

Kendrick, Walter M. *The Thrill of Fear: 250 Years of Scary Entertainment*. New York: Grove, 1991.

Kevorkian, Jack. "A Brief History of Experimentation on Condemned and Executed Humans." *Journal of National Medical Association* 77, no. 3 (1985): 215–26.

Kimmel, M. S., and M. Mahler. "Adolescent Masculinity, Homophobia, and Violence: Random School Shootings, 1982–2001." *American Behavioral Scientist* 46 (2003): 1439–58.

King, Stephen. *Danse Macabre*. New York: Berkley, 1981.

———. *Night Shift*. New York: Doubleday, 1976.

Klimmt, Christoph. "How Players Manage Moral Concerns to Make Video Game Violence Enjoyable." *Communications* 3 (2006): 309–28.

Knauft, Bruce M. "Reconsidering Violence in Simple Human Societies." *Current Anthropology* 28, no. 4 (1987): 457–82.

Knox, S. L. *Murder: A Tale of Modern American Life.* Durham, NC: Duke University Press, 1998.

Kottler, Jeffrey A. *The Assassin and the Therapist: An Exploration of Truth in Psychotherapy and in Life.* New York: Routledge, 2010.

———. *Divine Madness: Ten Stories of Creative Struggle.* San Francisco: Jossey-Bass, 2006.

———. *The Language of Tears.* San Francisco: Jossey-Bass, 1996.

———. *On Being a Therapist.* 4th ed. San Francisco: Jossey-Bass, 2010.

———. *Private Moments, Secret Selves: Enriching Our Time Alone.* New York: Ballantine, 1990.

———. *Travel That Can Change Your Life.* San Francisco: Jossey-Bass, 1997.

Kottler, Jeffrey A., and D. Blau. *The Imperfect Therapist: Learning from Failure in Therapeutic Practice.* San Francisco, Jossey-Bass, 1989.

Kottler, Jeffrey A., and Jon Carlson. *Bad Therapy: Master Therapists Share Their Worst Failures.* New York: Routledge, 2002.

———. *The Client Who Changed Me: Stories of Therapist Personal Transformation.* New York: Routledge, 2006.

———. *Creative Breakthroughs in Therapy: Tales of Transformation and Astonishment.* New York: Wiley, 2009.

———. *Duped: Lies and Deception in Psychotherapy.* New York: Routledge, 2011.

Kottler, Jeffrey A., and David Chen. *Stress Management and Prevention: Applications to Daily Life.* Belmont, CA: Wadsworth, 2007.

Kruuk, Hans. *The Spotted Hyena: A Study of Predation and Social Behavior.* Chicago: University of Chicago Press, 1992.

Kurtz, H. "Murder Rates Drop, but Coverage Soars." *Boston Globe*, August 13, 1997, p. D8.

Lacks, Robin D., Jill A. Gordo, and Colleen M McCue. "Who, What, and When: A Descriptive Examination of Crowd Formation, Crowd Participation, and Participation with Law Enforcement at Homicide Scenes in One City." *American Journal of Criminal Justice* 30, no. 1 (2005): 1–20.

Last, J. V. "New Grand Theft Auto Next Generation of Violence." *Philadelphia Inquirer,* May 15, 2008.

Lawrence, Patricia, and Philip Palmgreen. "Uses and Gratifications of Analysis of Horror." In *Horror Films: Current Research on Audience Preferences and Reactions*, edited by James Weaver and Ron Tamborini. Mahwah, NJ: Lawrence Erlbaum, 1996, pp. 161–78.

Lee, L. *100 Most Dangerous Things in Everyday Life and What You Can Do about Them.* London: Murdoch Books, 2004.

Leonard, J. *Smoke and Mirrors: Violence, Television, and Other American Cultures.* New York: Free Press, 1997.

Lerner, Melvin. *The Belief in a Just World: A Fundamental Delusion*. New York: Springer, 1980.

Lester, D. *Questions and Answers about Murder*. Philadelphia: Charles Press, 1991.

Maisel, Ivan, A. Kim, and K. Kennedy. "Sport? Not a Sport? This Week: Bull-fighting." *Sports Illustrated* 96, no. 20.

Marche, Stephen. "Aren't We Enjoying All This Celebrity Death a Little Too Much?" *Esquire,* December 2009, p. 98.

Marechaux, Laurent. *Outlaws: Adventures of Pirates, Scoundrels, and Other Rebels*. Paris: Flammarion, 2009.

Masinick, Jonathan P., and Hualiang (Harry) Teng. *An Analysis on the Impact of Rubbernecking on Urban Freeway Traffic*. Charlottesville, VA: Center for Transportation Studies, 2004.

Matthews, Rupert. *The Age of Gladiators: Savagery and Spectacle in Ancient Rome*. Edison, NJ: Chartwell, 2003.

McGowan, Kathleen. "Seven Deadly Sentiments." *Psychology Today*, January/February 2004.

Meijer, Fik. *The Gladiators: History's Most Deadly Sport*. New York: Thomas Dunne Books, 2003.

Miller, Alan S., and Satoshi Kanazawa. *Why Beautiful People Have More Daughters*. New York: Perigee, 2007.

Moss, Jason, and Jeffrey A. Kottler, *The Last Victim: A True Life Journey into the Minds of Serial Killers*. New York: Warner, 1999.

Murray, John P. "Media Violence: The Effects Are Both Real and Strong." *American Behavioral Scientist* 51, no. 8 (2008): 1212–30.

Nell, Victor. "Cruelty's Rewards: The Gratifications of Perpetrators and Spectators." *Behavioral and Brain Sciences* 29 (2006): 211–57.

Newton, Michael. "Written in Blood: A History of Human Sacrifice." *Journal of Psychohistory* 24, no. 2 (1996): 104–31.

Nixon, H. L., and J. H. Frey. *A Sociology of Sport*. Belmont, CA: Wadsworth, 1996.

Norris, Joel. *Henry Lee Lucas: The Shocking True Story of America's Most Notorious Serial Killer*. New York: Zebra Books, 1991.

Osofsky, Michael J., Albert Bandura, and Philip G. Zimbardo. "The Role of Moral Disengagement in the Execution Process." *Law and Human Behavior* 29, no. 4 (2005): 371–93.

Patterson, James. *Cat and Mouse*. New York: Warner, 1998.

Pinedo, Isabel C. *Recreational Terror: Women and the Pleasures of Horror Film Viewing*. Albany: SUNY Press, 1997.

Pinker, Steven. "A History of Violence." *New Republic*, March, 19, 2007. http://www.tnr.com/article/history-violence-were-getting-nicer-every-day (accessed April 21, 2010).

Pittman, F. "Chivalry for the 90's: New Heroes for Old Fantasies." *Family Therapy Networker*, November/December 1990, pp. 73–75.

Pizzato, Mark. *Theatres of Human Sacrifice: From Ancient Ritual to Screen Violence.* Albany: SUNY Press, 2005.

Pompilio, Natalie. "Lessons Learned from School Shootings Past." *American Journalism Review* (June 1999): 10–11.

Potier, Beth. "Once Upon a Time . . ." *Harvard Gazette*, April 10, 2003.

Potter, N. N. "Shame, Violence, and Perpetrators' Voices." *Behavioral and Brain Sciences* 29, no. 3 (2006): 237–38.

Potter, W. James. *The 11 Myths of Media Violence.* Thousand Oaks, CA: Sage, 2003.

Potton, E. "Gore with the Wind." *Times of London*, July 11, 2009.

Rainer, P. "First Blood: It's Rocky versus the World." *Los Angeles Herald Examiner*, October 22, 1982.

Ramsland, Katherine. "Serial Killer Groupies." http://www.trutv.com/library/crime/criminal_mind/psychology/s_k_groupies/4.html (accessed November 20, 2009).

Raney, A. A., and A. J. Depalma. "The Effect of Viewing Varying Levels and Contexts of Violent Sports Programming on Enjoyment, Mood, and Perceived Violence." *Mass Communication and Society* 9 (2006): 321–38.

Raney, Arthur A., and William Kinnally. "Examining Perceived Violence in and Enjoyment of Televised Rivalry Sports Contests." *Mass Communication and Society*, no. 12 (July 2009): 311–31.

Roach, Mary. "Slow-Moving Vehicle." *New York Times*, August 10, 2008.

Ross, Winston. "Cracking Down on Cockfighting: Why the Bloodsport Remains a Thriving Industry." *Newsweek*, March, 24, 2008.

Rountree, Mark. "Violence Helps Sell Extreme Fighting." *Mixed Martial Arts Weekly*, September 30, 2005.

Russell, Jamie. *Book of the Dead: The Complete History of Zombie Cinema.* Surrey: FAB Press, 2005.

Samuels, Jonathan. "Thousands Download Illegal Ultra-violent Game." *Sky News*, February 27, 2008.

Sapolsky, Barry S., and Fred Molitor. "Content Trends in Contemporary Horror Films." In *Horror Films: Current Research on Audience Preferences and Reactions*, edited by James B. Weaver and Ron Tamborini. Mahwah, NJ: Lawrence Erlbaum, 1996, pp. 33–48.

Sapolsky, Barry S., Fred Molitor, and S. Luque. "Sex and Violence in Slasher Films: Reexamining the Assumptions." *Journalism and Mass Communication Quarterly* 80 (2003): 28–38.

Savage, Joanne. "The Role of Exposure to Media Violence in the Etiology of Violent Behavior: A Criminologist Weighs In." *American Behavioral Scientist* 51 (2008): 1123–36.

Scharrer, Erica. "Media Exposure and Sensitivity to Violence in News Reports: Evidence of Desensitization." *Journal of Media Communication Quarterly* 85, no. 2 (2008): 291–310.

Schechter, Harold. *Savage Pastimes: A Cultural History of Violent Entertainment.* New York: St. Martin's Press, 2005.

Schmid, David. *Natural Born Celebrities: Serial Killers in American Culture.* Chicago: University of Chicago Press, 2005.

Shaw, Rachel. "Making Sense of Violence: A Study of Narrative Meaning." *Qualitative Research in Psychology* 1 (2004): 131–51.

Sherry, John L. "Violent Video Games and Aggression: Why Can't We Find Effects?" In *Mass Media Effects Research: Advances Through Meta-analysis,* edited by Raymond Priess et al. Mahwah, NJ: Lawrence Erlbaum, 2007, pp. 245–79.

Shreeve, Jimmy L. *Human Sacrifice: A Shocking Expose of Ritual Killings Worldwide.* Fort Lee, NJ: Barricade, 2008.

Simon, Robert I. *Bad Men Do What Good Men Dream: A Forensic Psychiatrist Illuminates the Darker Side of Human Behavior.* Arlington, VA: American Psychiatric Press, 2008.

Smith, S. L., K. Lachlan, and R. Tamborini. "Popular Video Games: Quantifying the Presentation of Violence and Its Context." *Journal of Broadcasting and Electronic Media* 47 (2003): 58–76.

Smith, W. L. "Unrequited Love: Women Who Love Serial Killers and Men on Death Row." *Ezine,* 2007. http://ezinearticles.com/?Unrequited-Love—Women-Who-Love-Serial-Killers-and-Men-on-Death-Row&id=645902 (accessed April 22, 2010).

Smolej, M., and J. Kivivuori. "The Relation between Crime News and Fear of Violence." *Journal of Scandinavian Studies in Criminology and Crime Prevention* 7 (2006): 211–27.

Spiering, Frank. *Lizzie.* New York: Random House, 1984.

Spines, Christine. "Horror Films and the Women Who Love Them." *Entertainment Weekly,* July 31, 2009, pp. 31–33.

Staub, E. *The Roots of Evil.* Cambridge: Cambridge University Press, 1989.

Stine, Scott. "The Snuff Film: The Making of an Urban Legend." *Skeptical Inquirer* 23 (1999). http://www.csicop.org/si/show/snuff_film_the_making_of_an_urban_legend/ (accessed April 20, 2010).

Stoudt, J. P. "A Nation of Gawkers." *Albright Reporter,* 2009. http://www.albright.edu/reporter/spring2009/gawkers.html (accessed November 6, 2009).

Taibbi, Matt. "Why Sports Are for Losers." *Men's Journal,* December 2010, p. 78.

Tait, Sue. "Pornographies of Violence? Internet Spectatorship on Body Horror." *Critical Studies in Media Communication* 25, no. 1 (2008): 91–111.

Tamborini, Ron. "A Model of Empathy and Emotional Reactions to Horror." In *Horror Films: Current Research on Audience Preferences and Reactions,* edited by James B. Weaver and Ron Tamborini. Mahwah, NJ: Lawrence Erlbaum, 1996, pp. 103–24.

Tamborini, Ron, and James B. Weaver. "Frightening Entertainment: An Historical Perspective of Fictional Horror." In *Horror Films: Current Research on Audience Preferences and Reactions,* edited by James B. Weaver and Ron Tamborini. Mahwah, NJ: Lawrence Erlbaum, 1996, pp. 1–14.

Tatar, Maria. *Annotated Classic Fairy Tales.* New York: Norton, 2002.

Thornhill, Randy, and Craig T. Palmer. *A Natural History of Rape: Biological Basis of Sexual Coercion*. Cambridge, MA: MIT Press, 2000.

Tierny, Patrick. *The Highest Alter: Unveiling the Mystery of Human Sacrifice*. New York: Penguin, 1989.

Tiger, Lionel. "Torturers, Horror Films, and the Aesthetic Legacy of Predation." *Behavioral and Brain Sciences* 29, no. 3 (2006): 244–45.

Trend, David. *The Myth of Media Violence: A Critical Introduction*. Malden, MA: Blackwell, 2007.

Tyree, J. M. "Splatter Pattern." *Film Quarterly*, Fall 2008, pp. 82–85.

US Department of Justice. *Homicide Trends in the U.S.* 2007, http://www.ojp.usdoj.gov/bjs/homicide/race.htm (accessed April 21, 2010).

Vallejo, Justin, and Lauren Williams. "Family of Neil Gledhill Shocked at Callous Rubberneckers." *Daily Telegraph*, April 2, 2009.

Vanderbilt, Tom. *Why We Drive the Way We Do (and What It Says about Us)*. New York: Knopf, 2008.

Von Drehle, David. "Can Attack Dogs Be Rehabilitated?" *Time*, December 7, 2009, pp. 45–48.

Weiss, Joanna. "Fear of Fairy Tales." *Boston Globe*, September 21, 2007.

Weist, Julie. *Serial Killers as Heroes in the Media's Storybook of Murder*. Masters thesis, University of Georgia, Athens, GA, 2003.

Wells-Barnett, Ida B. *On Lynchings*. Amherst, NY. Humanity Books, 2002.

Wenegrat, Brant. *Sociobiology and Mental Disorders*. Menlo Park, CA: Addison-Wesley, 1984.

Wertham, Fredric. *Seduction of the Innocent*. New York: Rinehart, 1954.

Weyr, Tom. "Marketing America's Psychos." *Publishers Weekly* 12, April 1993, pp. 38–41.

Wiener, P. P., and J. Fisher. *Violence and Aggression in the History of Ideas*. New Brunswick, NJ: Rutgers University Press, 1974.

Wilson, Wayne, and Randy Hunter. "Movie-Inspired Violence." *Psychological Reports* 53 (1983): 435–41.

Woolf, Virginia. *The Essays of Virginia Woolf*. New York: Harcourt Brace, 1987

Wrangham, Richard, and Dale Peterson. *Demonic Males: Apes and the Origins of Human Violence*. Boston: Houghton Mifflin, 1996.

Wright, Robert. *The Moral Animal: Why We Are the Way We Are*. New York: Pantheon, 1994.

Yalom, Irvin. *Staring at the Sun: Overcoming the Terror of Death*. San Francisco: Jossey-Bass, 2008.

Zillman, Dolf, and Rhonda Gibson. "Evolution of the Horror Genre." In *Horror Films: Current Research on Audience Preferences and Reactions*, edited by J. B. Weaver and Ron Tamborini. Mahwah, NJ: Lawrence Erlbaum, 1996, pp. 15–32.

Zillman, Dolf, and James B. Weaver. "Gender-Socialization Theory and Reactions to Horror." In *Horror Films: Current Research on Audience Preferences and Reactions*, edited by J. B. Weaver and Ron Tamborini. Mahwah, NJ: Lawrence Erlbaum, 1996, pp. 81–102.

Index

multiple identification (from prey to predator), 193–94
mummies, 105
Mummy, The (movie), 104
murder, 247
"culture of murder," 176
decline in murder rates, 247
films including real-life murders, 204
Gebusi tribe of New Guinea having highest incidence of, 215–16
public executions as a spectator sport, 137–44
depersonalization of those conducting the execution, 151
See also killers; serial killers and mass murderers
Murder in the Red Barn, The (pamphlet), 55
Murders in the Rue Morgue (movie), 104
Murray, John P., 211–13
Myers, Michael (fictional character), 122
My Lai, 241, 252
MySpace, 259

"narrative or mild violence," 106
NASCAR, equivalent to chariot races, 45
National Catholic Office for Motion Pictures, 101
National Enquirer, 123
National Football League, 79
National Geographic Channel, 25
National Institute of Mental Health, 261
National Police Gazette (tabloid), 55, 56
Natural Born Killers (movie), 122–23, 244
naval battle, staged to win public popularity, 135–36
Nazis, 105, 145, 240, 242, 249
Nepal
animal sacrifice in, 49, 258
car crash in, 132–33
Nero (emperor), 138–39
Netflix, 259
New Guinea, 215–16

Newman, David, 101
newspapers and news broadcasts, 153, 256
covering violence and murder, 31, 58–59, 78, 87, 195
creating a market for violence, 123–24, 125, 190, 224
interest in high-profile cases, 133, 154
National Police Gazette mainly focusing on, 56
sensationalizing violence, 135, 145–46, 164, 191, 217, 243, 259
stories about human sacrifice, 49
use of suspense in reporting, 192
news junkies, 154, 190
looking for bad news, 135, 182, 190, 191, 217
news photographers' views on violence, 149–50
New Testament and human sacrifice, 48
Newton, Michael, 46–47
New York Times, 123–24
NFL. *See* National Football League
Ngorongoro Crater of Tanzania, 17–18
Nice Girls Don't Have Fangs (Jameson), 20
Nietzsche, Friedrich, 203
Nigeria, attempted suicide in, 146–47
Nightmare on Elm Street, A (movie), 19, 83, 98, 100, 108, 122
Night Stalker, 60, 120, 123, 125, 127, 128, 130, 176. *See also* Ramirez, Richard
9/11, 135, 146, 240
numb, becoming. *See* desensitization to violence

occupations of violence, 149–67
perspectives of a killer and a police officer, 153–61
"Old Sparky" (electric chair), 221
Old Testament, 48, 54

About the Author

Jeffrey A. Kottler, PhD, is the author of over eighty nonfiction books including the *New York Times* bestseller *The Last Victim: A True-Life Journey Inside the Mind of the Serial Killer*. He is one of the foremost psychologists in the world writing about issues related to human behavior. He has written dozens of classic texts and manuals for psychotherapists and teachers, as well as many others about complex phe-nomena related to crying (*The Language of Tears*), conflict (*Beyond Blame*), solitary behavior (*Private Moments, Secret Selves*), creativity (*Divine Madness, Creative Breakthroughs in Therapy*), deception and lying (*The Assassin and the Therapist, Duped*), social justice (*Changing People's Lives While Trans-forming Your Own*), and the inner world of practicing therapists (*On Being a Therapist, The Client Who Changed Me*). His books have been translated into two dozen languages.

Jeffrey is Professor of Counseling at California State University, Fullerton. He is also cofounder of Empower Nepali Girls, an organization that provides scholarships for lower-caste, at-risk girls in Nepal who would otherwise not be able to attend school.